Toni Morrison and the Geopoetics
of Place, Race, and Be/longing

MARILYN SANDERS MOBLEY

TONI MORRISON AND THE GEOPOETICS OF PLACE, RACE, AND BE/LONGING

TEMPLE UNIVERSITY PRESS
Philadelphia • Rome • Tokyo

TEMPLE UNIVERSITY PRESS
Philadelphia, Pennsylvania 19122
tupress.temple.edu

Copyright © 2024 by Temple University—Of The Commonwealth System of Higher Education
All rights reserved
Published 2024

Library of Congress Cataloging-in-Publication Data

Names: Mobley, Marilyn Sanders, 1952– author.
Title: Toni Morrison and the geopoetics of place, race, and be/longing / Marilyn Sanders Mobley.
Description: Philadelphia : Temple University Press, 2024. | Includes bibliographical references and index. | Summary: "In this interdisciplinary work of Literary Criticism, notable Toni Morrison scholar Marilyn S. Mobley endeavors to apply geopoetics toward establishing a new framework for understanding Morrison's famous call to create and allow for "spaces for the reader to come into the text.""— Provided by publisher.
Identifiers: LCCN 2024000274 (print) | LCCN 2024000275 (ebook) | ISBN 9781439924303 (cloth) | ISBN 9781439924310 (paperback) | ISBN 9781439924327 (pdf)
Subjects: LCSH: Morrison, Toni—Criticism and interpretation. | Geography in literature. | Black people in literature. | Belonging (Social psychology) in literature.
Classification: LCC PS3563.O8749 Z777 2024 (print) | LCC PS3563.O8749 (ebook) | DDC 813/.5409—dc23/eng/20240317
LC record available at https://lccn.loc.gov/2024000274
LC ebook record available at https://lccn.loc.gov/2024000275

9 8 7 6 5 4 3 2 1

Contents

Acknowledgments — vii

Introduction: Between the Text and the Reader:
The Word-Work of Toni Morrison — 1

1. Crafting Spaces for the Reader: The Geopoetics
   of Discursive Mediation — 22
2. Spatializing the Self: The Geopoetics of Emancipatory Spaces — 58
3. Circling the Subject: The Geopoetics of Narrative Rememory — 104
4. A Matter of Be/longing: Geopoetic Interrogations of Home — 140

Conclusion: Toni Morrison's Spaces for Readers:
The Geopoetics of the Dancing Mind — 165

Notes — 177
Bibliography — 195
Index — 205

Acknowledgments

The journey from the idea of this book to its completion has been long and circuitous, but I owe a debt of gratitude to many for inspiring me, walking alongside me, praying for me, and believing the project was worthwhile even when I sometimes wondered whether it would see the light of day. I want to acknowledge them in this space as best I can.

I am most grateful for my parents, Priscilla Lumpkins and Delbert Sanders, for inspiring me to have faith, love reading, value learning, and remain committed to social justice and serving others. Their memory blesses me daily, as does the memory of Professor Quandra Prettyman, who introduced me to the writing of Toni Morrison when I was a student at Barnard College. Her death and that of Professor Morrison on the eve that I found my earlier version of this manuscript were devastating, but their spirit motivated me to persevere.

I thank my mentor and friend Gary Lee Stonum for his insightful feedback on the early chapters and for recommending that I reach out to Robert Tally, whose scholarship in the field of spatial literary humanities would sharpen my thinking about geopoetics. I am grateful for other colleagues who took the time to read, comment, and share their insights about this book. I take responsibility for how I used the feedback, however. On the list of those who read different iterations of the manuscript and/or who offered comments about the project include Keith Clark, Amelia Rutledge, Wendi Manuel-Scott, Jeffrey Stewart, Thirty Umrigar, Chris Flint, Sara Gridley, Michael Clune, Maggie Vinter, and Thom Dawkins.

Over the years of my research, scholarship, and teaching, I have learned a great deal from my students, many of whom have become academic leaders, scholars, teachers, lawyers, writers, poets, and activists. Dr. Denise Douglas, Kenyatta Dorey Graves, Dr. Keysha Ingram Gamor, Chadra Pittman, Michael Parker, Cara Byrne, Makela Hayford, Teauna Felder, and Cielle Brady are just a few of my former students whose feedback has enriched my thinking about Morrison, Africana Studies, and related cultural, social, and political matters.

The Ford Foundation postdoctoral fellowship I received during my early years of thinking about this book and the faculty study leaves from George Mason University were most helpful. My sabbatical from CWRU gave me the intellectual and emotional time and space I needed to return to the manuscript in earnest with renewed focus and clarity.

I am forever indebted to the brilliant sisters of the Wintergreen Women Writers group, led by Joanne Gabbin, for being a safe space for our voices, our stories, our ideas, and our work in progress as we gave birth to manuscripts and various forms of artistic expression. I especially thank Opal Moore and Trudier Harris for reading and commenting on drafts of the manuscript and Maryemma Graham for publishing my article "Spaces for Readers," an early version of my ideas for this book, in her edited volume of essays on the African American novel.

I thank Carolyn Denard, founder of the Toni Morrison Society, for her vision in creating a community of scholars and readers devoted to the work of Toni Morrison. My service to the TMS as a member, speaker, president, and board member provided several opportunities for me to visit with Professor Morrison and share time and space with her at her home, at our conferences, and on telephone conversations with her each year on her birthday. I appreciate how Rene Boatman assisted me with these connections to Professor Morrison and with my visit to the archives at Princeton. My TMS friends are too numerous to name, and some have passed on, but those who have listened to papers, commented on excerpts of this manuscript, and given me phone, text, or email time include Adrienne Lanier Seward, Evelyn Schreiber, Dana Williams, Deborah McDowell, Angelyn Mitchell, Deborah Barnes, Herman Beavers, Henry Louis Gates Jr., Rene Boatman, Farah Jasmine Griffin, Valerie Smith, Hortense Spillers, Danille Taylor-Guthrie, Justine Tally, Tess Roynon, Kristine Yohe, John McCluskey, Audrey McCluskey, Cornel West, and Thadious Davis. I miss Claudia Tate, Cheryl Wall, Barbara Christian, Nellie McKay, Carmen Gillespie, and bell hooks, but consider it an honor that I got to know them as friends and sister scholars.

I am very grateful for the network of sister and brother scholars who continue to enrich my life with the intellectual exchange of ideas. Linda Williamson Nelson, Jeffrey Stewart, Michael Eric Dyson, Christine Stanley, Paulette Granberry-Russell, Jonette O'Kelley Miller, Rhonda Williams, Marsha Coleman-Adebayo, Patricia Miller, Kimberle Crenshaw, Ayesha Hardaway, Beverly Guy-Sheftal, Deborah Willis, Sharon Milligan, and Joy Bostic are part of this network.

I am also grateful for my church family at Arlington Church of God in Akron, Ohio, where my senior pastor, Rev. Dr. Charles Myricks, his wife, Sheri Myricks, Wellness and Grief Recovery Ministry members Dr. Angela Neal-Barnett, Dr. Daniel Sanders, and Maisha Green-McIntyre, my pastor laureate, Rev. Dr. Ronald J. Fowler, who always refers to Toni Morrison as "Sister Morrison," and my intercessory prayer team and prayer warriors have helped me "persevere, persist, and prevail," as my late pastor, Dr. Diana Swoope, once said in celebrating my milestone of becoming an ordained minister even as I was working to complete this book. I thank God for my prayer partners Sandra Roebuck, my cousin Crystal Darnell, Marion Hazly, Marilyn Barkley, Marilyn Vancant, and Olivia Demas, whose prayers have sustained me in my most challenging moments. My other minister friends, Rev. Cynthia Lee, Minister LeNettra Tomlinson, Rev. Marvin McMickle, Rev. Doris Crews, and Rev. Otis Moss Jr., have provided encouragement along the way.

I thank my Touch Tuesday family for the online support and safety net of love and prayer their text messages provide. Losing my best sister friend, the honorable Judge Sheila Abdus-Salaam, affected me profoundly because she was always my cheerleader for every project, including this book. Deborah Thornhill and my other Barnard Columbia JAM friends have been a real blessing during this last year of completing the book.

My weekly FaceTime calls with my sons, Rashad and Jamal, have given me the encouragement I needed when the work created doubt and loneliness. I love them more than words can express. I thank my daughter-in-law, Renita, my grandsons, Nyles, Nazir, and Carlton, and my great granddaughter, Olivia, for being sources of joy. My mother-sister-scholar-friend, Dr. Patricia Stewart, has nourished my mind and spirit throughout this project and remains a role model for me as a scholar activist and devout woman of faith.

I have nothing but profound gratitude and appreciation for my editor, Shaun Vigil, at Temple University Press for his unwavering support. He and Will Forrest, the editorial assistant and rights and contracts coordinator, helped me navigate the process of bringing my book project to completion with wise counsel and the grace I needed.

I hope anyone I omitted will charge the oversight to my head and not to my heart.

Most of all, I have heartfelt gratitude to Toni Morrison for being a "friend of my mind." This book is my humble testimony to that fact and is evidence of amazing grace.

Toni Morrison and the Geopoetics
of Place, Race, and Be/longing

Introduction

Between the Text and the Reader

The Word-Work of Toni Morrison

> Every literary work *faces outward away from itself,* toward the listener-reader, and to a certain extent thus anticipates possible reactions to itself.
> —Mikhail Bakhtin, "Discourse in the Novel"[1]

From *The Bluest Eye* (1970) to *God Help the Child* (2015) and all the writing in between, the work of Toni Morrison solidified her reputation as a major writer in the United States and around the world. Her success was about not only the strong social and political themes of African American life and culture but also the ability of her novels to speak to the reader and to invite the reader to speak back to her texts. With few exceptions, however, critical attention to the novels of Morrison has focused primarily on thematic concerns and cultural politics and less on matters of literary aesthetics or narrative poetics. The preoccupation with themes or *what* her novels mean has reductively neglected the matter of the network of discourse into which her texts enter or *how* her texts invite the reader to discern these themes. The distinction between *what* and *how* is reminiscent of the distinction the narrator makes in *The Bluest Eye* when she states, "*Since* why *is difficult to handle, we must take refuge in* how" (9). For the most part, Morrison's readers and critics have focused more on the *what* than the *how* of her writing. As a result, there has been limited focus on her expressed narrative intention of writing (to give her fiction the "oral quality" of Black vernacular language) and there has been even less focus on her other authorial intention of writing (to "provide spaces so that the reader can participate") in terms of how her texts operate in and comment on the cultural moment into which they enter.[2] This study explores themes of place, race, and belonging through the lens of her expressed narrative intention of providing "spaces for the reader."[3] Moreover, it is inspired by the clarion call in Morrison's 1988 lecture, "Unspeakable Things Unspoken," for critics who would consider unexplored approaches to her work, who address "*how* as well as *what* [my emphasis] . . . [and] who identify the workings as well as the work."⁴ This study attempts to respond to Morrison's call for critics who would "identify the workings" of her work by reading it through the interdisciplinary lens of geopoetics.

Morrison's statement in her 1993 Nobel Prize lecture that "word-work is sublime" is a related call, though of another sort, to listener-readers, including literary critics, to consider the generative qualities of the interconnectedness between politics and poetics not only in her work but in the human experience.⁵ She seemed eager to have readers understand that to focus on one and not the other is to underestimate the overarching power of what she brought to the work and art of writing. Teasing out the implications of the interconnections between the what and the how, the intersection between the politics and the poetics of her writing offers us new ways to approach, read, and interpret her work.

Although literary critics in general and reader-response critics in particular have raised legitimate questions about using an author's expressed narrative intentions as a basis for interpretation or literary analysis, the powerful implications inscribed within Morrison's words invite speculation, nonetheless, beyond matters of authorial intention to critical matters of reading, narrative poetics, cultural interpretation, and the political spaces into which her texts enter.⁶ For example, when we consider that Morrison says not only that she writes so that the reader can participate in the construction of meaning in her texts but also that she writes for Black people rather than in response to the white gaze, how do we account for the changes in Morrison's readership over time? Does the fact that some Black readers claim that her writing became increasingly difficult and inaccessible alter how we interpret her authorial intentions? To what extent does the identity of the reader matter, in terms of race, gender, class, place, or any other category of difference? How is it that some audiences who once followed her writing religiously began to complain that she was too hard to read, as one Black woman openly said to Morrison after a reading at Princeton University and even as professed fan Oprah Winfrey was known to say?⁷ How do we simultaneously interpret this change in her readership in the context of the growing body of scholarship on her novels and acceptance of her work in the academy, where she is routinely taught in secondary schools and on college campuses around the country and indeed around the world?⁸ In what way is analysis of Morrison's work informed by the intersection of Black studies and cultural studies with feminist studies, and in what ways has this intersection offered new theoretical models for reading late twentieth- and early twenty-first-century culture? How does the spatial turn in the humanities enable additional insights into her work? Finally, in what ways are her own ideas about place and space, race and identity, and house and home a kind of articulation of a theory of reading that illuminates the narrative poetics and cultural politics at work not only in her novels but also in her nonfiction and numerous public lectures? How can analyzing her work through the lens of geopoetics help us understand the narrative strategies at work in Morrison's writing? *Toni Morrison and the Geopoetics of Place, Race, and Be/longing* is a modest attempt to answer such questions and others that have emerged from this overarching reconsideration of her work.

In *The Source of Self-Regard* (2019), her last publication of selected essays, speeches, and meditations before her death, are statements that begin to provide possible answers to some of these questions. One of the most telling articulations of how place, race, and belonging are interconnected appears in the essay "The Foreigner's Home," in which she speaks of "a ubiquitous blur, a rattling of the concept of home," "our own fraying sense of belonging," and a feeling "of being exiled in the place one belongs."[9] This "rattling of the concept of home" is integral to "destabilizing the text and reorienting the reader," which Morrison articulates as goals of her work.[10] In other words, if we begin our consideration of Morrison's work from the perspective of the positionality or situatedness of the reader who is in the space of exile, and if we begin by considering that Morrison wrote primarily—but not solely—with that reader in mind, then we can begin to understand the participatory role she sought for the reader. Moreover, we can see that her artistic goal was to deploy narrative strategies that "disturb, rattle, and engage the entire environment of the reading experience" that would make demands "that the reader not just participate in the narrative, but specifically help to write it."[11] In regard to her narrative strategies, she elaborates on her "reliance for full comprehension on codes embedded in black culture, [her] effort to effect immediate co-conspiracy and intimacy (without any distancing, explanatory fabric), as well as [her] attempt to . . . transfigure the complexity and wealth of Afro-American culture into a language worthy of the culture."[12] Given her preoccupation with viewing herself as a reader who became an artist, she once wrote that "the words on the page are only half the story. . . . The rest is what you bring to the party."[13] Using such statements as a point of departure, this study offers a map back into and through Morrison's work through the lens of geopoetics to unpack and shed light on how she presents and represents place and space, racial and ethnic identity, being and belonging and on how Black subjects imagine life, living, and humanity in the midst of the forces designed to contain, marginalize, and oppress them. Agreeing with Morrison's suggestion in her essay "Goodbye to All That: Race, Surrogacy, and Farewell" that we dispense with the bifurcated view of politics and aesthetics, this study connects the two through the lens of geopoetics.[14] Put another way, the tool this study deploys for navigating this connection between politics and aesthetics is the analytic of geopoetics.

What is geopoetics, why geopoetics, and how can it assist us in reading and rereading Morrison's work, especially as it relates to place, race, and be/longing? As an analytic, geopoetics has its origins in the geocritical theoretical work of Kenneth White, who proposed in the 1970s that there is a connection between geography and poetics that can be made by looking at the writings of such authors as Walt Whitman and Henry David Thoreau.[15] Borrowing from the general field of geopoetics but deploying it to ruminate on place, identity, and belonging, I am using the term to refer to an analytic that will enable us to return to Morrison's work to determine how she portrays Black subjects who read the places and spaces in which they find themselves. Viewing Morrison's texts themselves as "sites of memory," to use the title of one of her most important essays, this study returns to the site of her texts to excavate, expose, and explore the ways in which she locates Black subjects in various places, represents their ways of navigating race (i.e., their racial identity) in those places, and crafts language and narrative to enable her readers to navigate the interior spaces of their humanity.[16]

Informed by the work of such critics as Katherine McKittrick, Kathleen M. Kirby, Thadious Davis, Rashad Shabazz, Christine Sharpe, Saidiya Hartman, and Dionne Brand, I am attempting to explore the connection between place and race, identity and imagination, and geography and narrative poetics in Morrison's writing. Reentering Morrison's work using geopoetics as an analytic for discovering and unpacking her narrative strategies helps us see new levels of meaning and understand her preoccupation with place in her metaphors of house and home, or what Trudier Harris refers to as depictions of "homespace."[17] In many respects, Morrison is not as interested in physical spaces as she is in what Raymond Williams refers to as "structures of feeling" or what she identifies as "the interior life" that could provide the "revelation of a kind of truth."[18] This study interrogates how these structures of feeling that make up the interior life show up as an "aesthetics of belonging" in Morrison's work. References to house and home and other places become sites for exploring the protocols of reading that Black subjects use successfully and sometimes unsuccessfully to attain the refuge aligned with their yearnings for spaces for being and belonging. I'm interested in how Morrison writes about the "both/and" spaces (i.e., both interior and exterior as opposed to either one or the other) in which Black subjects find themselves, how her subjects read those spaces, and how they successfully or unsuccessfully mediate and create ways of being that satisfy their desires for belonging. The lens that best serves as a reassessment tool or heuristic for this new reading of Morrison is one I am identifying as geopoetics, in that it both focuses on a broad definition of place (geography) and on her narrative aesthetics (poetics). Thus, this study reenters her work through geopoetics to reveal how an aesthetics of belonging shows up and operates in and through the spaces she creates through her representations of Black subjectivity beyond the exterior dimensions defined by the white gaze to the interior spaces where desire, yearning, and the imagination hold sway.

Unlike White and the earlier thinkers in the field of geopoetics, I have an interest in geography that is inclusive of but not limited to thinking about the earth and natural environment as the only material reality. Instead, my references to geography are in keeping with the ideas of such scholars as Homi Bhabha, Edward Soja, Brand, McKittrick, Hartman, and others, whose use of geography is about the multivalent spaces in which subjectivity is defined and/or created in the environment in terms of material and even metaphysical places. In my references to geography, therefore, I am as interested in interior spaces as I am in material ones. For example, *The Bluest Eye* begins with a prenarrative excerpt from an elementary school primer that contains a description of home as a physical space that is a normalized space of whiteness. The novel opens, however, with the narrator's reading of and feelings about what has transpired in her home, in the home of Pecola Breedlove, and inside the Black and white spaces of their Lorain, Ohio, community. In turn, Pecola's reading of and feelings about the community's reading of her leads her to a tragic turn inward to a space of self-loathing that inspires her to crave an aesthetic of beauty and belonging outside of the skin in which she was born. Interrogating Morrison's narrative choices in her telling of Pecola's story through Claudia's reading of it opens new ways of understanding the power of this first novel and how Morrison develops and hones her interest in the aesthetics of belonging over the course of her career as a writer. Rather than engaging in a rereading of each of the eleven novels and all her nonfiction, however, this study acknowledges how selected works of Morrison lend themselves to this geopoetic focus and point the way to using such a focus even more broadly.

As the following pages illustrate, my approach to Morrison's work, though eclectic, is heavily indebted to African American literary criticism, Black feminist criticism, critical race theory, cultural studies, and spatial literary criticism. What this book attempts to contribute to scholarship on Morrison by drawing on these distinct but related fields of study is an approach to her fiction that is as interdisciplinary, intersectional, nuanced, and complex as the works themselves—an approach that combines textual analysis with an analysis of her cultural politics and narrative poetics and connects both with a consideration of the discursive space into which her texts enter into dialogue with her readers. Moreover, because Morrison established her reputation not only as a highly acclaimed literary artist but also as a cultural critic and public intellectual whose commentary is now recorded in interviews, lectures, essays, introductions, speeches, literary criticism, and documentaries, it seems appropriate to turn critical attention to an overarching view of her literary/cultural production.[19] By so doing, we can begin to illuminate the multiple ways in which her work not only engages with history but also intervenes significantly, with an unflinching honesty that is reminiscent of James Baldwin, in the present political moment and interrogates how we might think about ourselves, our cultural locations, and the future we are imagining and creating in the midst of various contentious political realities.

What I believe we discover throughout the body of her work are what Mae Henderson refers to as "counternarratives" or Hartman calls "counteraesthetics" that destabilize received hegemonic narratives, expose misrepresentations and devaluations of Black life, and act as cultural critiques of issues ranging from race and gender, to class and ethnicity, to family relations and the African diaspora.[20] And with her familiar pronouncement that "the best art is political and you ought to be able to make it unquestionably political and irrevocably beautiful at the same time," Morrison challenges the old lie that literature is a priori somehow aesthetically pure until tainted by ideological interpretations of it.[21] The significance of this much-quoted pronouncement was that Morrison—at what was approximately the mid-career point—was asserting an ideological position that had already shaped her first four novels. While the interpenetration of art and politics is now the accepted terrain on which literary studies has become cultural studies, Morrison's pronouncement was exemplary of how the feminist and Black cultural studies perspectives that inform her writing have always understood their ideological underpinnings and already operated in the public sphere. As Gayatri Spivak asserts:

> Ideology in the critical sense does not signify an avowed doctrine. It is rather loosely articulated sets of historically determined and determining notions, presuppositions, and practices, each implying the other by real (but where does one stop to get a grip on reality?) or forced logic, which goes by the name of common sense or self-evident truth or natural behavior in a certain situation. What I have been talking about . . . has been the displacing of the ideology of our discipline of literature.[22]

In the counternarratives that shape the body of her literature, Morrison is engaged in various forms of displacement of traditional American literary studies. How she has produced these counternarratives through her fictional and nonfictional reimaginings and counteraesthetics of place and identity and how these counternarratives and counteraesthetics represent how Black subjects read and create emancipatory spaces as interpretive communities of readers are central areas of focus for this book.

In addition to illuminating how Morrison creates these emancipatory spaces for herself, her characters, and her readers, this study seeks to link multiple spaces of her contribution to American life and letters. It participates in ongoing dialogues in cultural studies and spatial humanities by illuminating how Morrison's fiction and nonfiction intervene in the lived life circumstances of her readers and offer readings of those circumstances that merit deeper analysis and understanding. In this regard, the body of writing that she has produced is not only beyond what has ideologically been regarded as belles lettres or literature; it has also engaged her readers through her geopoetics in a series of call-and-response opportunities to interrogate the public and private spaces of our lived lives. In Morrison's cultural commentary, of which her 1993 Nobel lecture is a primary example, she speaks from a position within the African American community, informed by that community's multivalent ways of knowing and reading the world, and uses the space of that global stage to comment self-consciously and unapologetically about the very tools that have made her celebrity possible, fully aware that she was intervening in ongoing debates that have emerged from the binary oppositional either/or thinking around issues of gender, age, race, identity, nationhood, education, and the like. Her courageous and bold intervention in such debates, born out of an awareness of the oppressive limitations and liberating possibilities inherent in them, gives her fiction and commentary their unique quality. The dynamics of this quality that I call *discursive mediation*—that is, both/and thinking, or what Eve Tavor Bannet refers to as "the logic of both/and"—are intrinsic to Morrison's worldview and, as such, are crucial to this study.[23] This space of discursive mediation is similar to what Bhabha, Soja, and others refer to as a *Third Space*— that is, a space of articulation and translation where we are forced to recognize and interrogate the mutual influences on any given moment and where we release ourselves from the limits of binary oppositional epistemologies.[24] I am also indebted to how Edouard Glissant and Elijah Anderson help us interrogate the racial dynamics that shape how Black subjects navigate white space.[25] This project involves, therefore, an interrogation of Morrison's fictional and nonfictional practices and the theoretical implications of these practices to suggest a viable model for mapping the intersection of spatial literary studies and the lived lives of Black people reading the text of the space called the United States of America and the African diaspora.[26] Reading her work through a spatial lens requires an analysis of another "both/and," and that is what Neil Smith refers to as the "mutuality of material and metaphorical space."[27] An analytic of geopoetics enables us to map the ways in which Morrison's narrative aesthetics illustrate and even influence how we read her Black subjects engaged in reading these in-between third spaces in which they find themselves.

This book is informed by a Black studies and critical race theory framework that a text enters a discursive space, not a vacuum. Indeed, a text can potentially intervene, comment on, and even disrupt the ongoing dialogues of which it is a part. Consequently, I am interested not only in the history and memories upon which Morrison's books are grounded but also in the highly contested spaces into which they enter from the moment they are read, reviewed, discussed, and taught. Hence, I am interested in the cultural work her books do, particularly in communities of color.[28] I am moving beyond the concept of dialogism in the text, however, which, according to critic Claudia Tate, was a given of literary and cultural studies, to Mikhail Bakhtin's concept of dialogism among readers—a concept that suggests that a text, especially one that foregrounds issues of race, gender, and class, enters a discursive space that has been shaped by numerous contending forces and that is still in the process of cultural formation.[29] For example, while we know that Morrison consistently foregrounds Black subjects and invokes historical dialogues from the distant and recent past, her writing also speaks to contemporary iterations of the Black and feminist struggle for social justice such as Black Lives Matter and other anti-racist movements.[30]

As Morrison's texts enter these spaces, the counternarratives she creates offer a new space that speaks back to, contradicts, revises, and often reimagines and transforms earlier narratives, especially America's narratives about itself, both past and present. As Michel Foucault says in *The Archaeology of Knowledge and the Discourse on Language*:

> The frontiers of a book are never clear-cut; beyond the title, the first lines and the last full stop, beyond its internal configuration and its autonomous form, it is caught up in a system of references to other books, other texts, other sentences: it is a node within a network . . . As soon as one questions the unity, it loses its self-evidence; it indicates itself, constructs itself, only on the basis of a complex field of discourse.[31]

Each novel produces a counternarrative to each historical moment into which it enters and thus comments on that moment through Morrison's reading of it and through the spaces her texts create for readers, irrespective of her position or narrative intentions as author. Thus, this study follows critic Deborah McDowell's lead in considering the value of "a dialogic method of reading" African American texts, especially those by Black women novelists.[32] Indeed, this study is an attempt to engage in the very "sort of private and broader inquiry" that Hortense Spillers felt was called for in response to McDowell's nuanced reading of *Sula*.[33] By considering a focus on the space populated by diverse communities of readers, we can gain new insights into how Morrison's writing intervenes and participates in the public sphere.

Although the concepts of counternarrative and counteraesthetics have been useful frameworks for thinking of Morrison's work, this study attempts to propose a new term that captures a return to her oeuvre with a different perspective: *narrative rememory*. In a sense, the word *counternarrative* seems ultimately unsuccessful in moving the Black subject from margin to center. In fact, there's a way in which it inadvertently participates in a reification of the power relationships of narrative rather than the destabilization that I believe Morrison's writing seeks to achieve. While she was writing *Beloved*, the novel in which her character Sethe uses the vernacular expression *rememory*, Morrison offers a statement that might explain how the term *narrative rememory* enables a new way of naming how her fiction affects the reader. In "The Site of Memory," she writes:

> How I gain access to the interior life is what drives me. . . . It's a kind of literary archaeology: on the basis of some information and a little guesswork you journey to a site to what remains were left behind and to reconstruct the world that these remains imply. What makes it fiction is the nature of the imaginative act . . . my reliance on the image—on the remains—in addition to recollection, to yield up a kind of truth. . . . By "image" I simply mean "picture" and the feelings that accompany the picture.[34]

By the time she completes *Beloved*, what we have in the words of Sethe is a fictional manifestation of how the shift from image to memory works when she explains:

> I used to think it was my rememory. . . . Some things you forget. Other things you never do. . . . Someday you walking down the road. . . . A thought picture. But no. It's when you bump into a rememory. That belong to somebody else. . . . It's . . . going to always be there waiting for you. (36–37)

The first time *rememory* is used, it is vernacular for *memory*, the noun that describes the mental activity of recollecting experiences and information. The second time, it is also used as a noun, but in this case, the word resides outside the body, outside the interior space of the mind, and is available for recognition by those subjects familiar with the experiences and information that constitute the memory. These two iterations of the term are combined in what I'm naming *narrative rememory* to describe Morrison's fiction. Rather than simply being counternarratives, narrative rememories are fictional texts that tap into history, lived life, and the imagination to create new representations of Black subjectivity. Thus, narrative rememories move blackness to the center in ways that counternarratives do not and invite readers into the text in ways that hegemonic narratives cannot. Though readers of diverse racial, ethnic, linguistic, and cultural backgrounds have and will continue to read her work, the ways in which her writing produces narrative rememories shape a new category of fictional theorizing that emerges from this rereading of her fiction.

Beloved takes the reader back in time and space to the period of enslavement and the unique excesses of parental love that emerged from the peculiar institution for Black people, in general, and Black women. On one hand, this novel is about Sethe and the implications of her act of infanticide for her own life, the lives of her surviving children, and the communities that bore witness to and had knowledge of her act. On the other hand, the text creates spaces for multiple modes of analysis and readings of American and African American history and cultural memory. Moreover, it moves the reader beyond notions of the physical realities of enslavement to interior spaces and considerations of the psychic implications of not owning one's own body or one's own children. What constructions of subjectivity and understandings of being and belonging could exist under the circumstances and in the space of such horrible oppression and how these constructions could best be represented are at the center of the text. Yet, because of Morrison's geopoetics in *Beloved*—that is, her style of representing Black interiority and moments of intersubjectivity, her prose, which foregrounds Sethe's narrative practice of "circling the subject" to avoid the psychic pain inherent in the telling, and her negotiation of the space between the past and the present—her readers have multiple points of entry into the text. In addition, *Beloved* invites an interrogation of enslavement from several perspectives—from a gendered perspective, from the perspective of the enslaved and the enslaver, and from that within the community of the enslaved. This novel appeared at the precise moment in American culture when the African American community was facing new versions of old challenges of the nation's racial dilemma. Intraracially, the late 1980s and early 1990s were a moment of diverse public opinion within the Black community. The historical claims for unity had given way to multiple perspectives that called into question what such notions of unity might look like in reality. The education of African American children in many underprivileged neighborhoods was calling into question the nation's commitment to educate all children.[35] And Afrocentricity was becoming a significant ideological perspective both within and outside of the academy at the same time that some Black public intellectuals were agreeing with many white people, according to Khalil Gibran Muhammad, in questioning the continuing significance of race in American culture.[36]

Into this network of discourse, *Beloved* enters, offering a narrative rememory of self-love to negate the growing sense of nihilism that Cornel West describes in *Race Matters* (1993).[37] Into a cultural milieu of despair over continued oppression and white supremacy and a dizzying number of responses to them, Morrison's novel narrates a story of agency, an intervention through the geopoetics of intersubjectivity, and redemption from the excesses of love and self-sabotage through self-acceptance, redemptive love, and reimagined spaces of belonging. The novel operates, therefore, especially for many Black readers who navigate their way through Morrison's complex narrative, as a balm for the nihilism that characterized the historical moment at which it was published. As I argue elsewhere, the novel disturbs "domestic tranquility," just as Margaret Garner's act of infanticide exposed the contradictions between her identity as property and the court's assertion that she should be tried for murder under the law, even though the three-fifths clause of the Constitution negated her full humanity.[38] At the same time, it creates spaces for all readers, regardless of their race, to interrogate the meaning of a moment in history about which many have been miseducated, uneducated, or undereducated. As Brand argues, "To enter Toni Morrison's fiction is to enter her rewriting of the myth of America, and so it is also a conversation . . . against the official American narrative."[39] The problem remains, however, that Morrison's narrative poetics and cultural politics both enabled the very readings for which she hoped at the same time that the sheer artifice of her poetics encouraged some readers to distance themselves from the novel and thereby miss how the text was not only a commentary on the past but also an engagement with the present.[40]

Likewise, Morrison's 1993 Nobel lecture raises some of the same issues about the reader, the text, and the connection between the two. On one hand, the lecture is a marvelous tour de force on the positive and negative power of language, the positive and negative uses to which language and narrative have been put, and the possibilities inherent in narrative for making us at the same time that we engage in the act of narration. The lecture is a magnificent example of Morrison's statement that "word-work is sublime."[41] Yet, the intergenerational dialogue between the old, blind Black woman and the two young people who accost her, or so she thinks, with their apparent ruse of asking her whether the bird in their hands is alive or dead exposes all kinds of political, cultural, and ethical questions. Morrison takes the august moment of receiving the Nobel Prize in Literature in Stockholm not simply to express gratitude for the honor but also to challenge an international audience of readers to interrogate what it is we do and do not do with language. Within the space of this intergenerational dialogue, she analyzes the policing powers and oppressive uses of language and the destructive stories we tell ourselves about ourselves and the other. Morrison uses the occasion and the location of the global stage not just to accept the congratulations on receiving the prestigious literary award but also to challenge all readers of all texts—both literary and nonliterary—to explore the consequences of language use and the radical power of narrative to subvert oppressive practices. The implications of the two spaces at once—the space of the global audience of readers and the narrative space imagined in the dialogue—are critical to this study.

A closer look at the Nobel lecture through a geopoetic lens offers an example of what is at stake in considering place, race, and be/longing in Morrison's work. While the text does not reveal for the reader the precise physical location where this intergenerational encounter takes place, what we do know is that for a designated moment in time, the old, blind, Black woman and one of the young people who says "I hold in my hand a bird. Tell me whether it is living or dead,"[42] occupy the same marginalized space and engage in dialogue that begins as a kind of narrative standoff and ends in a genuine connection made. What we do know is that the woman "lives in a small house outside of town" and that she is honored as far away as "the city where the intelligence of rural prophets is the source of amusement."[43] Morrison acknowledges that the tale appears in the lore of many cultures but insists on her version of the familiar moral tale and uses the occasion to challenge readers' presuppositions about race, gender, ability, language, and narrative all at once.[44] While the old woman harbors suspicions of their intentions, the young visitors harbor their presuppositions about her ability to know theirs. What ensues is Morrison's descriptions of the old woman's thoughts about the bird—which she chooses to read "as language and the woman as a practiced writer" (12), and her response to their query with the words, "It is in your hands" (11). The young people read her response as a dismissive stance and as an attempt to "keep . . . her distance, enforce . . . it and retreat . . . into the singularity of isolation, in sophisticated, privileged space" (24). Annoyed with her response, the young people fill the silence "with language invented on the spot" (24). They challenge her by asking her to consider their young lives rather than presuming that they wish to do her harm. They plea with her "to make up a story" (27), to acknowledge that "narrative is radical, creating us at the very moment it is being created" (27). They then do just that—make up a story and narrate it into her hearing. They also remind her:

> You, old woman, blessed with blindness, can speak the language that tells us what only language can: how to see without pictures. Language alone protects us from the scariness of things with no names. Language alone is meditation. Tell us what it is to be a woman so that we may know what it is to be a man. What moves at the margin. What it is to have no home in this place. To be set adrift from the one you knew. What it is to live at the edge of towns that cannot bear your company. (28–29)

By the time the young people move from this plea to the invented language of a scene they create in real time, the old woman has relinquished her suspicion of them and responds by saying, "I trust you now. I trust you with the bird that is not in your hands because you have truly caught it. Look. How lovely it is, this thing we have done—together" (30).

Morrison's version of the tale ends on a note of "be/longing." Between the elder's suspicion of the young people and their suspicion of her is a third space of narrative that they have mutually created and that is informed by both of their perspectives on the power of language. By the end of the tale, they have shifted from their accusatorial stances of the other and the "structure[s] of feeling" inherent in those stances to a third space characterized by an "aesthetics of belonging."[45] They suspend their distrust based on their lived identities and enter a third space of community, recognizing their common bond of being marginalized and their common capacity for resisting their marginalization and oppression through the power of the word and their mutual desire for recognition of the other from the other. As readers, we witness what Charles Taylor refers to as "the politics of recognition" play out through *nommo*, the African term for the power of the word.[46] In many respects, this study attempts to mark and map the multiple ways in which Morrison creates such spaces for her readers and for her Black subjects as readers of their own lives within the texts of her narratives, away from the white gaze and very much engaged in understanding life and living in terms mutually created.

In the metadiscursive moments that resonate in her sixth novel, *Jazz*, we have a striking example of language use that is both a generative and a resistant form of agency at one and the same time. The narrator self-reflexively says:

> They knew how little I could be counted on; how poorly, how shabbily my know-it-all self covered for helplessness. That when I invented stories about them—and doing it seemed to me so fine—I was completely in their hands, managed without mercy. I thought I'd hidden myself so well as I watched them through windows and doors, took every opportunity I had to follow them, to gossip about them and fill in their lives, and all the while they were watching me . . . they were busy being original, complicated, changeable—human, I guess you'd say, while I was the predictable one, confused in my solitude into arrogance, thinking my space, my view was the only one that was or that mattered.[47]

In some respects, this study reveals how the subjects onto which critics have cast their gaze—especially Black women and people of color—have indeed been engaged in their own forms of theorizing, constructing, and representing their subjectivity that must be figured into notions of culture. As the narrator in *Jazz* says, "Something is missing there. Something rogue. Something you have to figure in before you can figure it out."[48]

The combination of cultural studies, Black studies, and feminist studies in the context of more recent developments in spatial humanities and spatial literary studies offers us some new ways of reentering Morrison's body of work and exploring place, race, and belonging through the lens of geopoetics to figure out how she does what she does. Like Davis, I am seeking "an engagement with the politics of race, space, and representation," but I am doing so through the lens of geopoetics to explore Morrison's "aesthetics of belonging."[49] An aesthetics of belonging, like a "culture of belonging," to quote bell hooks, is characterized not by a denial of Black history and Black pain but instead by a mindful examination of how Black people read the circumstances of their lives, map "an oppositional world view," and affirm their humanity in spite of and because of the places in which they have found themselves.[50] Written in a way to reveal how Black subjects read the spaces of their lives and attempt to create spaces of belonging, Morrison's work invites us to interrogate how space has been theorized through her fiction. In many ways, this study is in dialogue with that of other scholars, including hooks, Hartman, and Kirby, who have been theorizing about what McKittrick refers to as "black women's geographies," on one hand and with such scholars as Brand, Kevin Quashie, and Christina Sharpe, who are engaged in interrogating blackness in terms of the everyday, quotidian ways Black people imagine and reimagine ways of being and belonging, on the other hand. My review of earlier studies on Morrison, including Valerie Sweeney Prince's *Burnin' Down the House: Home in African American Literature* (2005), Evelyn Jaffee Schreiber's *Race, Trauma and Home in the Novels of Toni Morrison* (2010), Yvette Christiansë's *Toni Morrison: An Ethical Poetics* (2012), and Herman Beavers's *Geography and the Political Imaginary in the Novels of Toni Morrison* (2018), informs my understanding of her fiction. Unlike these studies, however, this one attempts to reenter Morrison's body of work from another angle—that of geopoetics—to determine the kinds of narrative strategies at work in her representations of place, race, and belonging.

Reading Morrison through her geopoetics delineates the narrative strategies that undergird her work and invites a clarification of the three terms that are critical to this study—*place*, *race*, and *belonging*. Though my use of the term *place* is informed by Bhabha's "location of culture" and Hartman's "scenes of subjection," it is also informed by Yi-Fu Tuan's distinction between place and space.[51] As a geographer, Tuan was uniquely aware that the word *place* connotes a boundedness with dimensions of height, depth, width, color, and so on. *Space*, on the other hand, connotes how we experience a place, give it meaning, and understand ourselves in relation to it. Though the terms are sometimes used interchangeably, how we experience a place and how we are situated in relation to a place make all the difference.[52] Looking more closely at Morrison's representation of place invites us, therefore, to move beyond commonsense, taken-for-granted understandings of geographical locations to the networks of meanings that lie within and around them, especially for Black subjects. Using Doreen Massey's argument that place and space are always interconnected and part of a "dynamic simultaneity . . . in the production of social relations," we can interpret Morrison's geopoetics as a series of narrative strategies enabling us to read simultaneously how her characters are located in various places at the intersection of race, class, and gender and how they read those locations as spaces from which to construct their sense of Black subjectivity.[53] As one of the narrative strategies that reveals her geopoetics, discursive mediation is evident in the way Morrison draws our attention as readers from the places in which her characters are located to the ways in which they read those spaces to make meaning of their lives. Those spaces are never one or the other but always a hybrid reality of both/and—that is, a reality of how they interpenetrate or are mutually interconnected. The narrator of *The Bluest Eye* articulates how this interconnectedness of narratives works when she observes at the conclusion that the protagonist, Pecola, destroyed by self-loathing, rape, and the town's disregard, can still be seen at the edge of town, among the "tire rims and the sunflowers" (205). Between the discourses of place that shape the novel, Morrison crafts spaces for the reader to mediate between and among to prevent them from jumping too easily to conclusions as to where to cast guilt or blame for Pecola's undoing.

Like *place*, *race* is another term that has commonsense, taken-for-granted connotations that can benefit from some unpacking and clarification, not only for how Morrison references it in her fiction but also for how it is connected to her larger artistic project as an author and public intellectual. While an in-depth definition is both unnecessary and beyond the scope and focus of this study, as a baseline, I refer to *race* both as a socially constructed phenomenon and as a political concept that circulates in culture to shape identity and social relations. In other words, given that Morrison describes America as a society that is "racialized and race-conscious," how those realities show up in her representations of Black and white subjectivity are crucial to understanding how she uses discursive mediation as a geopoetic strategy.[54] As West argues, we must also be mindful that because race is connected to skin color and African phenotype as it operates in culture, "blackness is a political and ethical construct."[55] Thus, interrogating what Claudine Rankin describes as "the scene of race, taking up residence in the creative act" or what she calls the "racial imaginary," especially as it affects Black female subjectivity, is critical for our understanding of race in Morrison's work.[56] Morrison posits this concern in *Playing in the Dark* when she explains that she is deeply invested in understanding how "racial 'unconscious' or awareness of race enrich interpretive language, and when does it impoverish it?"[57] Moreover, to pay attention to the racial imaginary as it manifests itself in her fiction is also to pay attention to its intersectional dimensions and to how race always already requires that we take gender into account, as Kimberle Crenshaw reminds us in her frameworks for mapping the margins shaped by race and gender.[58]

While this study proposes that Morrison's readers bear witness to the spatial and racial imaginaries at work in her writing, it also argues that her geopoetics provide a lens into another related theme in her work: the theme of belonging. On one hand, belonging is a process that involves another kind of discursive mediation that Spillers aptly describes as "negotiating the ground between forms of exile and belonging."[59] Thus, belonging is connected to one's relationship to a place or a sense of place. In one novel after another, we read characters negotiating the terms of being treated or feeling in and out of various places, however it is defined by the powers that be. On the other hand, in Morrison's work, belonging also entails negotiating the terms of being and what Tate refers to as "desire and the protocols of race" that represent efforts to shape narrative spaces that require "the active complicity of a reader willing to step outside established boundaries of the racial imaginary."[60] Located between the exterior and interior are spaces of yearning and structures of feeling that are informed but not entirely defined by either. The term *belonging*, therefore, invites us to consider terms of connection between the self and the other, or what Jessica Benjamin refers to as the "paradox of recognition."[61] Or, as Taylor explains, the terms of mutual recognition are both public and private. In Morrison's work, her geopoetics of discursive mediation are reflected in her efforts to explore belonging as a public phenomenon of being and as a private struggle to shape the terms of one's subjectivity in ways that are consistent with one's values and desires. From her first novel to her last, this complex interplay of external and internal forces is apparent in how her characters understand belonging in the context of community and in the challenges to a sense of belonging that she creates for her readers.

Undergirding this study of Morrison as a writer and public intellectual are four narrative strategies that emerge from reading her through the lens of geopoetics: the ways in which her writing continuously engages in discursive mediation or the logic of both/and thinking to address the complexity of the third space of the interior lives of Black subjects that lies between binary oppositional either/or frameworks; the ways in which she creates emancipatory spaces for reading that destabilize received narratives of the dominant culture and spaces for Black subjects and those who attempt to "read" them; the ways in which she uses narrative rememory to illustrate how the past insinuates itself into the present for her characters and shapes their reading of the places where they find themselves as Black subjects and how they use the power of rememory to create spaces of belonging in the present; and the ways in which her representations and interrogations of house and home deromanticize and destabilize received notions of home to reveal the paradoxical properties of belonging found in domestic spaces that can both constrain them from being and enable them to be "both snug and wide open."[62] This closer scrutiny of the relationship between texts and readers reveals spaces for recuperating, affirming, and understanding the meanings of place in her work as an antidote to misrepresentations of Black life and culture that lock Black people solely in identities of the history of enslavement, collective trauma, or locations in marginalized spaces and consequently overlook the plenitude of cultural formations that have emerged from the very spaces designed to contain. As Black people in the church community often say, "we are not what we have been through," though we are not in denial that what we have been through has partly constituted who we are. Ultimately, my goal is to come to terms with a wider, more comprehensive way of reading Morrison's body of work by focusing through geopoetics on the spaces for the reader—both in and outside of her texts and the meanings of place, race, and belonging—that her writing invites us to enter, interrogate, understand, and reimagine.

Chapter 1, "Crafting Spaces for the Reader: The Geopoetics of Discursive Mediation," identifies Morrison's 1988 essay, "Unspeakable Things Unspoken," as a turning point in her career because it signals her growing respect for literary criticism and the ability of critics to produce meaningful responses to her work. In that essay, we see her both drawing on a wide body of interdisciplinary scholarship and engaging in a close reading of the first line of each of her novels. The implications of a living writer participating in such an active way in the interpretive discourse that surrounds her writing are explored in this chapter, but more importantly, we see her intentionally and meticulously crafting a place for the reader to enter her texts in what she hopes are nonconventional ways. Using a close analysis of place, race, and belonging in *The Bluest Eye*, Morrison's first novel, published in 1970, this chapter includes an analysis of *Song of Solomon* and *Tar Baby*. In the opening lines of the novel is a prenarrative excerpt from a preschool primer, the very kind of primer once used in early American preschool education to teach children how to read. Although most critics consider the lines "Quiet as it's kept" as the beginning of the novel, the excerpt from the primer that precedes the body of the narrative is ripe for analysis in terms of place, race, and belonging for understanding the context of the narrative inside the novel itself. In fact, it could be argued that the primer excerpt announces Morrison's lifelong agenda of challenging received ways of reading and knowing that have constituted an assault on Black subjects and their ways of being, reading, and making sense of their lives. This chapter also considers Morrison's 1993 afterword to the newer edition of the novel, which offers a retrospective glance at *The Bluest Eye* in terms of her authorial intentions and reader responses. I argue that Morrison created new spaces for her readers by mapping out the development of her poetic, cultural, and political concerns in that essay. These concerns had already been introduced artistically, however, in *The Bluest Eye*, a text that entered the public sphere by creating space for stories about racially and culturally tabooed subjects. This chapter also includes geopoetic reflections on *Sula*, *Song of Solomon*, and *Tar Baby* through the characterizations Sula, Pilate, and Jadine as examples of Morrison's theorizing about place, race, and belonging in her writing. While she was known for rejecting praise of her lyricism and of descriptions of herself as a "poetic writer," this chapter seeks to foreground, nonetheless, the aesthetic dynamics of her narrative fiction for their ability to illuminate the discursive mediation (that is, the movement and connection between binary oppositional thoughts) at work in the language and protocols of reading she represents in the art of her early fiction.[63]

Chapter 2, "Spatializing the Self: The Geopoetics of Emancipatory Spaces," builds on the geopoetic strategy of discursive mediation and argues that Morrison consistently presents characters who "read" their circumstances and set about imagining and creating alternative ways of being and belonging despite those circumstances. They create "third spaces" or emancipatory spaces. Through an analysis of selected female characters in *Sula*, *Jazz*, *Beloved*, and *Paradise*, I argue that Morrison's geopoetics offer ways of rereading history through the eyes of Black subjectivity. Including a discussion of *Beloved* in the trilogy on excesses of love as the novel about the horrors of the Middle Passage, the Transatlantic Slave Trade, enslavement in America, and a mother's infanticide as an act of love, this chapter interrogates Morrisons's geopoetics through the ways in which the narrative flows, through her representations of a Black community under duress, and through the ways of being and belonging they create to imagine, reimagine, and save themselves in the midst of the assault on their minds and bodies. It will examine the role of women through the ways in which they map spaces for themselves or attempt to do so and how those strategies speak back to ways of knowing, being, and belonging in contemporary American culture and society. In *Jazz*, recognizing how the Great Migration precipitated the need to reimagine the self and interrogating the strategies Black people used to create a new life in a new place are only part of what makes this novel an important text for rereading Morrison through a geopoetic lens. The novel also illustrates her very self-conscious narrative innovation through metadiscursive forays into the narrative—that is, the narrator—speaking back directly to the reader and calling her role into question. The second-guessing that the narrator engages in reinforces the paradoxical space in which Black people found themselves during the so-called Jazz Age, also known as the Harlem Renaissance. Morrison is not engaged in constructing a coherent narrative, however, but in representing the complex interior lives of women and men and the strategies they imagined and enacted to create spaces of being and belonging.

Chapter 3, "Circling the Subject: The Geopoetics of Narrative Rememory," argues that when Morrison discussed *Jazz*, *Beloved*, and *Paradise* as a trilogy about excesses of love, she was doing much more than that in each novel from a geopoetics perspective. Each novel in the trilogy engages in a kind of narrative aesthetic exploration of how to imagine and represent Black subjectivity in three different historical moments of extreme dislocation. This chapter moves from that trilogy to a consideration of memory in *Beloved*, *A Mercy*, and *Home* to interrogate how Morrison simultaneously creates the same disorienting experience for her reader that her characters experience as they navigate the spaces history has created. In each of these three novels, Morrison experiments with narrative and language in ways that disorient the reader in an effort to capture the historical sense of disorientation of Black people reading a new location, entering a new time and space, and determining how memory both constrains and enables a sense of being and belonging in a new situation.

Chapter 4, "A Matter of Be/longing: Geopoetic Interrogations of Home," examines the geopoetics at work in Morrison's representation of house and home throughout her work, especially in *Home, God Help the Child*, and the essay "The Foreigner's Home." Returning to Morrison's essay "Home," in which she shares the thinking undergirding the writing of *Paradise*, this chapter also attempts to place her preoccupation with reimaging home as a central concern of her geopoetics and work as a public intellectual. In some respects, *Paradise* is almost a sequel to the existential ideas introduced at the end of *The Bluest Eye* and a prequel to the existential ideas Morrison takes on in her collection of essays *The Origin of Others* (2017). This chapter also comments on her essay "God's Language" in *The Source of Self-Regard*, where she elaborates on the ideas about religion that she introduces in *Paradise*. I argue that Morrison is attempting at every turn to engage her readers in the serious work of reading against racial, gendered, and even spiritual presuppositions of home to explore what belonging could mean if read and understood through the spaces in which Black subjects have read and found themselves. How belonging matters and gets represented in her work through her representations of house and home constitute not just a political preoccupation of her writing but a geopoetics of interrogating notions of home in the racial imaginary.

The concluding chapter, "Toni Morrison's Spaces for Readers: The Geopoetics of the Dancing Mind," argues that from "Recitatif" to "The Foreigner's Home," Morrison's readers can discern how her narrative strategies constitute a geopoetics of concern with place, race, and belonging not only to illuminate the cultural politics that have shaped our lives but also to illustrate, through the very narrative strategies she deploys, how our work as readers is to discern alternative spaces to shape our own reading and understanding of our lives and the future we seek to create for ourselves and in relation to others. This chapter focuses on some of her nonfiction writing, such as the essay "Invisible Ink: Reading the Writing and Writing the Reading," where she ruminates on the work of the imagination in the act of reading, whether in the classroom or in private.[64] Readers must navigate the same inconsistencies, contradictions, and mental juxtapositions that plague her characters and, by so doing, rethink domestic and global notions of home, democracy, and freedom. As in "Recitatif," she creates what Lesley Larkin names "reading encounters" so that her readers are left to their own devices in attempting to establish a sense of equilibrium as they make meaning within the self and in community with others, regardless of the spatial arrangements that are shaping their lived lives.[65] In the panoply of lectures she gave and essays she wrote, Morrison demonstrated how the aesthetics of belonging and the work of the imagination were always the terrain of her intellectual work inside and outside of her novels. In many regards, whether inside the space of her novels or that of her speeches and essays, she was concerned with ways of knowing, being, and belonging that had been discredited but were valuable beyond measure to Black people and what Black people had contributed to the nation and the world. As she argues at the end of *The Source of Self-Regard*, however, in some respects, her journey was always connected to her desire to not be "a (raced) foreigner but a home girl, who already belonged to the human race" (345). *Toni Morrison and the Geopoetics of Place, Race, and Bellonging* maps the various ways in which her body of work created spaces for her journey but also for her readers, who she wanted to "work *with* the author in the construction of the book" and thereby engage in the "word-work" that shaped her oeuvre.[66] Ultimately, this study attempts to unpack some of the inner workings of Morrison's word-work in a new way.

1

Crafting Spaces for the Reader

The Geopoetics of Discursive Mediation

> The play between the exterior and intimacy is not a balanced one. . . . Our soul is our abode.
> —GASTON BACHELARD, *The Poetics of Space*[1]

The fact that Toni Morrison's very first novel, *The Bluest Eye*, begins with an epigraph from an elementary school primer is significant. In many respects, beginning her first work of fiction in 1970 with an excerpt from a text used to teach children to read is Morrison's earliest strategy for introducing her readers to what would be a lifelong concern with the art of writing and the act of reading. When we consider all the ways her work has been the subject of book bans and other forms of censorship, her early attention to the act of reading and to its potential to be racialized and politicized was prophetic.[2] Put another way, the novel is an introduction to what Anne Cheng refers to as Morrison's critique of "the pedagogy of racism" and what Baldwin refers to as "one of the paradoxes of education," which is that your education makes you feel compelled to change the society in which you find yourself.[3] In the sense that those early primers were also an introduction to American cultural values and ideas about race, it could be argued that Morrison's first novel is an intervention at the very site that contributes to the acculturation and subsequent psychic unraveling that happens to the protagonist of *The Bluest Eye*. In fact, one way of reading the novel is to view it as Morrison's foray into transforming what she calls "the race house" by destabilizing, dislodging, and deconstructing its representation of itself.[4]

By the time readers complete the novel, they may not even recall this unassuming prenarrative text or the significance of its strategic placement before the tragic tale of Pecola Breedlove. Nonetheless, Morrison uses it to begin theorizing through narrative fiction about American education, aesthetics, and culture. By placing this epigraph at the beginning of the novel as a kind of preamble, she illustrates how the cultural and aesthetic values promulgated in childhood are introduced at what Christiansë correctly describes as the site of the "acquisition of literacy" for the Black subject that Morrison identifies as "the most vulnerable member of society"—a female child.[5] Given that the site at which one acquires literacy was historically also the site at which one reads texts that excluded the Black female subject from self-recognition, the primer can be read as a site at which one was introduced to reading against oneself. Thus, the site of the acquisition of literacy for a black girl is also, to use Hartman's phrase, a space where there are "scenes of subjection."[6] This chapter seeks to interrogate how Morrison's geopoetics of discursive mediation in *The Bluest Eye*, *Sula*, *Song of Solomon*, and *Tar Baby* provide examples of her theorizing through narrative about the received notions of self and other colored by white supremacy, racism, sexism, and poverty. Within the spaces that her characters find themselves—between the two extremes of how they are perceived and how they read their own lives—are the ways in which they successfully and sometimes unsuccessfully create a plenitude of being and belonging from the spaces of lack and oppression. To quote Bhabha, Morrison creates "liminal signifying space" for her readers to reconsider the "strategies of selfhood" her characters deploy in the very places or "locations of culture" that have been overlooked, marginalized, or taken for granted.[7] Or, as Davis asserts, "writers of color claim the very space that would negate their humanity and devalue their worth," and by so doing, they offer readers new ways to read the "spatial-racial nexus."[8] A closer look at the discourse in Morrison's early fiction reveals how she intentionally mediates liminal spaces between dominant and marginalized subject positions.

The words that open *The Bluest Eye*—"Here is the house. It is green and white"—take readers into what Spillers refers to as Morrison's "house of fiction."[9] Beginning the novel with an epigraph from the apparently innocent location of a children's primer at the site of a generic house painted green and white is not so innocent or benign. What the epigraph from the primer suggests is that the use of the definite article *the* and the colors *green* and *white* is an aesthetic decision Morrison makes to escort her reader into the text. The definite article *the* directs the reader to the standard, normalized, official dominant narrative of whiteness through which all American readers have historically been introduced to the world of literacy, American culture, and the "racialized house" that is the subject of Morrison's critique. Introduced through the dominant colors of *green* and *white* at the intersection of capitalism and race, the primer reflects how such children's books though ostensibly texts for the acquisition of literacy, nonetheless historically introduced young readers to representations of place, race, and being, even before they had full conscious awareness of how their mindsets were being influenced.[10] So, it is not just the house of the childhood primer but the house of American culture to which the readers of these texts were being introduced. From the house as a physical place to the colors of green and white, Morrison's aesthetic choices foreshadow how capitalism flows and does not flow and how those who wield power share and do not extend power, knowledge, and resources to people of color, women, the poor, and other marginalized members of the community. The reader is set up, therefore, with this pristine and innocent though superficial "very pretty" representation of home in very sharp contrast to and against which to measure the neighborhood spaces where her characters live.

In other words, *The Bluest Eye* is Morrison's opening artistic salvo into her literary interrogation of the hegemonic aesthetics that have dominated the American narrative's representation about itself, its values, and its culture. Such an interrogation of what hooks refers to as an "aesthetics of space" is akin to delineating the "cognitive mapping" that Fredric Jameson describes as the process by which subjects use language in the "struggle with and for representation."[11] With this epigraph, Morrison invites the reader into her antiracism project by invoking and destabilizing the dominant official narrative to make space for a narrative category that reads against it and that places black subjects at the center of their own narrative.[12] Years after the publication of *The Bluest Eye*, in the 1988 essay "Unspeakable Things Unspoken," Morrison offers what amounts to a rationale for her narrative project of creating new spaces for readers when she says:

> We have always been imagining ourselves.... We are the subjects of our own narrative, witnesses to and participating in our own experience, and in no way coincidentally, in the experience of those with whom we have come in contact.... We are not, in fact, "Other." We are choices. And to read imaginative literature by and about us is to choose to examine centers of the self and to have the opportunity to compare these centers with the 'raceless' one with which we are, all of us, most familiar.[13]

It could be argued that even from the beginning of her career as a writer, then, Morrison was intentionally seeking to map the process and the consequences of the process of placing black subjects at the margin rather than the center of their lives. Thus, as early as *The Bluest Eye*, Morrison introduces her readers to her geopoetics of discursive mediation—that is, to her production of discourse that invites the reader to bear witness to and participate in the process of reading between official narratives and lived narratives, between the margin and the center, and between self and other. The discourse in the novel therefore invites the reader to mediate the spaces between these narratives by paying attention to how her characters do the same.

It also could be argued that the use of this excerpt from a childhood primer as the epigraph for the novel is in many respects a return to another place that Morrison could refer to as a "site of memory."[14] The epigraph represents an archival space to which she returns as an artist—not to rehearse all its superficial contours but to invoke its silences, absences, omissions, subtextual meanings, and effects. Thus, the epigraph is the *archive*, to use the Foucauldian sense of the word, through which Morrison represents the discursive texture of its subtextual meanings and quotidian effects of the previously unacknowledged space of the interior life of black subjects.[15] Through Morrison's imagination, the reader gains access to Claudia's reading of her own life, Pecola's life, and the life of their Lorain, Ohio, community. Thus, the primer becomes a form of originary site that must be deconstructed, resisted, and exposed for its omissions and its role in the pedagogy of racism. From the text of the primer, however, is another originary site to which Morrison returns: the site of the Black community in Lorain, Morrison's own birthplace. Represented as the site of her upbringing, both in the town and in the McTeer household, the domestic space in *The Bluest Eye* is the other originary space that constitutes the "in-between" or "third space" of Claudia's narrative, a space much like what Bhabha describes in *The Location of Culture*.[16] But the third space of Claudia's narrative is not only an index to her reading between the public and private spaces of her life but also a representation of her desire to read against received racial narratives, to call them into question, and to create a space for belonging out of her act of bearing witness and giving voice to what had been unspoken about Black selfhood.

In the economy of language that was characteristic of those early primers, Morrison uses a form of foreshadowing. The short passage from the primer refers to the mother, the father, and presumably their two children, Dick and Jane. Other than his name, there is no further mention of Dick. However, there is attention to Jane in several respects—namely, her clothing, her desire to have someone play with her, and the disregard for her from everyone in the household, including her mother, her father, the cat, and the dog. At every turn, Jane's desire for attention and for someone to play with is thwarted. Inside the space of her own household, she is ignored by her family and reduced to what she is wearing—"a red dress"—until her friend, who remains nondescript and unnamed, comes to play with her. So even in the presumed space of ideal normalcy, Morrison both invokes white normativity and deconstructs it. Put another way, Morrison calls into question the very notion of perfection that had been taken for granted in the space of the elementary school primers used to introduce American children to the reading process. Moreover, she foreshadows the more complex, complicated disregard at the intersection of racism and sexism that will shape the life of her novel's Black child protagonist.

Morrison continues the introduction to the family in the primer with the words: "Mother, Father, Dick and Jane live in the green-and-white house."[17] The lack of names for the parents and the hyphenated reference to the house illustrate Morrison's authorial intention to signal how the larger culture presents a hierarchical accumulation of power and wealth. What appears to be a simple narrative on the first page of the novel, however, begins to dissolve on the second page, where Morrison omits the punctuation and leaves spaces between the words of the text in the second representation of the primer excerpt. This second version of the text can be read as a foreshadowing of what is to come in the novel. In contradistinction to the neatly spaced and correctly punctuated text of the primer according to the rules and accepted structures of grammar, the second version of the text represents a rupture in the so-called normal order of things with the house and the people who occupy it. The punctuation disappears, and the names are presented in lowercase, representing another alteration to the received structures of place, people, and the order of things. By the time the reader gets to the third iteration of the text from the primer, it has devolved into one long string of words with no spaces between them, devoid of punctuation and recognizable meaning. The preamble to the narrative represents in stark aesthetic terms, therefore, the overarching structures, locations, and systems against which the Black subjects in the story of Pecola Breedlove will be presented in the novel. In many respects, therefore, it could be argued that the novel begins "in the break," as Fred Moten would suggest, "in the space between expression and meaning," in anticipation of a narrative that represents the disruption to childhood innocence that the intersection of racism and sexism is.[18]

But even before we meet Pecola, we enter the novel through the perspective of Claudia McTeer, the narrator, who begins by letting the reader in on how she has read the text of her life, of her family, of the family of Pecola Breedlove, and of the neighborhood in which they live. The words that begin the novel—"Quiet as it's kept"—indicate that Claudia has read the spaces of her environment in two ways at once. She has read what she has been told and what she has observed with her own eyes, even if it has not been told. In the interstitial space between the two is the difficult truth that even nature is revealing the story she is about to unfold for the reader, even if no one else was willing to share what Morrison calls the "unspeakable things unspoken."[19] As the novel states,

> Quiet as it's kept, there were no marigolds in the fall of 1941. We thought, at the time, that it was because Pecola was having her father's baby that the marigolds did not grow. A little examination and much less melancholy would have proved to us that our seeds were not the only ones that did not sprout; nobody's did.... It was a long time before my sister and I admitted to ourselves that no green was going to spring from our seeds.... It never occurred to either of us that the earth itself might have been unyielding. (5)

In this opening passage of the novel, Morrison introduces the reader to a kind of multiscale reading of the systems surrounding the narrator, the protagonist, and the community in which they live. The challenges to being and belonging in the spaces of home as house, neighborhood, and the environment of the very earth itself are all introduced in this passage. However, because the novel begins with gossip—that is, with the disclosure of a secret—the narrator implicates the reader from the beginning, as Morrison explains in the afterword she wrote to the novel in 1993, and thereby "distribute[s] . . . the weight of . . . problematical questions to a larger constituency . . . [and that is] the circle of listeners," or what I call the *community of readers*, who are now in on the secret.[20] Ironically, in 2001, on the occasion of her seventieth birthday, Morrison would describe her journey as a writer as one that began simply with a very personal desire to express herself, to write to see her own "dancing mind" in print; however, over time, that desire became other-directed toward readers, then toward critics, and ultimately toward the larger community of readers.[21] The author's retrospective statement of her overall intentions notwithstanding, readers of this first novel enter the narrative with both a knowing sense of implication and a desire to know precisely how they could possibly be implicated in such a disruption of the environmental and social order. By sharing a community secret, the narrator implicates herself and reveals that the narrative is as much about Pecola's demise as it is about her own loss of innocence. By using a vernacular expression known for its discursive mediation between what is known and who knows it, Morrison invites the reader into the text through familiar language about transgressive behavior and how it circulates within a community through spaces of so-called private conversations.

Morrison's interrogation of beauty through Pecola's desire for blue eyes is achieved with these three levels of reading at once—that of the reader, the narrator, and the community. But the text makes an early disclosure about the kind of narrative space being created for the reader. It clarifies that *"since why is difficult to handle, one must take refuge in* how."[22] Another way to frame the binary of *why* and *how* is to read it as an example of discursive mediation. In other words, the reader is invited to consider both *why* and *how* and to mediate between the two, knowing that the narrator's focus will be constitutive of both dynamics of what happened and how it happened, just as this study attempts to explicate content and context, text and subtext, and politics and aesthetics all through the lens of geopoetics. The refuge that the narrator takes in *how*, however, signals a narrative device designed to provide space for the reader to engage in the more difficult work of determining causation and of interpreting the complex, multivalent tale that is at the center of her story.

The McTeer household is represented as a domestic space of relative normalcy in the Black community. Through Claudia's descriptions of her home, her parents, and their language with other adults, we learn of her efforts to read between the lines of adult conversations. She notes:

> Their conversation is like a gently wicked dance: sound meets sound, curtsies, shimmies, and retires. Another sound enters, but is upstaged by still another: the two circle each other and stop. Sometimes their words move in lofty spirals; other times they take strident leaps, and all of it is punctuated with warm-pulsed laughter—like the throb of a heart made of jelly. . . . We do not, cannot, know the meanings of all their words, for we are nine and ten years old. So we watch their faces, their hands, their feet, and listen for truth in timbre. (15)

The language, metaphors, movement, and sound that catch Claudia's attention can also be read as the author linguistically playing in her first novel with drawing the reader into what Claudia Brodsky called Morrison's acts of "aesthetic activity" that "cause the reader to join . . . in a specular relationship."[23] For Morrison, the activity is never just specular, however; it is also always oral. On one hand, we have the innocence of a child's attention to sound and the elusiveness of meaning. On the other hand, we have the author's attention to how language operates and creates "truth in timbre" or spaces for the reader to acknowledge their own subjectivity and tentative understanding of the text even as they read it. Morrison will return to this kind of metanarrative more explicitly in *Jazz*, but it is noteworthy that she was attentive, in a very self-conscious way, to the complex interplay between language and meaning for the reader in this first novel. The relative normalcy, safety, and comfort of the McTeer home is signaled not only by the innocent observations of a hypervigilant child but also by the role the family plays in taking in two homeless boarders partly to supplement their own income and partly to help neighbors in distress. The McTeers take in Mr. Henry Washington, a charming gentleman who apparently has no family who can take him in, and Pecola Breedlove, a child whose fate has been decided by the state after her father's incarceration results in their being evicted from their home. These two individuals—an unassuming boarder who turns out to be a lewd and lascivious child molester and an innocent child who is a victim of poverty, incest, rape, and eviction—set the stage for Morrison to interrogate the meanings of house and home, the aesthetics of beauty and Black subjectivity, and the ways in which Black subjects navigate the desire for belonging in a society that does not value their existence.

But even before we learn more about these two guests, we have an example of how the lens of geopoetics can enable a rereading of *The Bluest Eye*. In the following passage, Morrison situates the narrative as a site to interrogate how the Black community reads displacement and homelessness from within and apart from the gaze of the racial other:

> Outdoors, we knew, was the real terror of life.... There is a difference between being put *out* and being put *outdoors*.... The distinction was subtle but final. Outdoors was the end of something, an irrevocable, physical fact, defining and complementing our metaphysical condition. Being a minority in both caste and class, we moved about anyway on the hem of life, struggling to consolidate our weaknesses and hang on, or to creep singly up into the major folds of the garment. Our peripheral existence, however, was something we had learned to deal with.... But the concreteness of being outdoors was another matter—like the difference between the concept of death and being.... Knowing that there was such a thing as outdoors bred in us a hunger for property, for ownership. (17–18)

The distinction between being put out (the status of Mr. Henry) and being put outdoors (the status of Pecola Breedlove and her family) indicates early in the narrative the multiscale ways that place matters and that the conditions that lead to one's location matter as well. The novel illustrates in Morrison's painstaking, meticulous attention to detail the interdependence between the context of the community and the context of home for making meaning of the narratives of the lives of her characters. The narrator's reading of the two is significant for how they direct the reader to see not only the external forces shaping the McTeer and Breedlove households but also how they read the interior dimensions of their own lives. For example, the narrator states that the Breedloves lived in a dilapidated storefront house "because they were poor and black, and they stayed there because they believed they were ugly.... They had looked ... and saw nothing to contradict ... the ugliness" (38–39). Black subjectivity, therefore, in Morrison's first novel, is a matter not only of how her characters arrived at their spatial locations but also of how they read and cope with the locations where they find themselves.

In contradistinction to the Breedloves are those who owned their homes. To own a home, or, in the language of the text, to be "propertied black people" (18), was to imagine and attempt to concretize a space to shape one's identity on one's own terms and to protect oneself from the perceptions of the other. In just a few sentences, Morrison illustrates how Black people transformed spaces into what Erica Carter and others refer to as "places of cultural belonging."[24] In other words, in the same narrative space where she illustrates the vagaries and implications of homelessness for one's sense of identity in a racialized society, she describes the strategies that propertied people used to shore up their identities, even at the risk of being viewed as Black homeowners who "overdecorated everything; fussed and fidgeted over their hard-won homes ... painted, picked, and poked at every corner of their houses" (18). Rather than interpret these propensities as excesses of desire, however, Morrison presents them as examples of what Zora Neale Hurston calls "the will to adorn" and as an affirmation of Black imagination, self-expression, and subjectivity.[25] What at first glance could be read simply as excess to avoid the appearance of lack, therefore, in Morrison's representation of Black subjectivity is instead an excess of plenitude that simultaneously affirms a sense of place, being, and belonging shaped on one's own terms.

At the heart of the novel is Morrison's interrogation of beauty, the commodification of it, and the representation of Claudia's reading and resistance to that commodification. Through the lens of geopoetics, we can see how Morrison uses domestic and communal spaces to interrogate how Black female subjectivity is shaped in part by received notions of aesthetics represented in Shirley Temple and "the gift of dolls" (19). Pecola Breedlove's desire for blue eyes becomes the canvas for Morrison's literary exploration of how Black female subjects read and interpret cultural representations of beauty in relation to their bodies. This interrogation of beauty and the Black female body begins in her early fiction and extends through last novel, *God Help the Child*, published in 2015.[26] And even though the term had not yet come into the coherent currency in the late sixties that it now has in literary/critical/cultural studies circles, as early as her first novel, Morrison was introducing her readers to an intersectional analysis through her fictional representation of how racism and sexism are manifested in Black female subjectivity.[27] In the afterword to the

1993 edition of *The Bluest Eye*, published on the twentieth anniversary of the novel and in the same year that she was awarded the Nobel Prize, Morrison makes her narrative intentions explicit:

> Beauty was not simply something to behold; it was something to *do*. *The Bluest Eye* was my effort to say something about that. . . . Implicit in her [Pecola's] desire was racial self-loathing. . . . Who looked at her and found her so wanting, so small a weight on the beauty scale? The novel pecks away at the gaze that condemned her . . . [and] how something as grotesque as the demonization of an entire race could take root inside the most delicate member of society; a child; the most vulnerable member; a female. (210–211)

On one hand, Morrison was acutely aware that Black people across the nation and the African diaspora were engaged in the "reclamation of racial beauty" (210), a cultural and political project represented in such pronouncements as "Black is beautiful." On the other hand, she wanted to illustrate the contradistinction between the rhetoric of the historical moment and the lived lives of those Black people, especially Black girls, who had not internalized the positive message or been treated with the high regard their humanity deserved. In many respects, the novel attempts to eviscerate the very concept of beauty itself by painstakingly unpacking how white supremacist notions of beauty get introduced into the psyche of a Black girl in three ways—through language, images, and symbols, through marketing and merchandise, and through communal reinforcement.

The power of Morrison's narrative, however, is that it lays bare multiple strategies of resistance to white norms of beauty. The references to Shirley Temple signal this resistance. Recognized as a 1930s iconic blonde child actress who could sing and was known for dancing with Bill "Bojangles" Robinson, the famous Black male dancer, Shirley Temple personified a desirable standard of beauty of the era. When Claudia's sister welcomes Pecola into their home by offering her milk in a Shirley Temple cup, the narrative literally illustrates the consumption of an image of beauty that is paradoxically both outside and inside the Black community. When Frieda and Pecola gaze fondly at the image and express their adoration in "loving conversation" (19), Claudia muses on her hatred of the image. Her vehement pronouncement that she prefers "Jane Withers" to Shirley Temple signals her resistance to the iconic white image and her attempt to replace that image with one of her own choosing. As the dark-haired obnoxious costar of Shirley Temple, Jane Withers was an example of the Hollywood propensity to juxtapose light- and dark-skin-toned actors in assigning value and in foregrounding who to celebrate and who to demonize or look on with less favor.

But Claudia's rejection of the cultural icon goes further. Recognizing that she "had not yet arrived in the turning point in the development of [her] psyche which would allow [her] to love [her]"—that is, Shirley Temple—she connects the image to the dolls she and her sister received at Christmas (19). Her "unsullied hatred" (19) of Shirley Temple shows up in her propensity to "dismember" the very dolls "that the world said [were] lovable" (20–21). Dismembering the dolls becomes her strategy of resisting the images of all the dolls she received that "were supposed to bring . . . great pleasure, [but] succeeded in doing quite the opposite" (20). Her desire to dismember the dolls is explained as follows:

> I had only one desire: to dismember it. To see of what it was made, to discover the dearness, to find the beauty, the desirability that had escaped me, but apparently only me. Adults, older girls, shops, magazines, newspapers, window signs—all the world had agreed that a blue-eyed, yellow-haired, pink skinned doll was what every girl child treasured. . . . I could examine it to see what it was that all the world said was lovable. (20–21)

In the graphic description of how she dismembered the doll, the narrator illustrates her displeasure and her resistance to how her family has colluded in the conspiracy against her self-worth. From within the domestic space of house and home, the community's standard of beauty and the consumerist regime of manufacturing beauty insidiously conspire to produce varying levels of self-loathing. The way this regime operates in Claudia's understanding of what the larger community and her family value does not produce the same level of self-loathing in Claudia as it does in Pecola, but Morrison's methodical unpacking of how it occurs is no less striking. The education in beauty and self-regard that Claudia learns reminds us of Patricia Williams's statement that "hate learned in the context of love is a complicated phenomenon."[28] In fact, Morrison illustrates how Claudia struggles with the paradox of her own identity in a context where the images that are valued outside her home influence the values that are exchanged inside her home. Her strategy of dismemberment, therefore, is a dual strategy of affirming her developing subjectivity against the values of the larger society and those of her community. At the intersection of place, race, and a girl's desire for belonging, Claudia makes use of the resistance strategy that was at her immediate disposal. Thus, through the representation of Claudia's reading of her situation is an illustration of discursive mediation as a geopoetic strategy for narrating both the exterior and interior life of Black female subjectivity.

Yet, the reader learns that Claudia's resistance as a child to the regime of white beauty is short-lived. She transfers her hatred for white dolls to a sadistic hatred for white girls. As she observes the "eye slide of black women" and the "possessive gentleness" of their touch as they handled them (22–23), she contemplates various ways to do physical harm to white girls. Much to her dismay, Claudia learns, however, that "disinterested violence" against white girls was not fully satisfying nor worth the trouble. Morrison describes another level of discursive mediation—the psychic shift from self-loathing to fraudulent love—in this way:

> When I learned how repulsive this disinterested violence was, that it was repulsive because it was disinterested, my shame foundered about for refuge. The best hiding place was love. Thus, the conversion from pristine sadism to fabricated hatred, to fraudulent love. It was a small step to Shirley Temple. I learned much later to worship her, just as I learned to delight in cleanliness, knowing, even as I learned, that the change was adjustment without improvement. (23)

It could be argued that this process is deeply Freudian in the sense that the very object that Claudia hates begins to infiltrate the psychic space of her mind, becomes the object of desire, and even judges the self for its previous hatred of the object.[29] Anne Anlin Cheng suggests in *The Melancholy of Race: Psychoanalysis, Assimilation, and Hidden Grief* that this process of exchanging hatred for the other to hatred of the self is part of how the racial imaginary develops.[30] Some readers might recall the doll test study by Black psychologists Kenneth and Mamie Clark that became part of the historic *Brown vs. Board of Education* case of 1954. In that study, we learn that Black children routinely preferred white dolls over Black dolls, a pattern that the Clarks argued was connected to acculturation and self-image.[31] Morrison's representation of how hatred for the other transforms into hatred of the self may have been informed by her knowledge of the influence that this doll study had on American public policy as it relates to the education of children. Beyond the issue of self-image, the reader is introduced to manifestations of grief and trauma that remind us of Morrison's master's thesis at Cornell University on the topics of alienation, suicide, and death in the work of William Faulkner and Virginia Woolf.[32] What is significant, however, is the recognition that Claudia's journey from hating Shirley Temple to worshipping her is yet another dimension of the discursive mediation that Morrison deploys in constructing a narrative about identity. Put another way, Morrison takes her reader from the image to the commodification and marketing of that image to the acceptance and promulgation of the image inside the self and the community.[33] While the larger narrative is a focus on what happens to Pecola Breedlove, the narrative is constructed as a kind of bildungsroman in the sense that we simultaneously bear witness to Claudia McTeer's education at the intersection of race, gender, and class in the context of her home and community. As she reads the tragic result of Pecola's education, she also reveals the psychic toll of racism on the development of her own interior life.

Claudia's education in the aesthetics of beauty as it relates to Black female subjectivity includes the intraracial dynamic of colorism that emerges in such later novels as *Tar Baby* and *God Help the Child*. When Maureen Peal, described as a "disrupter of seasons" and a "high-yellow dream child" (62), enrolls as a new student at the school that Claudia, her sister, Frieda, and Pecola attend, the reader learns how Black people's reading of skin color adds another dimension of Black female subjectivity that figures into being and belonging. Morrison includes this dimension to illustrate how self-loathing may originate from outside the community but gets internalized and circulates and contributes across gender and class to the internalization of those ideas within the self. When a group of boys begin to hurl epithets of "Black e mo" (65) at Pecola, Frieda and Claudia come to her defense and nearly come to blows with the offenders until Maureen's presence changes everything. Indeed, Claudia is convinced that a full-fledged fight does not ensue because the boys were "reluctant to continue under her springtime eyes . . . [and] watchful gaze" (66–67). The text invites the reader into the space of a childhood manifestation of how intraracial colorism is yet another example of blackness as a site that McKittrick describes as a "struggle with discourses that erase and de-spatialize their sense of place."[34] Morrison's description of this incident is an illustration of Black subjectivity in conflict with itself—one group of Black children engaging in an attack on another because of her skin color—but it is also an example of the simultaneous erasure that Pecola and by extension the narrator experience in the grip of the clash of values. The narrator experiences the implications of how the community's propensity to assign value along a continuum of beauty is directly connected to appearance and skin color issues both inside and outside of the space of home. Because the incident is one familiar to the Black community of readers—of the ways in which the community assigns value based on looks—the scene represents a site of memory and an instance of the specularity that Brodsky argues is emblematic of Morrison's aesthetics.[35]

The shift from the interior space of childhood psychic development and identity formation under the influence of exclusive regimes of beauty to the houses in which these two different representations of Black subjectivity reside deserves a closer look. In comparison to the McTeer home, which is described as "old, cold and green" (10) and becomes home to Pecola after her family is put outdoors, is the Breedlove storefront home that is described as the "debris of a realtor's whim" (34). The language of this description is loaded with powerful synecdoche for what many Black readers recognize as geographic shorthand for the disregard of Black, brown, and poor citizens in neighborhoods like Lorain during and since the 1930s. In fact, in his article "The Case for Reparations," journalist Ta-Nehisi Coates describes the inequitable ways in which the federal government, banks, and real estate agencies colluded in redlining and shaping the housing options available to Black people during and after the 1930s.[36] Caught between the socioeconomic realities of their resources and the racist whims and policies of the marketplace, the Breedloves were left with few housing options other than the storefront house in which they find themselves.

Morrison returns to this theme of race and geographic space in each of her novels in one way or another. Through this image of the storefront house and the surrounding descriptions, she pulls the reader into the multiscale spaces that mitigate being and belonging. The text reads:

> The Breedloves . . . slipped in and out of the box of the peeling gray, making no stir in the neighborhood, no sound in the labor force, and no wave in the mayor's office. Each member of the family in his own cell of consciousness, each making his patchwork quilt of reality—collecting fragments of experience here, pieces of information there. From the tiny impressions gleaned from one another, they created a sense of belonging and tried to make do with the way they found each other. (34)

The language used to describe the aesthetic dimensions of these two households provides a window for the reader into the spaces where Pecola comes into puberty and a meager sense of herself as a subject. The reader gains insight into the forces both inside and outside the domestic space of her home and to the struggle to make meaning despite the forms of lack that surround her. As we navigate our way through these passages, we learn the contours of neglect at the intersection of race, gender, and class that shape Pecola's consciousness and that of her parents. Thus, the sparse description of the space in which the Breedloves reside, which is related to the low regard given to their humanity, is directly connected, in Morrison's geopoetics, to their self-regard. The text elaborates on the connection between where they reside and how they regard themselves in the following language:

> The Breedloves did not live in a storefront because they were having temporary difficulty adjusting to the cutbacks at the plant. They lived there because they were poor and black, and they stayed there because they believed they were ugly. Although their poverty was traditional and stultifying, it was not unique. . . . Then you realized that it came from conviction. . . . They had looked about themselves and saw nothing to contradict the statement; saw, in fact, support for it leaning at them from every billboard, every movie, every glance. (38–39)

The description of the Breedlove household illustrates how the regimes of wealth, power, and beauty conspire against Black subjects, seep into the consciousness of Black subjectivity, and begin to shape the way each character navigates what Beavers refers to as the "tight spaces" in which they find themselves.[37] Given how the gaze of others, combined with the domestic violence that decorated her life and that of her family, constrained and contained the options available to them for self-regard, it is no wonder that Pecola begins to vacillate between wanting to make herself disappear and wanting the blue eyes she believes will make her beautiful. In her mind, "she belonged to them" (45)—her family, that is. The third space of her interior life, however, becomes what Sharpe describes as the "orthography of the wake," the space between "non-Being" and being that was her only option for imagining an alternative way of being and belonging in the world.[38] Indeed, as the title of the novel suggests, she goes from desiring blue eyes to being the manifestation of what the lack of blue eyes produced—a "bluest eye" in the subject position of "I." The title of the book, therefore, refers to both a phenotypic eye color and the condition of the blues—a condition Houston A. Baker Jr. calls a "matrix" characterized as "a mediational site where familiar antimonies are resolved" simultaneously by lament and signifying on the circumstances that created the condition.[39]

The geopoetics of discursive mediation also offer us a way to reread Morrison's description of Pecola's mother, Pauline. Outside of the confines of her own home, she enters the white space of her employer's home, where she can fantasize about another form of subjectivity for herself, as a domestic worker. Morrison makes the connection between a sense of self and a sense of place through the characterization of Pauline in several ways. For one, the fact that her employer refers to her as "Polly" rather than by her name Pauline is indicative of the power dynamics and racial relations at the time. The diminishment of her given name through the façade of familiarity ironically transferred to Pauline a sense of ownership of a house she did not own and a sense of belonging in a home where she did not live. While working there, she could escape the violence of her husband, Cholly, and the ugly discomfort of her family, home, and children that diminished her sense of self-regard. As the text explains:

> It was her good fortune to find a permanent job in the home of a well-to-do family whose members were affectionate, appreciative, and generous. . . . She became what is known as an ideal servant, for such a role that filled practically all of her needs. . . . Soon she stopped trying to keep her own house. . . . Here she found beauty, order, cleanliness, and praise. . . . Pauline kept this order, this beauty, for herself, a private world. (127–128)

Morrison's geopoetics are at work in multiple ways in this passage. The opportunity that Pauline's labor creates in her workspace substitutes for the diminished sense of self she experiences at home. The home of her employer becomes a space where she experiences "respectability" (128) and the "meaningfulness of life" (128) that she lacks at home. Her experience as a domestic worker destabilizes her self-loathing with a fabricated sense of subjectivity and privilege that emerges from occupying a space that contains the very accoutrements of identity she lacks. The passage also illustrates that in the space between her public and private world is a subjectivity inspired by both. On one hand, she must endure forms of abasement in the private space of the home she shares with Cholly, where his violent assaults are "breaks in routine that were themselves routine, where . . . she could display the style and imagination of what she believed to be her own true self" (41). On the other hand, there is the public space of the movie theater, where the reader sees the implications of the interior life that she has constructed for herself. As the text describes it:

> There in the dark her memory was refreshed, and she succumbed to her earlier dreams. Along with the idea of romantic love, she was introduced to another—physical beauty. Probably the most destructive idea in the history of human thought. Both originated in envy, thrived in insecurity, and ended in disillusion. In equating physical beauty with virtue, she stripped her mind, bound it, and collected self-contempt by the heap. . . . She was never able, after her education in the

movies, to look at a face and not assign it some category in the scale of absolute beauty, and the scale was one she absorbed in full from the silver screen. (122)

The reader discovers, then, how both Pauline, the mother, and Pecola, her daughter, read the spaces they inhabit—both public and private—under the influences of registers of beauty outside of themselves. The education that they both receive from these external sources—primers, Shirley Temple, and Mary Jane candy wrappers for Pecola and movie screens where the adult counterpart to Shirley Temple is the image of Jean Harlow that Pauline consumes—illustrates the assault to the third space of interiority that defines the subjectivity for each of them. In language that is precise in its specificity and ornate in its style, Morrison defines the self as a site of the struggle to belong. Between being and belonging, however, is the recurring theme of longing or desire that connects the narrator to the protagonist and to her mother.

The novel ends, however, as suggested earlier, by placing Pecola's demise in a larger societal context. The domestic space of home, already illumined as a site of struggle against violence for Pauline, is also a site of struggle against violence for Pecola. Her father's rape and impregnation of her are examples of themes that Morrison will revisit in *Sula* and *Song of Solomon*, where home is not a space of "domestic tranquility" but a site of transgression. Indeed, the topic of home as a complex site of transgression will be discussed in other sections of this study. While *The Bluest Eye* points to Cholly's own struggles around racial violence and identity as part of his passage into adulthood, Morrison is seemingly more focused on how the intersection of race, gender, and class shapes Black female subjectivity. To be more specific, Black male subjectivity is represented in contradistinction to Black female subjectivity in terms of racial/spatial relationships. While the Black male character focuses on forces outside of the home that account for his behavior, Morrison's Black female characters focus on forces both inside and outside of domestic space. Black male subjectivity is represented as a house assaulted by racial and economic forces external to the self and the Black community. Black female subjectivity, however, is represented as a both/and condition in which forces external to the self and Black community are illustrated along with those forces inside the space of home as a site of transgression. As Gaston Bachelard suggests, an interrogation of the "poetics of space" inevitably requires an interrogation of "intimate space."[40] In Morrison's rendering of house and home, intimate spaces at the intersection of race, gender, and poverty are often sites of struggle where the distinctions between how female subjects and male subjects internalize pain and read their lives are fully transparent. It can be argued that this difference obtains in the writing of several Black male writers in contradistinction to the writing of most Black female writers, but that point is beyond the scope of this study. Morrison's interrogations of home as an example of her geopoetics will be discussed as the focus of the fourth chapter of this study. What is critical here, however, is the reality that Morrison's representation of Cholly does not neglect the ways in which he is a victim of racism, nor does she represent his victimization as an excuse for the sexual assault of his own daughter. Instead, she focuses on the consequences of the multiple sources of assault that intersect and culminate in Pecola's demise and how meaning for the reader comes through a discursive mediation between and inclusive of both gendered perspectives.

The novel ends on a dual note of discursive mediation between redemption and condemnation. Claudia's narrative of Pecola's story provides a glimpse into her own education and reeducation as a Black female subject. As a witness who discloses her community's unspeakable thing and her own rite of passage from ignorance to knowledge of the forces that colluded against her, her community, and Pecola, she represents a kind of prophetic voice. She bears witness to the forces outside of and within the community and narrates the story of how both mitigate her own and Pecola's sense of belonging. But because Pecola's demise looms larger than anything and is the point of her narrative, she concludes by laying bare how the community bears the ultimate blame for what happens to Pecola. The conclusion begins with the words "The damage was total" (204). The damage done to Pecola lies in three domains—in how the community perceived her, in how they avoided her, and in how they used her as a scapegoat. Moreover, the knowledge of this damage and the failure to act are what make the community complicit and the narrative tragic. The brown house "on the edge of town" is where Pecola and her mother reside at the end, not in a space of warmth or belonging but in one of desolation and neglect "among all the waste and beauty of the world" (205). On one hand, we have the image of Pecola's null-and-void sense of subjectivity. On the other hand, Claudia makes it clear that her sense of subjectivity is flawed though enriched by her enlightened sense of what has transpired. In describing her identity as one that is lodged between binary oppositional dimensions of subjectivity, Claudia describes her thoughts about the inevitable ethical conundrum that ensues from the injustice of demonizing the other in these words:

> All of our waste which we dumped on her and which she absorbed. And all of our Beauty, which was hers first and which she gave to us. All of us—all who knew her—felt so wholesome after we cleaned ourselves on her. We were so beautiful astride her ugliness. Her simplic-

ity decorated us, her guilt sanctified us, her pain made us glow with health, her awkwardness made us think we had a sense of humor. Her inarticulateness made us believe we were eloquent. Her poverty kept us generous. Even her waking dreams we used—to silence our own nightmares. (205)

Through prose that methodically mediates the spaces between opposing forms of agency, opposing measures of value, and opposing states of being, Morrison concludes the novel with language that assesses the damage done to the psyche of the protagonist, the narrator, and the community. As if this description were not enough, the narrator attempts to illustrate just how all-encompassing the complicity of the community was in destroying Pecola. From Soaphead Church, the fraudulent preacher who deceived her, to Cholly, her father who raped and impregnated her, to the community that withheld love and concern, the narrator suggests that these silences that deprived Pecola of her humanity also deprived them of their humanity. The language of the text continues the assessment and explains:

We honed our egos on her, padded our characters with her frailty, and yawned in the fantasy of our strength. And fantasy it was, for we were not strong, only aggressive; we were not free, merely licensed; we were not compassionate, we were polite; not good but well behaved. We courted death in order to call ourselves brave, and hid like thieves from life. We substituted good grammar for intellect; we switched habits to simulate maturity; we rearranged lies and called it truth, seeing in the new pattern of an old idea the Revelation and the Word . . . on the edge of my town, among the garbage and the sunflowers of my town, it's much, much, much too late. (206–207)

Morrison ends her first novel with a narrative strategy of discursive mediation that uses an exquisite sequencing of binary oppositional descriptions of the spaces that mitigate being and belonging, not only for Pecola but also for Claudia and, by extension, for the reader. Juxtaposing frailty and strength, compassion with the lack of it, lies with truth, Morrison delineates the polarities between which a community of people attempts to make sense of their lives at the expense of Pecola's. Between the external spaces of poverty, abuse, and neglect and the interior spaces of desire, longing, and imagination, Morrison begins her literary career by theorizing through fiction how subjectivity is shaped and how it shapes our reading of the other.

In *Sula*, published three years after *The Bluest Eye*, Morrison shifts her focus from Black childhood to Black female identity in adulthood but begins the narrative with familiar themes about how the configurations of space influence Black individual and collective subjectivity. Her theorizing about place, race, and be/longing begins not with the Black female character for whom the novel is named but with an artful description of how racism and white deception are responsible for the social location in which the Black community of Medallion finds itself. The novel begins with the words "In that place, where they tore the nightshade and blackberry patches from their roots to make room for the Medallion City Golf Course, there was once a neighborhood. . . . It is called the suburbs now, but when black people lived there it was called the Bottom" (3). By her own admission, Morrison brings "a very strong sense of place . . . in terms of details, feeling, [and] the mood of the community" to the opening description of the geographical landscape, and in just three sentences, she signals to the reader how the "racialization of space," to use the language of George Lipsitz, occurs and how the connection between geography and race matters, as Shabazz argues in *Spatializing Blackness*.[41] In just three sentences, Morrison presents a literary representation of the process of gentrification that has historically torn Black people from the places where they have made their homes "to make room" for white people to claim those same spaces as their homes. The insidiousness of the dislocation process in Medallion, however, is represented by the promise made to an enslaved man and then broken by a so-called "good white farmer," by the disparity between the land the Black people once lived on and the town they are forced to occupy, and by the disproportionate expenditure of resources to secure privileged space for the white community, while the Black community is left to "make do" with the less preferable "hilly land" (5).

The racial logic that motivates white people to dislodge Black people from their land is exposed for its insidiousness, but Morrison shifts the focus from white behavior to Black people and how they imagine and reimagine their oxymoronically named space "up there in the Bottom" (6). The information used to invite the reader into the text bears the meaning and timbre found in Black vernacular and ways of naming in such place names as "Time and a Half Pool Hall," (3) . . . "Irene's Palace of Cosmetology, where women used to lean their heads back on sink trays and doze while Irene lathered Nu Nile into their hair . . . [and] Reba's Grill where the owner cooked in her hat because she couldn't remember the ingredients without it" (4). They could take "small consolation in the fact that every day they could literally look down on the white folks" (5), but reading their spatial location in this way helped them preserve their dignity and reflected their desire to reverse and subvert the power relations at play. What Morrison achieves in these opening passages is a shift from the racial logic and its racist hierarchies of value to the cultural logic of Black communities and the economies that sustained them despite segregationist practices. Her geopoetics of discursive mediation enables her to illustrate the dynamics at work as Black people attempt to navigate what Michel de Certeau refers to as the transformation of "places into spaces or spaces into places" and the practice of everyday life between "the poles of experiences" created.[42] Having established the racial context in which her Black subjects find themselves in the early pages of the novel, Morrison proceeds to shift to the interior life of the Black community in Medallion to tell a narrative of a community whose subjectivity is shaped by how Black subjects read and imagine their lives on their own terms. The novel also tells the story of how the Black community mediates the spaces between their lives and that of Sula, the woman whose return represents both a source of evil and a balm of grace.

The geopoetics of discursive mediation is most apparent, however, in the way Morrison represents the friendship between Sula and Nel at the center of the novel. Though Nel and Sula begin as childhood friends, Morrison takes great care to represent the distinctions between them. For one, Nel is described as the daughter of Helene Wright, a mother whose strict meticulousness "drove her daughter's imagination underground" (16), in contradistinction to Sula, whose mother, Hannah, is described as "sooty" (25), whose house is described as "woolly" (25), and whose sexual habits taught her daughter "that sex was pleasant and frequent, but unremarkable" (37–38). What connects these two girls at first is their joint knowledge that creating a third space would be the way to navigate the binary oppositions they had already perceived at a young age:

> Because each had discovered years before that they were neither white nor male, and that all freedom and triumph was forbidden to them, they had set about creating something else to be. Their meeting was fortunate, for it let them use each other to grow on . . . they found in each other's eyes the intimacy they were looking for. (44–45)

The space of intimacy and closeness between them is further described as "a friendship so close . . . [that] they themselves had difficulty distinguishing one's thoughts from the other's" (72). The point here is not to rehearse the twists and turns of the plot of the narrative but to show how the friendship metamorphizes over time because of the choices the women make. It is only after Nel chooses a more traditional role of marriage to Jude and Sula chooses a less traditional path away from the town of Medallion to attend college in Nashville that they begin to read their lives and their friendship in different ways. Indeed, when Sula returns, the reader must navigate the spaces that emerge between them as adult women rather than the spaces that shaped them as girls. Described as a woman who "was distinctly different" (104) and felt "no obligation to please anybody unless their pleasure pleased her" (104) and as a woman with "no center, no speck around which to grow" (103), Sula had "an idle imagination" (105). Consequently, "like any artist with no art form, she became dangerous" (105). She viewed married women and their husbands with disregard.

Through Sula's skepticism of marriage and Nel's acceptance of it, Morrison invites the reader into an interrogation of the institution, its role in Black female subjectivity, and its effect on the unique friendship between these two women. Morrison portrays Nel as a woman who embraces marriage and what it represents fully in contrast to Sula, who, when her grandmother asks, "When you gone get married? You need to have some babies. It'll settle you" (79), responds, "I don't want to make somebody else. I want to make myself" (80). Written in the early 1970s, the novel's stark pronouncements about gender, marriage, and the choices available to women offer readers another clear example of how Morrison's geopoetics of discursive mediation mirror and delineate the very gender divisions that were emerging in the culture at large. Through the geopoetics of discursive mediation, the reader can discern the developing wedge between these two friends and the vagaries of marriage as it is construed in American culture. While Sula remains "completely free of ambition, with no affection for money, property or things, no greed, no desire to command attention or compliments—no ego" (103), Nel chooses marriage, motherhood, and conventional ways of ordering her life and views her husband as her unique possession. Thus, in Sula's eyes, Nel has abandoned their friendship and become "one of *them*" (103) and "belonged to the town and all of its ways" (104). Having traveled from one city to another after college in Nashville, Sula views Nel's capitulation to conventional ways of being a woman as a major disappointment and an abandonment of the third space that their friendship created for them both. And while Nel views Sula in the same way that the rest of the town does—as a woman "free of any normal signs of vulnerability" (100) and as a "pariah" (105)—after Sula sleeps with Jude and Jude leaves her, Nel begins to experience feelings of abandonment because of the loss of her husband but also because of the loss of the unique friendship she had once treasured with Sula.

At the end of the novel, after Sula's death, as Nel walks toward the Black section of the cemetery, the reader learns the depth of her sorrow over the loss of her friend. As she walks away from the cemetery, "a soft ball of fur broke and scattered like dandelion spores in the breeze" (140). The reader is immediately reminded of the "gray ball . . . quiet, gray, dirty . . . fluffy but terrible in its malevolence" (93) that represents the sorrow Nel is unable to face, both in the loss of her marriage and in the loss of Sula, whose transgression against marriage was also a transgression against her understanding of herself. It can be argued that the gray ball represents the liminal space between these two women who lead binary oppositional adult lives. Indeed, like Nel, the reader's task is to mediate the space that emerges between them from childhood to their adult lives. When the "loss pressed down on her chest and came up into her throat," it is expressed first as a memory ("We was girls together") and then as a cry ("girl, girl, girlgirlgirl") (149). Moreover, just as the opening of the novel illustrates the vagaries of race that shaped places and spaces for Black people, even as Nel walks through the cemetery, she thinks of place, race, and belonging as she notices the grave markers for the Sula Peace family:

> With the same disregard for name changes by marriage that the black people of Medallion always showed, each flat slab had one word carved on it. Together they read like a chant: PEACE 1895–1921; PEACE 1890–1923; PEACE 1910–1940, PEACE 1892–1959. They were not dead people They were words. Not even words. Wishes, longings. (146–147)

Thus, just as Sula realizes sex was about the "endings of things: an eye of sorrow in the midst of all that hurricane rage of joy" (106), Nel realizes that her loss was beyond Jude and the end of their marriage. In opting for received notions of gender and identity, she had lost out on an opportunity to gain an understanding of herself and the third space that female friendship offered. As Gurleen Grewal asserts, while the other women of the town "were heaping their anger" on Sula as a scapegoat for their own shortcomings, Nel comes to a new understanding of how her friend's presence was both a curse and a blessing.[43] Through the geopoetics of discursive mediation, Morrison enables the reader to ruminate on the spaces of race and identity, self and community, feminine subjectivity and masculinity, singleness and marriage, joy and sorrow to explore the third space of the interior life of these two women, where they ultimately grow to read friendship as a space of being and be/longing.

As a narrative strategy, discursive mediation also appears in Morrison's third novel, *Song of Solomon*, which was her first work of fiction to receive national acclaim almost as soon as it was published in 1977. In its ostensible shift in focus from female protagonists to a male protagonist, it also shifts in length and scope from her previous two novels, drawing on African American myth and folklore in ways that the substantially shorter previous novels did not. As I argue in my previous study on Morrison, she revises the form of the bildungsroman by illustrating that the Black male "journey from ignorance to self-knowledge" is not only an individual journey but one that illustrates the communal cultural function of narrative.[44] Building on that perspective, by using a lens of geopoetics to return to *Song of Solomon*, we can gain new insights into how Morrison creates spaces for the reader to see how discourses of power shape how a community names itself, how male subjectivity is contingent upon female subjectivity, and how female subjectivity is influenced by resistant readings to constructions of identity that would attempt to contain and define. In my earlier reading of the novel, I focused on the character of Milkman, his relationship with his property-owning father, his journey from naïve middle-class privilege to a recognition of his complex history, and his coming to terms with his relationship to his family, women, and his community. But in this return to the text through geopoetics, the focus is not so much on Milkman, per se, but on the narrative strategies Morrison deploys to enable readers to see how subjectivity is interconnected, intersectional, and ultimately interspersed with contested sites of being and belonging. As in the first two novels, Morrison painstakingly connects places to the meaning that Black subjects give them, but in the third novel, male subjectivity is constructed in various contexts and spaces through interconnections to Black female subjectivity. This inordinate attention to place and the meaning attached to it illustrates the value of a geopoetic lens for reconsidering these novels and enables a focus on the multiple ways in which Morrison returns to sites of cultural and political memory to illuminate Black subjectivity. To be more specific, though *Song of Solomon* is ostensibly about a male protagonist, Milkman Dead, Morrison's characterization of Ruth, his mother, Hagar, his cousin whom he has an affair with, and Pilate, his aunt, provides the reader with an alternate way of seeing how she extends her narrative project about American life and culture to an intersectional perspective as it relates to place, race, and be/longing.

Considering that discursive mediation, as this study asserts, is one of the geopoetic strategies that Morrison deploys in her fiction, it is not surprising that *Song of Solomon* begins *in medias res*, a narrative technique that becomes a characteristic trademark of Morrison's fiction. Literally meaning "in the middle or midst of things," as a literary tool, *in media res* locates the reader, as M. H. Abrams reminds us, in a place of discomfort with few points of reference for making meaning.[45] "A place of discomfort" is exactly where Morrison wants her reader for the story she is about to tell. In other words, she does not want her reader to look for an Aristotelian "continuous sequence of beginning, middle, and end" for the comfort of their reading experience.[46] Peter Brooks identifies this desire for a particular narrative sequencing as a readerly desire shaped "in the course of our schooling . . . [as] a low form of activity."[47] Seeking to dislodge the reader from the comfort of a linear plot that flows with such a predictable logic of reading, Morrison intentionally destabilizes the plot so that the reader is forced to come to terms with the multiple layers of narrative and the multiple ways of reading them that shape time and space at any given moment. Reading against such preconceived notions of plot and having to dislodge even their presuppositions of what to expect, readers of a Morrison text must continually confront the existential disruptions that have shaped the lives of African American people on American soil.

At the beginning of the novel, the reader has no idea who the insurance agent is who is about to leap from the roof of Mercy Hospital, where Ruth, the mother of the protagonist, is about to give birth to the first African American child to be born in that hospital. Thus, Morrison begins the novel in the middle of crisis. The novel opens by connecting Ruth's identity to a place of significance to how the Black community identifies itself. As the only child of "the only colored doctor in the city" (4), Ruth is aware of how community history is tied to racial history and racist practices of exclusion. The reader learns that the townspeople named Mains Avenue "Doctor Street" in homage to Ruth's father and in recognition of the racial discrimination that prevented him from having hospital privileges at Mercy Hospital, which Black people renamed "No Mercy Hospital" (4). A geopoetic lens lets us see the humor and significance in Morrison's representation of space as a site of struggle where city legislators try to undermine Black communal naming practices with official language and geographic specificity that attempts to forbid unofficial naming. For the Black residents, however, the official municipal notice that the street "would always be known as Mains Avenue and not Doctor Street . . . was a genuinely clarifying public notice because it gave Southside residents a way to keep their memories alive and please city legislators as well. They called it Not Doctor Street and were inclined to call the charity hospital . . . No Mercy Hospital" (4), names which represented their signifying practices of exercising agency, subverting authority, and embracing subjectivity on their own terms.

Morrison's illustration of these subversive naming practices shows how Black subjectivity is represented by the creation of a third space between the dominant official narrative and the narrative of their lived lives. This third space, a space of agency and subversive signifying on those in power, as Henry Louis Gates would argue, becomes a way that Ruth's community affirms its identity despite the racialized structures and systems of power that attempt to control it.[48] It can be argued that Ruth's knowledge of this history and her father's role in securing a privileged life for his family partly account for her son being born into privilege. Ruth's marriage to Macon Dead further solidifies that privilege because of his status as the town's well-to-do landlord—that is, "a colored man of property" (23)—who was known for carrying "the keys to all of the doors of his houses (only four true houses; the rest were really shacks) and he fondled them from time to time as he walked down Not Doctor Street" (17). Ruth's husband's name, "Macon Dead," is also connected to race and place. The reader learns that his name is the result of a mistake—a "literal slip of the pen" on the part of a "drunken Yankee in the Union Army" who obviously "couldn't have cared less" (18). So, the confusion between place of birth—Macon—and status of his father—Dead—results in a name that gets passed down to succeeding generations without correction. Embedded in the narrative, therefore, is the serious reality of how two significant sites of identity—birth and freedom—get distorted in the act of registering his formerly enslaved father with the Freedmen's Bureau, when a drunken soldier writes all the pertinent information "in the wrong spaces" (53). By introducing these characters through these twists and turns of identity and contested sites of power, Morrison seeks to expose how Black subjectivity has historically been constructed through racial violence and indifference out of which Black people have nonetheless imagined ways of being and belonging that placed them at the center of their own narratives.

Ruth is significant in the novel because of her status as Milkman's mother but also because of how her habits of being as a mother account for his being known by his nickname of Milkman rather than his birth name of Macon Dead III. Ruth's propensity to nurse Milkman at her breast far beyond the age that it was considered socially acceptable to do so accounts for his name and for his father's "disgust and . . . uneasiness" (16). Beyond Macon's response to this practice is the symbolism of how it represents two distortions of identity at once—Ruth's arrested development at the point of her necrophiliac obsession with her deceased father and Milkman's arrested development and reluctant passage into adulthood. In a conversation with Milkman in which she explains the circumstances of his birth and allegations of her unnatural attraction for kneeling beside her father's dead body at the cemetery, she asserts that she also prayed for him "every single night and every single day" (126), a practice she shares to allay his misgivings about her by attaching it to the question "What harm did I do you on my knees?" (126). With this disconcerting representation of Milkman's mother, Morrison again represents the domestic space of home as a contested site where being and belonging are conflicted and sometimes at odds with efforts to come into subjectivity on one's own terms. In fact, Ruth's own explanation for who she is and why she behaves as she does offers even more information about this conflict:

> I am a small woman. I don't mean little; I mean small, and I'm small because I was pressed small. I lived in a great big house that pressed me into a small package. I had no friends, only schoolmates who wanted to touch my dresses and my white silk stockings. But I didn't think I'd ever need a friend because I had him. . . . Later it was just important for me to know he was in the world. When he left it, I kept on reigniting that cared-for feeling that I got from him. (124)

She goes on to share the story of Macon's responsibility for her father's death by throwing away his medicine and of his decision to sleep in another room apart from the conjugal bedroom when she threatened to go to the police rather than lose access to her family's money. She explains that her trips to the cemetery, therefore, were her way of dealing with the lack of touch from her husband, the "need to talk to somebody who wanted to listen and not laugh" and to have someone she could "trust" (125). While this explanation does not assuage Milkman's concerns, it provides the reader with another example of Morrison's interest in Black female subjectivity beyond stereotypical representations. Ruth's trips to the cemetery are a return to a site of memory as well as a literal return to the archive where her sense of identity felt intact.

As if the convoluted narrative of his birth and his mother's life were not complex enough, the challenge of coming into manhood for Milkman is further exacerbated by his loss of respect for his father and his romantic relationship with his cousin Hagar. After disrupting his father's physical assault on his mother by literally assaulting him in return, he begins to view sleeping with Hagar as an act of generosity, "or so he thought, wide-spirited. Or so he imagined. Wide-spirited and generous enough to defend his mother, whom he almost never thought about, and to deck his father, whom he feared and loved" (69). The reader gets a glimpse into his interior life when he looks in the mirror at himself and realizes that his image "lacked coherence, a coming together of the features into a total self. It was very tentative, the way he looked, like a man peeping around a corner of someplace he is not supposed to be, trying to make up his mind whether to go forward or to turn back" (69–70). Milkman views his father's justification for his behavior and treatment of Ruth as a "way out tale about how come and why" (76), and his rendezvous with Hagar becomes the escape from the domestic space of the familial home and the stories of his color-struck grandfather who "hated black skin" (76–77), although he apparently tolerated Macon's darker skin to allow him to marry Ruth. Milkman reads the space of his relationship with Hagar not as one of intimacy but as one of lust and private self-indulgence. When he first sees her, he falls "in love with her behind" (43), but those feelings quickly turn to boredom. He finds that her "eccentricities were no longer provocative and the stupefying ease with which he had gotten and stayed between her legs had changed from great good fortune . . . to annoyance at her refusal to make him hustle for it" (91). Thus, for Milkman, Hagar becomes "the third beer. Not the first one, which the throat receives with almost tearful gratitude; not the second one that confirms and extends the pleasure of the first. But the third, the one you drink because it's there, because it can't hurt, and because what difference does it make?" (91). Morrison's description of the deterioration of Milkman's relationship with Hagar is an example of how the narrative explores Black subjectivity through a return to the domestic space of family and to the presumed space of intimacy as a site where both male and female identity are vulnerable to exploitation of genuine desire for belonging. In Morrison's narrative theorizing, these characters are to be understood not only as racial beings but as Black subjects whose sense of self-regard is shaped by histories at the intersection of race and gender and at the intersection of being and belonging, where the reader gets glimpses into the third space of their interior life.

Morrison makes Pilate—Hagar's grandmother and Reba's mother—the most significant person in Milkman's passage into manhood. We know from earlier parts of the novel that Pilate is also the eccentric sister of Mason Dead, who has alternately embraced and disowned her, as she is generally considered a "regular source of embarrassment" (20). In fact, he forbids Milkman to go near her and shares unequivocally that "Pilate can't teach you a thing you can use in this world. Maybe the next, but not this one. . . . The one important thing you'll ever need to know: Own things. And let the things you own own other things. Then you'll own yourself and other people too" (55). In the company of Pilate, however, Milkman learns that his father's individualistic embrace of capitalism cannot teach him what he needs to know for survival in this world; he also finds that there is another way of reading the world that requires him to learn precisely what only his aunt Pilate can teach him about the connection between his history and his identity. When Milkman goes to visit her on one occasion to get two bottles of wine, he encounters Hagar summoning Pilate to come break up a domestic dispute between Reba and her new male suitor. Hagar's frantic summons interrupts Pilate from the "fourth-grade geography book she was reading" (93). What Pilate represents for Milkman is a return to a site of memory by the very way she has constructed her identity. Pilate is known for an itinerate life and for carrying a "green sack" of her deceased father's bones that she calls her "inheritance" (97), and her story in the novel is an illustration of narrative rememory, a geopoetic strategy that Morrison develops more extensively in *Beloved*. Unlike her brother Macon, who attempts to disassociate from his past and instead deploys his identity as a landlord as a status symbol, Pilate is the griot figure who demonstrably connects memories of her history to her identity. Ironically, Macon's collection of houses does not give him a sense of home anywhere, whereas Pilate's generosity of spirit gives her a sense of home wherever she finds herself. To the question that Milkman ponders after an argument with his friend Guitar—"What would they [black people] do if they didn't have black and white problems to talk about. Who would they be if they couldn't describe the insults, violence and oppression that their lives (and the television news) were made up of?" (107–108)—Pilate represents an answer.

Not needing or being willing to separate her history from her identity but viewing herself as a Black female subject whose subjectivity is constitutive of both where she has been and how she has imagined her own unique way of being, Pilate becomes the very person to Milkman that his father could not have anticipated. Born without a navel and regarded by other women as "something God never made" (144), Pilate shares that "everyplace I went I got me a rock" (142), that she learned from root workers, and that she has reconciled herself to being "cut off . . . early from other people" (142). The reader learns that her name originated from an old Black tradition of naming your child from wherever the parent's finger landed in the Bible and that she carries her "name folded in her ear" (147) in a brass box with a wire as an earring. Except for her daughter, Reba, and later her granddaughter, Hagar, she was "without family . . . further isolated from other people, for . . . every other resource was denied her: partnership in marriage, confessional friendship, and communal religion" (148). She takes the realities of her life in stride. As the text explains, "when she realized what her situation in the world was and what would probably always be she threw away every assumption she had learned and began at zero" (149). From this place of zero, Pilate creates a life for herself as a root worker, winemaker, and natural healer and becomes yet another example of Black subjectivity created in the interstices of others' perceptions and one's reading of those perceptions to imagine being and belonging on one's own terms. With references to her reading a geography book and to the rocks she carries in her sack that represent the places she has traveled, Morrison includes Pilate as a figure in the tradition of the African griot, one who represents a unique and expanded interpretation of place that includes the untold stories of a place. Locating her sense of identity on those terms makes her the most valuable resource Milkman could have for understanding how to read himself, his place in the world, and the spaces of community, family, and relationships that shaped his life.

By the end of *Song of Solomon*, Milkman has gained more information about his history, the history of family, and his African ancestors. With Pilate as his guide and others he meets on his journey back to the South, he "listened to gossip, stories, legends, speculations. His mind . . . with what . . . [was] said, what he knew, and what he guessed, he put it all together" (323). The reader learns that the song he overhears has more meaning than he suspected. He learns that the very song he had discounted was critical to his identity and that "these children were singing a story about his own people" (304). Through his return to the archival sites of his familial past, he is persuaded to relinquish his self-centered disregard for any and everyone else and to gain a healthy respect for why "Pilate had taken a rock from every state she had lived in—because she *had* lived there" (329). He learns that the very names of people and places that he had mocked out of ignorance were names that had meaning and expressed "yearnings, gestures, flaws, events, mistakes, weaknesses. Names . . . bore witness" (329–330). He also learns that the very places he wants to escape and/or discount are those he needs to read and understand. In a real sense, in this third novel, Morrison creates spaces for readers to do just that—bear witness to Black subjectivity and the ways of knowing, being, and belonging that emerge from it on its own terms. The spaces she creates for her readers become sites of cognition and/or recognition that they must navigate to understand and make meaning. Like the biblical love song from which the name of the novel is taken, the text is an example of a chorus of voices, multiple images, and songs that point to human connection and love. And like the "Song of Solomon" in the Old Testament, the song that Milkman learns to decipher is about not only a romantic connection between a man and a woman but also a divine connection that would deepen his relationship to his biological family, the larger narrative of his people, and the geographical spaces that shaped their lives.

In her fourth novel, *Tar Baby*, Morrison's geopoetics of discursive mediation becomes most explicit in her representation of the love affair between two nomads. She situates the central conflict of the novel in a place that forces the reader to come to terms with the actual geographical location and its history at the same time that she introduces the reader to the antagonist, a stowaway named Son. His romantic entanglement with the protagonist, Jadine, the Sorbonne-educated former model, exposes larger cultural conflicts that arguably are what motivated Morrison to write the novel in the first place. The epigraph to the novel, taken from the New Testament scripture in 1 Corinthians 1:11, says, "For it hath been declared unto me of you, my brethren, by them which are of the house of Chloe, that there are contentions among you."[49] In selecting a scripture that contains her birth name for the epigraph—"Chloe"— Morrison is virtually winking at the reader with an announcement that her "house of fiction" is about to disclose just what those contentions or cultural conflicts are. And as innocuous as it may seem, the opening statement of the book exposes the first conflict as one between seeing and believing. The words "He believed he was safe" (3) immediately thrust the reader in the same space between uncertainty and knowing, danger and safety, where Son, the antagonist, finds himself. In her comments in the 2004 foreword about the tar baby folktale for which the novel is named, Morrison states that she views the "tar figure . . . as the sticky mediator" between binary opposites.[50] Thus, these words confirm that part of the appeal of the folktale was that it could assist her in creating the narrative context for mediating the cultural discourses that were mitigating place, cultural identity, and belonging as she understood them in the late seventies, early eighties.

In Morrisonian style, the novel opens in a setting that appears to be the middle of nowhere but is somewhere off the coast of a Caribbean Island she names Isle des Chevaliers. Morrison begins *Tar Baby* with a description of the stowaway making his way in the water toward the shore of the island in language that is poetic, lyrical, and lush with detail about the sky, the water, and the scents and sights that strike Son as he navigates his way toward a boat that he later discovers belongs to Margaret and Valerian Street. At the beginning of the novel, however, even before we know who Son is or how his life will be entangled with the lives of the Streets, Ondine and Sydney Childs, who work for them, or their niece, Jadine, who they have adopted and helped achieve a life of privilege, we learn an important piece of history. The opening section ends unceremoniously and in a matter-of-fact way with the words "he was gazing at the shore of an island that, three hundred years ago, had struck slaves blind the moment they saw it" (8). Juxtaposing the previous description with this final phrase before the first chapter of the book is Morrison's way of not only historicizing the place but also orienting the reader to a both/and framework. That is, the novel begins in a historical moment that is clearly long after the enslavement of Africans on the island and in the hemisphere had ended, and yet the reference to enslaved people serves as a reminder of the cultural, political, and even existential ways in which the effects of the earlier period are still present enough in contemporary time to be part of the contentious competing forces at work in human interactions on the island and elsewhere in the African diaspora. In many respects, the entire novel can be summed up as Morrison's dramatization through a series of discursive mediations between the Caribbean and the West as represented by the United States and Europe, between Black and white, between rich and poor, between female and male, and between those who have achieved a sense of belonging and those who are still struggling, at an existential level, with where and to whom they belong and owe cultural allegiance.

Morrison calls attention to time, place, geography, and space in Chapter 1 with a declarative statement: "The end of the world, as it turned out, was nothing more than a collection of magnificent winter houses on Isle des Chevaliers. When laborers imported from Haiti came to clear the land, clouds and fish were convinced that the world was over" (9). The irony of this language and the implication of the human intervention into the natural and animal worlds emphasize Morrison's desire to simultaneously narrate and comment on how a human presence, namely the white presence of power and privilege, disrupted the received "order of things," to use Foucault's term, with Black labor and established an empire and hierarchy of human interaction.[51] Her use of personification in describing trees as "serene," clouds watching "the river scuttle around the forest floor . . . until exhausted, ill and grieving," and orchids spiraling to the ground to join fallen "champion daisy trees" (9–10) signals her desire for the reader to experience how the earth itself was bearing witness and anticipating the human response to the destruction that had taken place. Although early reviewers of *Tar Baby* were not overwhelmingly appreciative of her elaborate and sometimes ornate prose, it is clear that they understood that the critique of race, gender, and class inequities at play in the novel was also meant as a critique of how those same inequities were at play in the lived lives of her readers.[52] In a real sense, using the multiple disruptions in nature to signal the unexpected, Morrison sets the stage for her reader to expect *in medias res* to be the order of things for the unfolding of the narrative. The geopoetics of discursive mediation, therefore, between the natural environment and the imposed order of a palatial home where uprooted plants and flowers were replaced by "graceful landscaping" (11) signal the mediation between the binary opposition of the owners and the laborers, between rich and poor, and between the educated and uneducated. Moreover, as the love affair develops between Son and Jadine and the cultural conflicts between the life she has lived and the life he has chosen not to live play out throughout the novel, it becomes clear that Morrison wants the reading experience itself to be a kind of "tar baby," no matter how disconcerting.

If we understand discursive mediation to be a narrative geopoetic strategy that Morrison uses to juxtapose binary oppositional forces to reveal both how the apparent line between them is blurred and how the space between them can be read as an index to the third space of the interior life of her characters, then nowhere is that phenomenon more apparent than in the characters of Jadine and Son. By giving her what were considered to be the coveted attributes of being a Black woman who was "intelligent and lucky" (45) with beauty, skin, and hair to earn a place on the cover of *Elle* fashion magazine, an aunt and uncle who had secured patronage from their employer to send her to the Sorbonne for a degree in art education, and Ryk, a white boyfriend in Paris who had proposed to marry her, Morrison prepares her reader to acknowledge how privilege and power have worked for Jadine. Yet, when the African woman with "skin like tar" (45) in a "long canary yellow dress" (45) crosses her path and spits toward her in the grocery store, she suddenly feels "lonely and inauthentic" (49). Though Jadine has just appeared on the cover of the world's most coveted fashion and beauty magazine, she regards the African woman in yellow as "a woman's woman . . . that mother/sister/she; that unphotographable beauty" (46) that called all her presumed beauty into question. Morrison then explores the space between them by sharing the thoughts that trouble Jadine and have her literally stuck in her tracks as she reflects on her engagement to Ryk, the meaning of the accolades she has just received (including passing her oral examination for a doctoral degree), and the privileged life she has been fortunate to live, thanks to her aunt and uncle's hard work and the patronage of her white male benefactor. Morrison lets the reader shift from the life she has lived and the reaction of the Black woman in her presence to the third space of her interior life, where she finds herself questioning the terms of her interracial relationship:

> I guess the person I want to marry is him, but I wonder if the person he wants to marry is me or a black girl? And if it isn't me he wants, but any black girl who looks like me, talks and acts like me, what will happen when he finds out that I hate ear hoops, that I don't have to straighten my hair, that Mingus puts me to sleep, that sometimes I want to get out of my skin and be only the person inside—not American, not black—just me? (48)

With the knowledge that her physical beauty has helped her navigate spaces unintended for Black women and her return to a life where she is caught between the white world of her patron and the Black world of her aunt and uncle, Jadine inhabits a consciousness that questions the racial cultural imaginary that leaves her feeling orphaned in more ways than one. The interrogative voice—coupled with the words *I guess* and *I wonder*—emphasizes the lack of certainty and belonging that color her consciousness with self-doubt. Her references to stereotypical ways of identifying her blackness and femaleness and her question of being "just me" signify Morrison's desire to interrogate racial and cultural identity through the third space that this character occupies between blackness and whiteness, Europe and America, and essentialist notions of blackness and authentic ones. Her return to the Caribbean, itself a kind of third space between Africa and America, to sort things out only gets more complicated when Son, the person she is least likely to be attracted to, is attracted to her.

Based on the African American folktale of a farmer who uses a tar figure to snare a rabbit who has been eating his lettuce and cabbage, the novel *Tar Baby* is replete with analogies to the simultaneous attraction and danger that Jadine experiences in her relationship with Son. In fact, Morrison admits that her writerly desire in her characterization of Jadine is to create "a reader's sense of vertigo."[53] Thus, the dizzying effects of an interracial love affair pale in comparison to the intraracial love affair that ensues when Son invades the palatial home of Jadine's aunt and uncle and her white benefactor, Valerian Street. Even the ornate architecture and the spatial arrangements inside the island home reiterate the contentions that emerge from power relations, racial dynamics, and gender conflicts. While Jadine's sleeping quarters are upstairs on the same level as that of her benefactors, her aunt and uncle's quarters are on a lower floor of the home. These spatial locations are not lost on Son, the interloper who walks in on Jadine as she exits the shower and whose inquisitiveness about her life as an accomplished model leads him to speculate beyond what her life would be like in his world:

> He used to slip into her room . . . and lie still and dream steadily the dreams he wanted her to have about yellow houses with white doors which women opened and shouted Come on in, you honey you! And the fat black ladies in white dresses minding the pie table in the basement of the church and white wet sheets flapping on the line, and the sound of a six-string guitar plucked after supper while children scooped walnuts. (119)

Thus, the reader experiences the dizzying effect of an interloper entering the world of a Black woman who identifies herself as an orphan who belongs to only herself but who also owes her education, fame, and place in the household to her white patrons. Son is attracted to Jadine and the world she inhabits at the same time that he fantasizes about living with her elsewhere, in Eloe, Florida, in the world he himself misses yet has abandoned. Likewise, she is attracted to him yet resents the fact that he "had jangled something in her that was so repulsive, so awful, and he had managed to make her feel that the thing that repelled her was not in him, but in her" (123). While it may be tempting to view Son as the tar baby, Morrison feminizes the character to illustrate how her presence offers her readers an opportunity to interrogate the very questions about what constitutes blackness that were circulating in the culture. The temptations to land on one definition versus another, therefore, are thrown into question even as the love affair takes shape and ultimately dissipates.

The challenge to Jadine's identity and to the questions raised in her own interior life are most apparent in the words of Son, whose love gradually makes her vacillate between feeling orphaned and "unorphaned" (229) but whose words, amid an argument, reveal the competing realities at work in his mind and hers when he says:

> The truth is that whatever you learned in those colleges that didn't include me ain't shit. What did they teach you about me? What tests did they give? . . . Did they tell you what was in my heart? If they didn't teach you that, then they didn't teach you nothing, because until you know about me, you don't know nothing about yourself. (264)

Again, the interrogative voice exposes the liminal spaces between binary oppositional forces in their lives, but this time, the questions are not only those that Son is posing to challenge Jadine but also the same ones that are circulating in the culture between what is taught and what is not taught about Black people, Black history, and Black culture. In fact, at an earlier point in the novel, even Michael, the only son of the Streets who never shows up for Christmas as his mother had hoped, accuses Jadine of abandoning her "people" and her culture and for being more interested in European things than American or Black things. She thinks to herself that "without melanin, they were all reflection, like mirrors, chamber after chamber, corridor after corridor of mirrors . . . until the final effect was color where no color existed at all" (74). The reader is led to vacillate between these perspectives but ultimately to view the merits of Michael's critique that leads Jadine to say:

> "Picasso *is* better than an Itumba mask. The fact that he was intrigued by them is proof of *his* genius, not the mask-makers'. I wish it weren't so, but . . . " She gave a tiny shrug. Little matches of embarrassment burned even now in her face. (75)

In some respects, Jadine's thoughts signify the way the narrative moves beyond the tar baby figure in the folktale, per se, to explore the vacillating images between mirrors and masks and what they represent for identity, culture, and subjectivity.[54] Ironically, the biggest argument between her and Son occurs in Eloe, Son's Black hometown, where the difference between the two of them becomes most apparent. Jadine's thoughts are the very sort that had once led Valerian to describe Michael as "a cultural orphan who sought other cultures he could love without risk or pain" (145).[55] The novel juxtaposes multiple spaces—the island home of the Streets and the Southern community of Son's family, the Philadelphia home of the Streets, where the candy empire began, and the streets of Paris, where Jadine lived apart from those who raised and loved her and those who made her education possible. The novel also exposes the contradictions between Jadine's aunt and uncle, who, like the women in Eloe, believe Jadine has forgotten her "sacred properties" (183) and do not understand that a daughter is not about biology but relationship. As Ondine explains, "a daughter is a woman who cares about where she come from and takes care of them that took care of her" (281). The novel itself, therefore, becomes the sticky terrain. Morrison's reader must navigate the spaces between the spaces where her characters find themselves and engage in mediating the discourses that emerge from those spaces and self, identity, and culture. At the very cultural moment when African Americans and other people of color were navigating a new understanding of the African diaspora both in the United States and around the world and when colleges and universities were grappling with needed revisions to the curriculum to address the omissions and marginalization that racism and white supremacy had created, Morrison writes *Tar Baby*, crafting spaces for her readers to contemplate these large and small cultural conflicts—not to resolve them but to reveal how they have shaped and are continuing to shape our consciousness and the contours of our interior lives, even when we have not yet recognized or articulated what those contours might be.

Discursive mediation is the narrative strategy that enables Morrison to begin the mapping of these contours and the cultural spaces for the reader that they signify in her fiction. In Morrison's oeuvre, it becomes clear that binary oppositional either/or thinking forms the very set of contentions and competing terms of thought that she seeks to expose and disrupt—not only for reading her texts but also for enabling us to read the texts of our lived lives. Between the spaces of this either/or propensity of thought, she seems to suggest, is what Bhabha refers to as an "interstitial space" of "both/and" that may uncomfortably complicate our understanding but that may nonetheless teach us new ways of making meaning after all.[56]

2

Spatializing the Self

The Geopoetics of Emancipatory Spaces

> Deep space and the poetics of landscape add new contours to geographic inquiries . . . asking us to take seriously the ways in which spatial expressions are wrapped up in everyday struggles and critiques.
> —Katherine McKittrick, *Demonic Grounds*[1]

When we reread Morrison's work through the lens of her geopoetics, particularly at the intersection of race and gender, we begin to see how she shifts the focus from exterior places to the interior spaces of her Black female subjects and their reading of the places in which they find themselves. She is mindful, as Shabazz argues, that "space . . . plays a role in the production of identities," as she writes to mitigate the extent to which physical space is regarded as the sole determinant for how to represent the interior lives of her characters and their understanding of their subjectivity.[2] Through discursive mediation between the exterior and interior, she creates a third space that is similar to what Quashie refers to as "a poetics of being," where the focus is on "the text itself, a choral subjunctive that exemplifies but does not plead" and that creates "a quality of being . . . a manner and aesthetic, a feeling . . . circuits in an atmosphere."[3] In other words, Morrison creates characters who read the landscape between the binary oppositional terms set for their existence and deploys narrative strategies to engage her readers in seeing how her characters interrogate and imagine that in-between space as a third space in which to create a way to be on their own terms. Beginning with Sula, the protagonist in her second novel, who "operated from her own imagination," and with Pilate, the griot and guide in her third novel, who, "when she realized what her situation in the world was and would probably always be . . . threw away every assumption she had learned and began at zero," Morrison experiments with representing Black female subjects outside of established, prescribed social norms.[4] As suggested in the previous chapter, she uses the narrative strategy of *in medias res* to interrupt reader expectations and presuppositions and show how her characters navigate the confines of history, oppression, and marginalization signified by binary oppositional structures and systems. But she goes a step further by representing the ways in which the interior life of her characters becomes a new location to explore Black subjectivity both politically and aesthetically, especially through the imagination of her characters. She creates female characters who imagine their lives outside the confines of their physical location in time and space to emancipate themselves and to create new ways and spaces of being. Or, as Elizabeth Alexander frames it, they find ways to "of imagining the racial self unfettered, racialized but not delimited."[5] This chapter focuses on those emancipatory spaces as a manifestation of Morrison's geopoetics and how they illuminate themes of place and identity at the intersection of race and gender, being and belonging, not only in her early fiction but also in the set of novels she referred to as "the *Beloved* trilogy" about excesses of love—that is, *Beloved*, *Jazz*, and *Paradise*.[6]

Morrison's artistic propensity to create characters who read the spaces of their circumstances and imagine a life outside of them is apparent in one novel after another. While it has been historically accurate for hooks and others to characterize Black female subjectivity on the margin, when hooks refers to the margin as a "space of radical openness," she describes what I believe is the emancipatory space beyond the limits of the margin.[7] In other words, I am arguing that in suggesting that Black female subjects choose to situate themselves differently from how those in power have attempted to situate them, Morrison provides an alternative conceptualization outside of the margin/center binary with a third space of emancipated being and choice. In her essay "The Source of Self-Regard," published in the collection of essays by the same name, she argues that "imagination fosters real possibilities: you can't imagine it, you can't have it. And a third thing grows, where despair may have been, or even where the play lay whole and wouldn't let go. And it is this *third thing* [my emphasis] that jazz creates and that creates itself into these spaces and intersections of race and gender" that interests her.[8] This third space is an interstitial space, comparable to what Moten references as "in the break" but constitutive of the exterior and interior dimensions of the self, "between the word and sound, between meaning and content," where the imagination has power.[9] For example, unlike Nel, who "belonged to the town and all of its ways" (104), Sula was a "pariah" (105), an outlaw figure whose "craving for the other half of her equation was the consequence of an idle imagination" (105). Although Morrison represents her as "dangerous" and like an "artist with no art form" (105), the danger resides primarily in the fact that the freedom she created for herself is not aligned with the presuppositions of others about how a woman of her color, age, and status should conduct herself. Sula creates emancipatory spaces for herself by the way she chooses to live. As the novel states,

> with a twist that was all her own imagination, she lived out her days exploring her own thoughts and emotions, giving them full reign, feeling no obligation to please anybody unless their pleasure pleased her . . . hers was an experimental life. . . . She had no center, no speck around which to grow. . . . She was completely free of ambition . . . no greed, no desire to command attention or compliments—no ego. For that reason she felt no compulsion to verify herself—be consistent with herself. (102, 103)

Written in the late 1960s and published in the early 1970s, at the intersection of the feminist and Black power movements, *Sula* was a vehicle for Morrison to introduce her readers to Black female friendship, a topic she observed had not yet been explored in fiction at the time. She notes in the foreword of the 2004 edition of the novel that she wrote *Sula* to examine

> What is friendship between women when unmediated by men? What choices are available to black women outside their own society's approval? What are the risks of individualism in a determinedly individualist, yet racially uniform and socially static, community?[10]

As McDowell and Spillers suggest, Morrison answers this question with representations of Black female subjectivity that are transgressive and dismissive of established norms and boundaries. Consequently, her writing offers an example of how the historical moment empowered her to emancipate herself and her reader from established norms.[11] According to McDowell, Morrison's representation of Sula challenges the "reader's expectations" and thereby invites the reader to transgress boundaries and experience the freedom of reading Black female subjectivity in an unmediated way as well.[12]

With the character of Pilate in *Song of Solomon*, Morrison continues her literary project of creating emancipatory spaces both for her characters and her readers. Pilate is similarly transgressive and dismissive of boundaries and norms, but unlike Sula, whose individualistic ways of disregarding the feelings of others, even those of Nel, her best friend, separate the community from her, Pilate is a woman who mindfully and intentionally strategizes how she will be and operate in the space of her community. Morrison represents this intentionality by having Pilate interrogate herself:

When am I happy and when am I sad and what is the difference? What do I need to know to stay alive? What is true in the world? Her mind traveled crooked streets and aimless goat paths, arriving sometimes at profundity, other times at the revelations of a three-year old . . . the knowledge she had . . . kept her just barely within the boundaries of the elaborately socialized world of black people . . . her respect for other people's privacy . . . was balancing. (149)

Inside the interstices between her lived life and her life with others is the space of her own interior life, where her "mind traveled" across space and time in ways not mediated by her family, her community, or anyone. This interrogation of the self by her character inside the text of the novel invites Morrison's readers to interrogate themselves about the texts of their own minds and engage in a process that is consistent with what Robert Scholes argues are the protocols of reading, where textual matters simultaneously lie between the pages of the book and within our consciousness.[13] Morrison describes Pilate as a "natural healer" who "sometimes mediated a peace" (149, 150), which, despite her pariah status, made her a force for good within and outside her family, even when they thought she was strange. Between the rocks she carries from one space to another and the geography book she reads, Pilate is characterized by Morrison as a nomadic woman leading a "wandering life" (148), as one who navigates various spaces of her community as an emancipated self. She is a woman who "make[s] the road by walking," to quote the title of the book by Myles Horton and Paulo Freire.[14] Morrison uses characters such as Sula and Pilate to not only represent what Rosi Braidotti refers to as "nomadic subjectivity" but also to mirror the kind of disruptions to protocols of reading she seeks to engender in her readers.[15] Foregrounding not just how they show up in various spaces but also the internal dialogues they have within themselves, Morrison illuminates the interior spaces of her characters through narrative strategies of interrogation and declarations of emancipation that become hallmarks of her writing.

Nowhere is this spatializing of the self more apparent than it is in *Beloved*, the first novel of Morrison's trilogy. On more than one occasion in speaking about the origins of *Beloved*, Morrison attempted to situate herself both as a reader of history in search of answers that the official narrative of American history had never addressed to her satisfaction and as an artist attempting to wrestle, armed with the power of her imagination, not just with that history and its embedded narratives of Black bodies but also with how one could imagine different narratives of the same historical moment. What she argues in the essay about the need to return to "The Site of Memory" is very much what Hartman describes as a "return to the archive" and what Foucault describes as a process that requires a kind of "discursive archaeology" to discover the layers of subjectivity and interiority buried beneath official narratives and the complex power relations that led to them.[16]

Viewing Baby Suggs's sermon in the Clearing as a metaphor for the kinds of discursive interventions that reflect Black ways of reading, knowing, remembering, and imagining beyond the oppressive spaces of containment, we can see what Morrison means when she argues that her task was to engage in a kind of "literary archaeology" designed to "fill in the blanks that slave narratives left" and move from the "image to the text."[17] In a real sense, a geopoetic lens enables us to read the Clearing as an emancipatory space, as a third space within the Black community, as a site of resistance, as a space for the reclamation of the self, and as a space characterized by what Robin Kelley refers to as "radical imagination."[18] The Clearing represents a spatializing of the self that is not individualistic but communal, not just transgressive but radical in its power to transform the consciousness of the members of the enslaved community. In a real sense, for the enslaved, going to the Clearing, that "wide-open place cut deep in the woods nobody knew for what" (87), every Saturday to meet Baby Suggs was a survival strategy for embodying emancipation and for liberating their spirits, even while they were yet in physical bondage. The Clearing is where the enslaved learn from Baby Suggs that "the only grace they could have was the grace they could imagine" (88). It is a location for liberation that they can create for themselves.

The idea that the journey to the Clearing is a survival strategy is most explicitly illustrated and articulated in Baby Suggs's sermon there. Morrison incorporates the Clearing as a space in the narrative—not just as a physical location for the self in an alternative physical place set apart from the oppressive location of the plantation but also as a sacred space in the woods among the trees that takes on a generative life of its own. As Charles Baudelaire once wrote, "Nature is a temple . . . forests of symbols . . . as vast as darkness, as vast as light, perfumes, sounds and colours . . . which chant the ecstasies of the mind and senses."[19] So Baby Suggs summons the women, men, and children to a space not made with human hands to inspire them to visualize the sacredness of what has been oppressed, abused, and misused—their bodies. Moreover, in urging them to visualize the sacredness of their "inside parts" (88)—that is, their hearts—she also inspires them to value and protect the very dimension of their subjectivity that their oppressors could not touch, unless they succumbed to internalizing their oppression. Baby Suggs's sermons are designed to ward off the internalization of feelings that they were less than they were divinely created to be. What the enslaved hear, what they experience, and how they reimagine themselves in the Clearing become the substance of what transforms it from being an ordinary place in the woods into a sacred space that they imagine in their hearts and minds. The Clearing is a geolocation where they experience what social scientists refer to as a "sense of belonging."[20] Through Sethe's return to the site and her memory of it, Morrison enables the reader to bear witness to Baby Suggs's unique ability to use her voice and the spoken word to empower her people to love themselves despite and beyond their circumstances. Thus, the Clearing represents a space of agency and self-actualization that Baby Suggs both embodies and teaches others to value. As Sethe remembers Baby Suggs's sermons in the Clearing, she thinks, "in the Clearing, along with the others, she had claimed herself. Freeing yourself was one thing; claiming ownership of that freed self was another" (95). Moreover, by introducing Baby Suggs's message to the enslaved community as a sermon, Morrison illustrates how the spiritual practices of an enslaved woman invoked and signified on biblical imperatives the enslaved would have heard from their slave masters in a totally different light. She is not preaching to them "to clean up their lives or to go and sin no more" (88), as Jesus says to the woman caught in adultery in John 8:11; rather, Morrison's reference to the scripture through the character of Baby Suggs illustrates how Black spaces were spaces of rereading and reinterpreting the Bible in ways that confirmed and affirmed their humanity.[21] As the founder of Black Liberation Theology, James H. Cone, argues in *God of the Oppressed*: "In view of their social situation of oppression, black people needed liberating visions so that they would not let historical limitations determine their perception of black being."[22]

Baby Suggs summons the enslaved community to a space where they can collectively shape a counternarrative of faith and spiritual empowerment in contradistinction to the dehumanizing narratives of condemnation and self-loathing she knows they may have internalized from the slave masters' religion. Recognizing their need for a place to bring their whole selves and for a safe space to express the wellspring of emotions their oppression attempted to contain, she institutes an intergenerational ritual of healing and renewal in the Clearing with these words:

> Let the children come.... Let your mothers hear you laugh.... Let the grown men come.... Let your wives and children see you dance.... Finally, she called the women to cry. For the living and the dead. Just cry.... It started that way: laughing children, dancing men, crying women and then it got mixed up. Women stopped crying and danced; men sat down and cried; children danced, women laughed, children

cried until exhausted and riven, all and each lay about the Clearing damp and gasping for breath. In the silence that followed, Baby Suggs, holy, offered up to them her great big heart. (87–88)

Through this intergenerational sacred ritual in the Clearing, Morrison invokes yet another Black cultural archive, the hush harbor—the sacred space the enslaved created for themselves, by themselves, among themselves to survive the racial horrors that threatened their lives on a daily basis. Recognized in religious and theological scholarship on the African American church and even referenced in the eulogy that President Barack Obama gave in June 2015 at the Emanuel AME Church, where a white supremacist murdered nine Black worshippers, the hush harbor was "a secluded informal structure . . . set in places away from masters so slaves could meet in to worship in private."[23] The enslaved regarded the hush harbor not only as a place to worship on their own terms but also as a place where they were free to value their belonging to the human family on their own terms. Historically, hush harbors were sites of spiritual resilience and political empowerment where the enslaved could shape their freedom struggle. In the Clearing, at a physical distance from the plantation where their bodies were under constant surveillance, assault, and trauma, Morrison represents a sacred strategy in a specific kind of geographical location that had physical and spiritual meaning for the enslaved community. The journey to the Clearing was a journey to a space in the natural environment not governed by the dominance of the oppressive structures on the plantation. Morrison uses this place in the narrative to offer an example of how the enslaved exercised agency and control over their bodies, emotions, and souls in a location where they could be by themselves and be free to be themselves. As Bhabha explains, they enter a "space of intervention" in the cultural interstices of their lives.[24] Or, put another way, under the guidance and ministry of Baby Suggs, they spatialize themselves to save themselves. From a geopoetic perspective, the Clearing is not just a setting or backdrop to a plot; instead, it is constitutive of the space where they imagine and experience the very emancipation they are seeking. For Morrison, therefore, it is a conscious narrative strategy to illustrate for her reader the kind of day-to-day interventions that were possible in the midst of oppression and under the direst of challenges to Black subjectivity.

The summons to the Clearing begins with Baby Suggs's recognition of their humanity, the reality of the emotions they have internalized to keep themselves sane, and their need for psychic release in a safe space where Baby Suggs could minister to their physical and spiritual needs that had not been acknowledged or valued elsewhere. Indeed, the self-love that she teaches and the ethic of care that undergirds her sermon constitute a "form of resistance" but also serve as an antidote to the physical and spiritual brutality of enslavement:

> "Here," she said, "in this here place, we flesh; flesh that weeps, laughs; flesh that dances on bare feet in grass. Love it. Love it hard.... And O my people they do not love your hands. Those they only use, tie, bind, chop off and leave empty. Love your hands! Love them. Raise them up and kiss them. Touch others with them, pat them together, stroke them on your face 'cause they don't love that either. *You* got to love it, *you*! And no, they ain't in love with your mouth. Yonder, out there, they will see it broken and break it again. What you say out of it, they will not heed. What you scream from it they do not hear.... No, they don't love your mouth. *You* got to love it. This is flesh I'm talking about here. Flesh that needs to be loved.... And O my people out yonder, hear me, they do not love your neck unnoosed and straight. So love your neck; put a hand on it, grace it and stroke it and hold it up.... And your inside parts that they'd just as soon slop for hogs.... More than your life-holding womb and your life-giving private parts, hear me now, love your heart. For this is the prize." (88–89)

In prefacing her sermon by telling them that "the only grace they could have was the grace they could imagine" and that "if they could not see it, they would not have it" (88), she instructs them on how to actualize their faith by acknowledging that she knows the specificity of their struggle in a strange land. Moreover, Morrison gives Baby Suggs the word *here* in contradistinction to the understood *there* that the community of the enslaved know so well. She uses language aligning herself with them in this place not only with the place marker but also with the first-person plural pronoun in Black vernacular—"we flesh" (88). Through her voice, her words, and her familiarity with their pain (because it is also hers), Baby Suggs transforms the very "groundlife [that] shuddered under their feet" (87) into sacred ground and space to facilitate their healing. Like Harriet Jacobs's garret in *Incidents in the Life of a Slave Girl*, the Clearing is paradoxically a third space of freedom between the inside and the outside of the boundaries of enslavement, concretized by a woman elder who chooses to remind the community of their true value beyond the white supremacist gaze.[25] Similar to McKittrick, who asserts in *Demonic Grounds: Black Women and the Cartographies of Struggle* that this ability to read the text of the Black body at the intersection of race and gender is beyond the concept of the margin, Barbara Christian identifies this ability as a critical Black feminist move that "opens up other geographic imaginations, poetic and otherwise."[26]

Moreover, in calling attention to the womb, in particular, Baby Suggs's sermon in the Clearing calls attention to another third space—the space M. Nourbese Philip references as the space "between the legs," the space that the Black enslaved woman did not and could not control, given that her body was the site of both production and reproduction.[27] The geopoetic lens enables us to see the Clearing in all its complexity as a strategic space for reading and rethinking Black subjectivity, as a communal space for remembering the dead and the living, and as a healing space for celebrating resilience and creativity in the midst of the struggle for freedom. The sermon in the Clearing suggests instead that Morrison's fictional representation of slavery offers a powerful portrayal of how Black people survived a system that could have utterly destroyed them. The love that Baby Suggs preaches into the hearing of this "beloved community," to use the phrase Martin Luther King Jr. made famous, is a radical, healing form of empathic love that inspires self-love and love for the enslaved others to whom they were connected as a balm for pain and self-loathing.[28]

The sermon that Baby Suggs delivers in the Clearing also reflects the ways the Black church was and has been a site of resistance that operates outside the boundaries of other political and social constraints on Black life and culture in America. Unlike W.E.B. Du Bois's *Souls of Black Folk* (1903), which sought to remind the nation that those who had been regarded merely as Black bodies for free unpaid labor indeed had souls or a spiritual nature that had not been duly acknowledged or understood, Morrison's fictional representation of the Black preacher as an "unchurched" holy woman signifies on the self-loathing of the Black body that slavery produced, and she introduces a counternarrative of self-love that is not selfish but communal in its place.[29] By naming the site of this communal resistance "the Clearing," Morrison locates agency and the desire for healing from oppression as a space of belonging outside of and between the domestic spaces that benevolent white powers (represented by Mr. Garner, who allegedly treated his male slaves like men) and malevolent white power structures (signified by Schoolteacher, who treated the enslaved of both genders as if they were subhuman) could not police. Likewise, as an open space outside of the slave master's control, the Clearing represents "a place where you could love anything you chose—not to need permission for desire . . . *that* was freedom" (162). Thus, the Clearing is also a site of desire and a political space of community. Sethe remembers with longing the feeling

> of being part of a neighborhood . . . all that was long gone and would never come back. No more dancing in the Clearing or happy feeds. No more discussions, stormy or quiet, about the true meaning of the Fugitive Bill, the Settlement Fee, God's Ways and Negro pews; antislavery,

> Manumission, skin voting, Republicans, Dred Scott, book learning, Sojourner's high-wheeled buggy, the Colored Ladies of Delaware, Ohio, and the other weighty issues that held them in chairs. (173)

The Clearing operates in this novel, then, as both a communal site of claiming and reaffirming one's subjectivity and a space for giving voice to one's reading of a world that has attempted to circumscribe the terms of existence. Ironically, the Clearing is an intraracial, subversive space of resistance that the enslaved created for themselves.

After the reader has already met Baby Suggs in the Clearing through Sethe's memory of her, we meet her from another perspective in another passage—as a Black female subject whose interior life represents the space of personal interrogation of the self. The passage reveals how enslavement had distorted notions of self-knowledge and self-love that one would associate with identify formation. At one point early in the novel, in a moment of reflection, the text shifts from exterior space—that is, the physical location of the Sweet Home plantation that "wasn't sweet and it sure wasn't home" (14) but was itself a distortion of domestic tranquility—to the interior space of Baby Suggs's own mind, for

> the sadness was at her center, the desolated center where the self that was no self made its home. Sad as it was she did not know where her children were buried or what they looked like if alive, fact was she knew more about them than she knew about herself, having never had the map to discover what she was like. . . . Could she sing? (Was it nice to hear when she did?) Was she pretty? Was she a good friend? Could she have been a loving mother? A faithful wife? Have I got a sister and does she favor me? If my mother knew me would she like me? (140)

Through this set of interior interrogations, Morrison reveals how the conditions of enslavement foreclosed on Black female subjectivity and on ways of knowing oneself that might otherwise have been readily available. The use of the word *map*, for example, suggests that beyond the exterior life of the plantation, there was an interior mindscape that she may have been able to help others navigate but could not fully navigate herself. Unlike more familiar historical, factual, nonfictional representations of slavery, Morrison's fiction offers both a map and an intimate portrait of the psyche of one of the strongest members of the Sweet Home community to suggest the vulnerability of those who were not as strong. The passage also signals another level of interiority—the desire for intimacy with one's own subjectivity. As Tricia Rose says, *Beloved* "explores the painful connection between the brutality of American slavery with its hatred of black flesh, and the urgent need for black self-love as a survival strategy and form of resistance."[30] Thus, the Clearing is not a deterministic setting but an emancipatory space where the assault on minds and bodies could be healed, if only for a time. Morrison's representation of this other dimension of Baby Suggs, where, for all her ability to know and minister to others, she was still grieving the losses of her loved ones and those whose connection to her were critical to her sense of self, provides a kind of map for exploring the diverse, complex dimensions of Black subjectivity during and after enslavement.

Beloved is part of a trilogy that Marc C. Conner says is a "meditation on love."[31] While it is indeed the first in the trilogy, it is not simply about love but more specifically about excesses of mother love and how the manifestations of those excesses show up in and affect the individuals and the community. The novel comments on love that would empower a mother to love her children enough to save them from enslavement by killing them, even if to do so would create public scandal and community shame. Yet the novel does not romanticize mothering.[32] Instead, it portrays motherhood through Sethe's thoughts as "Needing to be good enough, alert enough, strong enough" (132). As a free woman living out the psychic consequences of the infanticide she committed while enslaved, Sethe sums up her feelings by thinking "motherlove was a killer" (132). So, through this portrayal of presence and absence, life and loss, Morrison represents how the emotional toll of slavery on mothers and families distorted the bonds of love one might otherwise expect in the domestic sphere. By shifting the locus of the story of enslavement away from the gaze of the white other to both an interrogation of and a meditation on the routine and courageous ways enslaved persons exercised agency, Morrison creates an emancipatory space for her reader to consider the psychic and emotional cost of slavery not only on mother love but also on other relationships and dimensions of identity. Indeed, as various critics have noted, the entire novel is a narrative of grief, mourning, and loss of life before enslavement and for the life after enslavement that was yet to materialize fully for formerly disenfranchised people.[33] Or, as Baby Suggs says, "Not a house in the country ain't packed to its rafters with some dead Negro's grief" (5). But it is critical to note that Morrison is not focused solely on the history as much as she is on the residue of emotional havoc that the history wreaked on the interior lives of Black subjects. Like the enslaved community, the reader is riveted to an interiority that is at the intersection of the already and the not yet in terms of America's reckoning with its past and the consequences of that past. The Clearing operates in this novel, then, as a communal site of claiming and reaffirming one's subjectivity and a space for giving voice to one's reading of a world that has attempted to circumscribe the terms of existence.

But there are two additional manifestations of how *Beloved* is not so much about the white presence as it is about Black subjectivity, being, and the desire for emancipatory spaces. One such manifestation of these desires is in the intersubjective moment among Sethe, Denver, and Beloved, the ghost. What Stamp Paid hears as "undecipherable" is a moment of the Black female subjects engaged in what Morrison represents as an interior monologue among three speaking subjects who communicate through their thoughts. Morrison situates the reader as an eavesdropper onto the conversation that the thoughts of Sethe, Denver, and Beloved have with one another. This section of the novel begins with Sethe's thoughts:

> BELOVED, she my daughter. She mine. See. She come back to me of her own free will and I don't have to explain a thing. . . . She had to be safe and I put her where she would be. (200)

The second set of thoughts are those of Denver:

> Beloved is my sister. I swallowed her blood right along with my mother's milk. . . . She was my secret company until Paul D came. . . . I love my mother but I know she killed one of her own daughters, and tender as she is with me, I'm scared of her because of it. (205)

And the third set of thoughts belong to Beloved:

> I AM BELOVED and she is mine. . . . I am not separate from her . . . there is no place where I stop . . . her face is my own and I want to be there in the place where her face is and be looking at it too . . . it is always now. (210)

Morrison's geopoetic rendering of this relationship reveals that when Beloved comes on the scene, she inspires this intersubjective love, recognition, and understanding of the interconnection between the past, present, and future that they collectively represent. Moreover, her presence in the story is a representation of the repressed past that Sethe attempts to beat back, but it also represents how the stories of Black lives from the Middle Passage to Post-Emancipation are interconnected in the real time of the present—the "always now." This intersubjective, intergenerational dialogue can be read aesthetically as a moment of reckoning outside of time and space but also within it, in what Bhabha identifies as a "fugue-like ceremony of claiming and naming through intersecting and interstitial" space.[34]

Morrison embeds this intimate dialogue as an enunciation into a liminal space that connects Sethe's memories, Beloved's sense of loss, and Denver's desire for the love of both her mother and her sister. Through the use of this narrative strategy of hybrid subjectivity and of a complex manipulation of punctuation, syntax, and possessive pronouns, Morrison disrupts the flow of the larger narrative to illustrate for the reader a new dimension of interiority that is outside of time and to give voice to what Bakhtin refers to as "audible echoes" of agency that represent consciousness between loss and desire that are out of the control of the author.[35] As Bhabha suggests, Morrison uses this intersubjective break in the narrative intentionally to introduce indeterminacy and to offer the reader new ways to consider how space reveals interconnections that had not previously been perceived or understood.[36] It is this same interconnectedness that the character Beloved exploits. She takes advantage of Sethe's trauma from Sweet Home, the grief and shame of infanticide, and the weight of guilt and loss to disrupt the modicum of domestic tranquility that Denver and Sethe had worked so hard to obtain inside the walls of their haunted home. As the novel says, "To Sethe, the future was a matter of keeping the past at bay" (42). When the past returns as memory, revenge, love, and desire all rolled into one, it appears as a major disruption in Sethe's life in the form of the ghost of the daughter she killed, but it reveals itself as the key to imagining a dimension of freedom she had not yet experienced.

The seventeen-page passage is also a major disruption in the flow of the novel. The reader must adjust to the disorienting presence of spaces and punctuation in unexpected places on the page of the text. It begins with Sethe's declaration—"BELOVED, she my daughter. She mine" (200)—and her thought that "her mind was homeless" (204). In Beloved's section, the narrative shifts back and forth from first-person singular to first-person plural—"we are all trying to leave our bodies behind" (210). The references to "crouching" (211) invoke not only the memory of giving birth, of her mother's escape, and of others attempting to escape enslavement on the Underground Railroad but also the sounds and scenes of the Middle Passage. Morrison places this poetic passage of intersubjectivity and Beloved's wrestling with her identity as a representation of the repressed past, as an insistent interrogative presence about that past, and as an all-consuming disruption to the uneasy domestic space of the present that drives Paul D away from 124. It could be argued that the intersubjective space that the three voices create is a poetic third space of an enactment of melancholia, especially if we understand melancholia as a space of "digesting loss," as Cheng suggests.[37] Morrison is creating a space for the reader to come into both the experience of mourning and loss and an understanding of the cost of denying that loss inside the sacred space of the soul. Beyond understanding the loss that enslavement has created and the infanticide that it provoked are the psychic consequences of beating back the past rather than coming to terms with it for all three female characters. The seventeen pages of poetic intersubjective narrative, described as the "unspeakable thoughts, unspoken" (199), are Morrison's attempt to represent her characters in the liminal space of their consciousness and to situate the reader to perceive a different understanding of the experience of enslavement through the mother-daughter bond. In the female-centered space that she creates through their thoughts, Morrison invites the reader to move outside of the subject-object binary with its trappings of ownership into an intersubjective space of mutual recognition that Benjamin says is a free space of "communion."[38] Near the end of the passage, the focus shifts from the specificity of relationship, regrets, and ownership to the elusive but inclusive language of communion, love, and belonging described as the desire for "the join" (213). The references to ownership shift to references of mutual belonging. Through their thoughts, we learn how they recognize that they belong to one another and are interconnected, despite their circumstances. The repetition and blurring together of the words "You are mine/You are mine/You are mine" (217) as the final utterances of the passage illustrate how the passage operates as what Quashie refers to as a "choral subjunctive."[39] In other words, Morrison uses her geopoetics to transport her readers from the familiar narrative mode of speaking about enslavement to a liberated space of imagination, free association, and stream of consciousness, where she can represent the implications of enslavement in a totally new poetic way, through voices speaking into and through one another in a kind of chorus to reveal a deeper truth of their being and interconnectedness.

Morrison creates another shift in the narrative, however, from the intersubjective space almost outside of narrative time back to the present, when Denver realizes that her mother's life is at risk. When Denver sees that Beloved's presence has begun to consume Sethe with grief both physically and spiritually, she realizes she must do the very thing she least wanted to do—abandon the comfort of their home and her sense of belonging to connect with the larger community outside of her home. In a real sense, she realizes she would have to expand her notion of belonging to recognize that the very community that had scorned, ostracized, and looked down on her mother and their family would be critical to her mother's deliverance, her emancipation from the trauma of the past, and the healing that would enable her to have a life on the other side of freedom. Moreover, she would have to abandon her own obsessive desire of Beloved to address the psychic consequences of her behavior on her mother. Denver realizes she must relinquish her dependence on the domestic space she shares with her mother to embrace the larger communal space in the company of the community of women. By invoking their spiritual power through song that is reminiscent of Baby Suggs in the Clearing, they can engage in a kind of healing ritual that will save Sethe. As Sethe hears the women singing, she remembers the sounds of the Clearing as a space

> where the voices of women searched for the right combination, the key, the code, the sound that broke the back of words. Building voice upon voice until they found it, and when they did it was a wave of sound wide enough to sound deep water.... It broke over Sethe and she trembled like the baptized in its wash. (261)

By engaging the community of women, Denver connects with yet another third space of belonging that represents her own psychic healing, not just her mother's. And just as the Clearing was a third space or hush harbor, it was also a space for what Du Bois refers to as "the sorrow songs" in *Souls of Black Folk*.[40] By representing the sorrow songs as coded music that could reach the interior recesses of the soul beyond the physical realm, Morrison reminds the reader of yet another history—the history of the sorrow songs as spirituals that were both an index to faith and a sign of resilience and resistance to oppression. In connecting the songs created in bondage from chattel slavery to the psychic bondage that remained in freedom, Morrison reminds the reader of spiritual resources embedded in Black history and culture. In many respects, the novel not only operates as a sorrow song or spiritual but also *is* a spiritual in the multivalent ways that it presents, as Karla F. C. Holloway argues, "innervision, the cognitive reclamation of our spiritual histories."[41]

At the end of *Beloved* is yet another third space beyond the desire for freedom, and that is the desire for love. Morrison inscribes this dimension of Black subjectivity to call into question normalized protocols of race in Black fiction that would limit representations to critiques of racism, enslavement, sexism, and other forms of oppression. Reading her narrative aesthetics and cultural politics through a mode of representation shaped by romantic desire and untainted sexual love enables us to see how Morrison employs the love affair of Paul D and Sethe to do a new kind of cultural work. The love between them is first discussed in terms of Sethe's reluctance:

> There were two rooms and she took him into one of them, hoping he wouldn't mind the fact that she was not prepared; that though she

could remember desire, she had forgotten how it worked; the clutch and helplessness that resided in the hands. . . . Her deprivation had been not having any dreams of her own at all. (19)

In fact, she later wonders "Would it be all right to go ahead and feel? Go ahead and *count on something?*" (38). In language that invokes the emotional reluctance and fear of trauma victims, Sethe gradually allows Paul D, one of the Sweet Home men, to come into her heart, into the interior space she had been guarding.[42] Morrison also includes a portrait of how Sweet Home and Schoolteacher affect him in the intervening years after enslavement. He says, "I wasn't allowed to be and stay what I was. . . . Schoolteacher changed me. I was something else" (72). But when Sethe begins lovingly rubbing his knee, he temporarily interrupts the sharing of his story, thinking, "Saying more might push them both to a place they couldn't get back from. He would keep the rest where it belonged: in that tobacco tin buried in his chest where a red heart used to be" (73). At the end of the novel, however, after Beloved has been exorcised from the house, Paul D returns and realizes there "are too many things to feel about this woman" (272). He thinks, "She is a friend of my mind. She gather me. . . . The pieces I am, she gather them and give them back to me in all the right order. It's good, you know, when you got a woman who is a friend of your mind" (273). Upon his return, he realizes, "Only this woman Sethe could have left him his manhood like that. He wants to put his story next to hers" (273). Most of all, he makes space in his own thinking for their relationship to be an intersubjective love when he reminds Sethe that she can be the subject of her own story and her own life. As Morrison says:

> We are the subjects of our own narrative, witnesses to and participants in our own experience, and in no way coincidentally, in the experience of those with whom we have come in contact. We are not, in fact, "other." We are choices. And to read imaginative literature by and about us is to choose to examine centers of the self and to have the opportunity to compare these centers with the "raceless" one with which we are, all of us, most familiar.[43]

Morrison concludes *Beloved* on a note of expectation that Sethe and Paul D will both remember that their individual and collective stories are not stories "to pass on" (275) and that they can have a new beginning with their commitment to create a third space, an emancipatory space, that combines both of their stories. Morrison suggests to her readers that only out of their combined stories is a new sense of self and a new understanding of freedom possible.

In the other two novels of the trilogy—*Jazz* and *Paradise*—Morrison continues her literary project of exploring identity through excesses of love. She again develops this theme through her geopoetics of creating and representing emancipatory spaces to interrogate the themes of place, race, and be/longing. The other two novels of the trilogy take place during two periods—the 1920s Great Migration of South to North and the 1970s, respectively. In *Jazz*, published in 1992, just five years after *Beloved*, Morrison shifts from the 1800s and the vagaries of maternal love during enslavement to the vagaries of romantic love that Violet and Joe Trace experience upon moving from Virginia to New York City. If *Beloved* can be read as a spiritual about the journey from enslavement to freedom, then *Jazz* can be read as a secular blues-like jazz riff on the journey from the oppressive Jim Crow South to the relative freedom of New York City and other Northern sites during the Harlem Renaissance. Morrison begins the novel *in media res* by suspending the reader in the middle of time and space and revealing the denouement of the plot in the very first paragraph. Like a jazz song, the entire tune is found in the opening notes on the first page of the novel, but it is the series of improvisations on the tune and the riffs over, under, around, and through those opening notes of the tune in the remaining pages of the book that make the song come alive and resonate with the listener. To use the words of Baker in his reference to the spirituals and jazz, it is the "terribleness and flair" that give the rest of the narrative its substance.[44]

The novel opens with the central information that a woman named Violet Trace (the female protagonist) has just gone to the funeral of an eighteen-year-old woman, Dorcas Manfred, with whom her husband, Joe Trace, has had an adulterous affair, with a plan go up to the casket "to cut her dead face" (3). A group of young men in attendance quickly interrupt her plan and throw her out of the church, after which she goes home and releases her birds, "including the parrot that said, 'I love you'" (3). What follows this dramatic introduction, told on the very first page of the novel, are two divergent forms of spatializing the self—that of a couple in an estranged marriage and that of the narrator. Between the two forms, Morrison introduces a new way to imagine and think about ordinary Black folk during the historical period we know of as the Harlem Renaissance, and she challenges the reader to reimagine what happens to their identity literally, intellectually, and emotionally in the space between the pages of a book.

After the startling introduction, Morrison begins unpacking the identity of the two characters, the status of their unraveling marriage, and the journey that led them from the South to New York City in the first place. Inspired by an actual photograph in the famous James Van Der Zee 1979 collection of photographs known as *The Harlem Book of the Dead*, Morrison's novel imagines an entire narrative behind the photograph of the young woman who refused to reveal, even as she lay dying, that her lover was the one who shot her.⁴⁵ Although this love affair and the image about it may have formed the kernel of the story that inspires the novel, what is more significant are the multiple angles Morrison introduces on the larger narrative of the journey of Violet and Joe to New York and how that journey from one place to a new geolocation changes each of them in ways they did not anticipate or fully understand. The intricate layers of each of their stories are examples of Morrison's narrative practice of going to the cultural archive, retrieving an image, and imagining the multiple underlying narratives that have brought it into being. Put another way, to use Sharpe's phrase "in the wake," the novel takes place in the wake of a love affair gone bad, in the wake of the disillusion that the migration from South to North created, and in the wake of a narrator's intrusive yet unreliable attempts to recount and explain all that has occurred.⁴⁶

With a foreword written by Morrison, *The Harlem Book of the Dead* is a compendium of photographs, reflections, and poetry representing the ways in which the Black community created and engaged in rituals of memorializing the dead. Morrison describes the book as a "remarkable concert of Black subject, Black poet, Black photographer and Black artist" that is significant for how it embodies the African proverb "The Ancestor lives as long as there are those who remember."⁴⁷ It could be argued that her use of the word *concert* was a form of literary telegraphing to a period thirteen years later, when she would provide for her readers not only the sites of the subject, poet, photographer, and artist but also the representations of the sound of the places and period that would encapsulate the music and aesthetics of jazz. As is true for the news clipping that is the archive that inspired *Beloved*, Morrison first encountered the photograph that inspired *Jazz* several years before she would create a fictional narrative around it. In many respects, as a source of information, an archive is, by its very nature, limited. As Hartman explains, "the archive dictates what can be said about the past and the kinds of stories that can be told about the persons catalogued, embalmed, and sealed away."⁴⁸ In addition to the photograph of the deceased young woman, Morrison also had Van Der Zee's annotation of it, which says:

> She was the one I think was shot by her sweetheart at a party with a noiseless gun. She complained of being sick at the party and friends said "Well, why don't you lay down?" and they taken [*sic*] her in a room and laid her down. After they undressed her and loosened her clothes, they saw the blood on her dress. They asked her about it and she said,

"I'll tell you tomorrow, yes, I'll tell you tomorrow." She was trying to give him a chance to get away.[49]

As a writer, then, Morrison not only had the photograph itself but also an annotative snippet from the archive of the Black female subject's life narrative as additional material from which to work and around which to imagine a narrative. Embedded in the annotation is what amounts to an aporia of a sort in which the dead girl, who is then an absence, speaks through a question that is rendered undecidable. The annotated photograph as archive, just like the newspaper clipping as archive, becomes, therefore, not only the site of memory around which Morrison would create fiction but also a site for narrative spatializing, where she would fill in the gaps to represent what the archive alone—that is, the dead girl—could not reveal. As Sharpe argues, the archive can simultaneously be the site of "imaging . . . and imagining . . . the fullness of Black life," especially when it is accompanied by the metadata of annotation.[50] Put another way, for an artist, the archive does *not* totally dictate what can and cannot be said. Instead, it serves as a both/and site, where Morrison the writer is free to imagine the site as both a point of entry and a point of departure and thus a "paradoxical space," to use Gillian Rose's term for this both/and quality.[51]

Morrison's goal in fleshing out the story behind the photograph and the words that commented on its origins was to imagine the interior life of the subjects and the narratives of their lives to explore the excesses of love that led to death and how various subjects navigated the complex spaces of loss and longing in their lives in the wake of leaving the rural South to live in a place known for its urban landscape. Morrison was aware, when she encountered the photograph as an archive, that by writing this narrative, she was undertaking a literary archaeological project of imagining, narrating, and creating spaces for the reader that the archive could not reveal. Moreover, almost as if channeling the dictum of poet Emily Dickinson to "tell all the truth but tell it slant," Morrison does not tell the narrative of *Beloved* or *Jazz* from the so-called beginning but instead follows her geopoetic, stylistic penchant of disorienting the reader by introducing the narrative *in medias res* and by structuring it in the meandering, nonlinear way that approximates the way the mind remembers and the way jazz improvises on a melody.[52] Her intentionality as an author in this regard was signaled as early as 1980, when she said:

> To make the story appear oral, meandering, effortless, spoken—to have the reader *feel* the narrator without *identifying* the narrator, or hearing him or her knock about, and to have the reader work *with* the author

in the construction of the book—is what's important. What is left out is as important as what is there.⁵³

Later, in a radio conversation with critic Michael Silverblatt, she elaborated by saying:

> The meaning of a novel is in the structure. The question of when the information is given, at what time, what you want the reader to not just know, but feel about this character. . . . Just writing the beginning, the middle, the end is one way to do it. It's not very interesting to me because it's not really life-like. I mean we don't live in plots. So the way in which the mind takes in the varieties of experiences of life and other people, has to be reassembled for its meaning and that's where the structure is, at least what I work very hard at, is the sort of deep structure, what is there underneath this activity. And then you see it from another person's point of view; not just one character but another's and how and when that information becomes available to the reader seems to me the real adventure.⁵⁴

These statements about her process suggest that she is interested in challenging the reader to forgo familiar and received "protocols of reading," whatever those may be, just as she has chosen, in her role of "the reader as artist," to disrupt narrative conventions to enter the story of a familiar place in a new way.⁵⁵

In a sense, Morrison expands one of the earlier Black protocols of reading that emerged from the Black aesthetic tradition of the 1960s that suggested that there was a single, predominantly male way to represent Black people.⁵⁶ Instead, her geopoetics point to a new way to enter the space of Black female and male subjectivity by interrupting reader expectations and presuppositions of a certain order. As Farah Jasmine Griffin notes, unlike her Black male predecessors, Morrison is not as focused in her fiction on Black masculinity as she is on the relationships between and among Black subjects—both female and male—and how they are connected to the time, places, and spaces where they find themselves.⁵⁷ The novel begins with references to not only the relationship of a married couple but also to the relationship between the narrator and the reader. Through a sound known for the intimacy it creates within the Black community—the sound of the narrator sucking her teeth with the arrogance of a gossip and represented with the words and tone of vernacular conversation: "Sth, I know this woman" (3)—Morrison begins the novel both by frustrating reader expectations and by building intrigue to invite the reader's trust and curiosity all at once.

By narrating the story not from the perspective of "The New Negro," as Alain Locke named what he thought was the representative Black person of the period—that is, the few well-known familiar artists and members of the Black and mostly male intelligentsia who popularized the history of the Harlem Renaissance—but from the perspective of those who lived in the quotidian shadow of those famous personages, Morrison sets out to fill in gaps in the national narrative about the people, the place, and the period.[58] As she explained in an interview with Salman Rushdie in 1992:

> What I was interested in was the concept of jazz, the jazz era, what all of that meant before it became appropriated and redistributed as music throughout the world. What was jazz when it was just music for the people, and what were those people like? That subject is highly contested—its origins, what it means, what the word's etymology is, and so on. The only thing that's consistent in the debate is the nature of improvisation—that one works very hard in order to be able to invent. It was that quality in these people's lives that I wanted to capture, moving from the South on into a city, where there were endless possibilities, of both security and danger.[59]

What this quote encapsulates are both her narrative poetics and cultural politics at once. On one hand, the quote captures Morrison's awareness of how the concept of jazz names a site of cultural commodification, appropriation, and contestation that capitalized on Black labor and artistic production at the expense of Black people having access to that production in places and spaces where white patrons could consume the music Black people produced. On the other hand, she also signals an awareness that the narrative of the Harlem Renaissance foregrounded one group of Black people and left another group entirely in the shadows. Against the backdrop of what Beavers refers to as the "two grand narratives" of the era—the Jazz Age and the Harlem Renaissance—Morrison's *Jazz* uses the archive of a Harlem Renaissance–era photo to recuperate, imagine, and improvise on the representation of the interstitial spaces of the narratives she referred to as "discredited" narratives from "discredited people" of the period that often omitted, marginalized, or invalidated their ways of being, belonging, and making meaning.[60] Thus, the narrative that shapes the novel is a third space between two well-known narratives about Black culture and Black aesthetics, a space where Morrison is then free as an artist to engage in improvisation by interrogating identity formation and subjectivity at a time of great upheaval, duress, and high aspirations.

In terms of content, it could be argued that the novel *Jazz* is a kind of fictional counterpart to Isabel Wilkerson's *The Warmth of Other Suns: The Epic Story of America's Great Migration*, the 2010 nonfiction national bestseller about the oral histories of the various individuals and families whose journey, known as the Black Migration from the South to the North, led to the Harlem Renaissance.[61] As a journalist and historian, Wilkerson describes Harlem as a "city [that] had a way of bringing out the best and . . . the worst in everyone," where people "had to learn to recognize that admixture" in themselves and those around them.[62] In the sense that it is a novel about migrants, their relocation, and the multilayered, multivalent, multivocal stories of their lives before and after migration, Morrison narrates *Jazz*, however, in the modernist tradition that Griffin describes as the "migration narrative" of the African American literary tradition.[63] As a migration narrative, it seeks to capture the modernist sensibilities of navigating the "creation of a new self" in a new geographical space.[64] In terms of style and poetics, the novel operates like jazz, the music that emerged from the Black modernist tradition that Baker associates with the Harlem Renaissance and that Moten describes as the tragic-erotic blues story that transforms itself into an improvisational melody or baseline of the entire tune, that not only incorporates death but "the sound that extends beyond the end of which it tells."[65] In his analysis of Duke Ellington's music, Moten describes the blackness of the avant-garde in language that is illustrative of Morrison's geopoetics in *Jazz* when he says:

> Such blackness is only in that it exceeds itself; it bears the groundedness of an uncontainable outside. It's an erotic of the cut, submerged in the broken, breaking space-time of an improvisation. Blurred, dying life; liberatory, improvisatory, damaged love; freedom drive.[66]

Morrison attempts to move beyond the linear grand narrative of epic stories and the Black subjects whose lives were shaped by dislocation and relocation to a meandering specificity about the deep psychic spaces that revealed the complexities of renegotiating the terms of living and loving in a new place in a new way.

Like *Beloved*, *Jazz* is imagined by Morrison as a story haunted by the death of someone whose absence has created a hyper-visible space of trauma, loss, grieving, mourning, and longing at the same time that it has created new ways for those left behind to imagine themselves and the larger context of their lives in the wake of loss. The ironic presence at the opening of the novel is the narrator who presumes an omniscience and who attempts to establish herself as a reliable source of information about the people and places of New York City in 1926. By the end of the novel, however, the reader observes that the narrator has on numerous occasions called her own omniscience into question and thereby abandoned the reader to the space of metanarrative and their own imagination as to what has transpired between the first and last pages of the novel. Thus, in some respects, to be explored later, this novel is a site where Morrison's project is improvisational narrative play, where she self-consciously experiments with the role of the author, the role of the narrator, and the complex, nuanced ways the reader is always at the mercy of both between the pages of the text. The narrator vacillates between establishing intimacy with the reader by claiming to let the reader in on information about the protagonists and communicating in language that intermingles objective narrative with her own biased, signifying vernacular commentary. For example, when the reader learns that Violet's first strategy for dealing with her grieving husband is to have an affair of her own in revenge, the narrator dismisses her actions by commenting, "That mess didn't last two weeks" (5). In its commentary on Violet's abbreviated, retaliatory love affair, the text becomes what Gates refers to as a double-voiced "speakerly text," in the sense that the narrator informs the reader of the affair and shifts, in the middle of doing so, from the Standard English of exposition to the Black vernacular English of signifying on it. Thus, she interrupts the narrative with clarifying information but subversive commentary, a disruptive pattern of improvisational narrative that continues throughout the novel.[67]

With the information of the failed affair established, Morrison proceeds into the body of the novel with a framework of Violet's determination to find out about the girl with whom her husband had had an affair and to "solve the mystery of love that way" (5). In response to her desire to solve the mystery of love, the narrator comments, as if speaking directly to Violet (and by extension, to the reader), "Good luck and let me know" (5). Violet begins her meticulous plan to discover more about her husband's teenage lover by placing a photo of the dead girl on the fireplace mantel so that she and her husband Joe Trace can both look "at it in bewilderment" (6). Violet's placement of the photo in the space between them signifies that Dorcas is the ostensible presence and absence with which both individuals must come to terms. In just a few pages into the novel, the narrator describes the circumstances that made the Trace home a space where "a poisoned silence floated through the rooms" and created "a mighty bleak household" (6). Morrison uses the remainder of the novel to fill in gaps in the narrative that led this couple into this third space of estrangement inside the walls of their own home. In a real sense, their home becomes a third space of longing, between the familiar landscape of the South that they had abandoned and the new landscape where they were still living after twenty years of attempting to understand life at the intersection of loss and love and the forces that mitigated both.

Morrison simultaneously places the narrator in the gap with the characters and gives her a voice to articulate her own impressions and perceptions of New York as a place. When the narrator exclaims, "I'm crazy about this City" (7), the capitalization of the word *city* personifies it and signals its major role in the narrative and in shaping Black subjectivity. The narrator removes any pretense of objectivity and establishes her identity as just another migrant attempting to come to terms with this urban space, just as the Black people who have migrated there are attempting to do. Situated between daylight and shadow, the narrator imagines that inside the buildings are combinations of "clarinets and lovemaking, fists and the voices of sorrowful women" (7), and forces that make her "dream tall and feel in on things. Hep" (7). Like Violet and Joe Trace, the narrator, therefore, is trying to read and understand the city and its effect on her experience of it. In contradistinction to the architecture left behind in the rural South are the tall buildings of Harlem that give the urban setting its paradoxical feeling of exclusion and inclusion. While the word *hep* names and describes the inclusion in the language of jazz, the word *feel* suggests that the narrator is imagining possibilities that are more likely the substance of dreams than fact. In fact, the narrator confesses that she is not really "in on things" (7) at all but remains a mere observer, a reader trying to read the signs and symbols like everyone else. And in the role of observer, she shares what she's heard and seen about the period in language that represents the third space between the two grand narratives:

> Here comes the new. Look out. There goes the sad stuff. The bad stuff. The things-nobody-could-help stuff. The way everybody was then and there. Forget that. History is over, you all, and everything's ahead at last. In halls and offices people are sitting around thinking future thoughts about projects and bridges and fast-clicking trains underneath. The A&P hires a colored clerk. Big-legged women with pink kitty tongues roll money into green tubes. . . . Regular people corner thieves in alleys. . . . Hoodlums hand out goodies. . . . Nobody wants to be an emergency at Harlem Hospital but if the Negro surgeon is visiting, pride cuts down the pain . . . the City can't hurt you. . . . I like the way the City makes people think they can do what they want and get away with it. (7–8)

On one hand, Morrison uses this passage to mimic the language of the period, even capturing the rhythm, beat, and flow of sound and music characteristic of the so-called Jazz Age that writers such as Langston Hughes and James Weldon Johnson tried to capture in their writing about the period.[68] On the other hand, the references to the racial dynamics of the period interspersed with the celebratory aspects of the city tell the other Harlem Renaissance story of the vagaries of when and where Black people were excluded from opportunities for belonging. In fact, it could be argued that Morrison uses the narrator's observations to illuminate the paradoxical both/and nature of the jazz aesthetic that accounted for its appeal and apprehension about its inevitable appropriation and commodification. But in the third space between these two is the space of Black subjectivity, of imagining possibilities of selfhood that go beyond what is said and not said, done or not done by those in power with their "future thoughts."

The use of the narrator as reader to develop the history of the period continues with references to Harlem's racial history. In other words, interspersed through the developing narrative of Violet Trace, her intricate plan to learn more about her husband's dead lover, and the story of their lives individually before and after marriage are the narrator's reading of the City and attempts to understand its appeal and decipher its effect on Black people. In sum, place and race are interconnected, and Morrison's geopoetics illustrate this interconnection at every turn. On one hand, the City exposes its emerging racial dynamics as "wealthy whites, and plain ones too, pile into mansions decorated and redecorated by black women richer than they are, and both pleased with the spectacle of the other" (8). On the other hand, the narrator takes note of how a "breeze stirs the white plumes of the helmets of the UNIA men" (8), a reference that points directly to the Black response of resistance to white supremacy. The United Negro Improvement Association, the organization founded by Marcus Garvey in 1914 that grew to over seven hundred branches by the 1920s, with its Black Nationalist agenda and "Back to Africa" movement, is an example, like jazz music, of a way Black people read and responded to how they were situated in Harlem and elsewhere. Moreover, the reference to it in the early part of the text suggests that there were multiple ways that Black people had already imagined their lives in response to the racial realities of living in Harlem. Morrison describes another response in this language: "[A] colored man floats down out of the sky blowing a saxophone, and below him, in the space between the two buildings, a girl talks earnestly to a man in a straw hat. . . . Do what you please in the City, it is there to back and frame you no matter what you do" (8–9). Morrison's narrator observes in one passage after another how the city has control over people:

> That kind of fascination, permanent and out of control, seized children, young girls, men of every description, mothers, brides, and barfly women and if they have their way and get to the City, they feel more like themselves, more like the people they always believed they were. Nothing can pry them away from that; the City is what they want it to be: thriftless, warm, scary and full of amiable strangers. (35)

Through her observant, seemingly omniscient narrator, Morrison provides a kind of geographical, cognitive, and emotional mapping with the music, thoughts, and narratives that shape the history not only of the Harlem Renaissance but also of Violet and Joe Trace.

Morrison represents Harlem from a Black perspective. At the same time that New York City is the site of this cultural transformation in music and dance, it is also the site of racial violence and where Black people navigated their lives in the midst of change in spaces designated for them. The only sound at the "silent march" was the sound of "the drums and the Colored Boy Scouts passing out explanatory leaflets to whitemen in straw hats who needed to know what the freezing faces already knew" (58). Although the words on the leaflets seem "crazy, out of focus . . . some great gap between the print and the child" (58), Alice hears the drums as a "rope cast for rescue" (58), as "an all-embracing rope of fellowship, discipline and transcendence" (60). With this language, the narrator transports the reader from the silent march on Fifth Avenue, to East St. Louis, to Europe, and back to Harlem. Unlike Dorcas, who was seduced by what was known during the era as "race music" (79), Alice represents a generational divide that

> heard a complicated anger in it; something hostile that disguised itself as flourish and roaring seduction. But the parts she hated most was its appetite. Its longing for the bash, the slit; a kind of careless hunger. . . . It was impossible to keep the Fifth Avenue drums separate from the belt-buckle tunes vibrating from pianos and spinning on every Victrola. (59)

In keeping with the metaphor of jazz as a form of improvisational reading, the individual song/stories of Alice Manfred and her deceased niece, Dorcas, are critical to Morrison's desire to reveal the multiple conflicting forces at play in shaping Black subjectivity in Harlem and elsewhere during the 1920s. Whereas Alice has read Harlem with fury and caution, Dorcas reads it with longing and a desire for freedom of expression outside the bounds of her aunt's protective policing of her coming and going. And, like the stories of various places where she has lived, the music holds within it spaces where her mind has negotiated how to create a life for herself as she attempted to raise her sister's child.

The song/stories of Violet and Joe, respectively, not only improvise and riff on the larger narrative of the allure and distraction of Harlem and the music of jazz but also develop the deep structure of love and loss, memory and desire that forms the substance of Morrison's distinct representation of the Harlem Renaissance. Given that the historical narrative of the Harlem Renaissance begins with the Great Migration, the story of how Violet got to New York City and became a freelance hairdresser is critical to connecting the narrator's observations to the specific journeys of the characters. Morrison's geopoetics alternate between two spaces—the interior life of Violet and the external realities of the other newly arrived immigrants and the specific sites of memory in Violet's life as a girl, as a young woman, and later as the object of Joe's affection. This alternating between interiority in the present and sites of memory from various moments of the past represents, for Morrison, how the mind operates but also serves as an invitation to the reader to consider an alternate route into the space of human history by exploring how a particular group of people handled and responded to the vicissitudes of change and racism. Early in the novel, the narrator even comments on these mental vacillations when she observes:

> While she sprinkles the collar of a white shirt her mind is at the bottom of the bed where the leg, broken clean away from the frame, is too split to nail back. . . . She thinks she longs for rest . . . but I don't think she would like it. . . . They are all like that, these women. Waiting for the ease, the space that need not be filled with anything other than the drift of their own thoughts. But they wouldn't like it. . . . They fill their mind and hands with soap and repair and dicey confrontations because what is waiting for them, in a suddenly idle moment, is the seep of rage. Molten. Thick and slow-moving. Mindful and particular about what in its path it chooses to bury. Or else, into a beat of time, and sideways under their breasts, slips a sorrow they don't know where from. (16)

Documenting in her observations of Violet the ways in which her mind and that of other women in Harlem move in and out of the interstices of thought and feelings from rage to sorrow, the narrator foregrounds daily ruminations that are as critical as doing chores, chatting with neighbors, or going to the movies. The novel, in many respects, offers an example of the "break" in jazz, that interstitial space where the melody or known tune is broken up, riffed upon, and presented as variations on itself and on a theme.

One space in the narrative where the reader must read through such interstitial space is in Violet's own interrogation of her behavior. On at least three occasions, the reader bears witness to her attempts to come to terms with her actions, her sense of herself, and the consequences of her actions. The most obvious example of this incongruity are her actions at the funeral. But there are two other moments that reveal her incongruity to both herself and her Harlem neighbors. In fact, this first incident occurs even before Joe meets Dorcas:

> Way, way before . . . Joe ever laid eyes on the girl, Violet sat down in the middle of the street. She didn't stumble nor was she pushed: she just sat down. . . . She slowly came around, dusted off her clothes, and got to her appointment an hour late. . . . It never happened again . . . the street sitting—but quiet as it's kept she did try to steal that baby although there is no way to prove it. (17)

The ease with which Morrison introduces these two examples of disconcerting and even disruptive behavior is an example of a narrative aesthetic designed to engage the reader in improvisational reading, of making sense of what does not necessarily make sense to the eye at first notice. Violet's attempts to navigate life in Harlem, therefore, are interspersed with these inexplicable behaviors, these episodes of "public crazinesses" (22) and what the narrator describes as her "renegade tongue" (24).

The contradistinction between the way she was in the South and the way she changes once she arrives in the North is introduced early in the novel and is part of the spatial logic at work in Morrison's geopoetics. In language that represents Violet's thoughts, the narrator observes: "She didn't use to be that way. She had been a snappy, determined girl and a hardworking young woman, with the snatch-gossip tongue of a beautician. She liked, and had, to get her way. She had chosen Joe and refused to go back home once she'd seen him taking shape in early light" (23). But once she arrives in Harlem, she understands herself as two people. The narrator describes her as "that other Violet" (89) and then lists a series of behaviors to contrast the Violet who could not seemingly predict the actions of "*that* Violet." The word *that* appears in italics nearly twenty times to describe a Violet that was out of sorts as she attempted to read herself as she was reading Harlem and the demands it made on her psyche and her ability to know herself. In words akin to "out of body" language to describe a self that one does not recognize as oneself, the reader learns about Violet's shift in and out of bizarre behavior and in and out of self-interrogation. At one point, as she sits in a drugstore having a malt, she begins "wondering who on earth that other Violet was that walked about the City in her skin; peeped out through her eyes and saw other things . . . [and] *that* Violet remembered what she did not" (89–90). She is very much aware that her behavior at the funeral prompts her neighbors to scorn her and to change her name to "Violent" (75), but beyond their assessment of her are the ways in which she reads her own newly spatialized identity and believes the city has taken "the power she used to boast of" (92) and alienated her from herself. The attention to this difference by the mere use of italics is yet another manifestation of Morrison's geopoetics of connecting place with meaning, feeling, and subjectivity.

In a similar fashion, Morrison illustrates how Joe is a different person in Harlem than he had been before he arrived. Ironically, like Violet, he works in the beauty industry, selling cosmetics. Through his thoughts, we learn that he, too, is wrestling with who he had been and who he had become—not only in his marriage and the affair but also in his understanding of his past. Embedding the complicated stories of Violet's life narrative with Joe's deepens the representation of subjectivity for each of them and connects the trauma of grieving and loss with the midlife crisis that complicates their marriage. Like the story of Hartman, both Violet's story and Joe's tell a "history tantamount to mourning" and to understanding that being a stranger somewhat to oneself and others "concerns not only matters of familiarity, belonging, and exclusion but as well involves a particular relation to the past."[69] At every turn, Morrison's geopoetics resist all reductive notions of time, space, history, and identity to reinforce her more nuanced, profoundly complicated intersectional understanding of Black subjectivity. The loss of her mother, literally by suicide at the bottom of a well, and Joe's inability to find his mother, Wild, only to learn she has chosen literally to live in the wild, complicate their respective sense of themselves and continue historical "representations of black maternity," as Sharpe describes them, at the intersection of life and death.[70] Moreover, as Demetrius Eudell argues, the move North represents a desire not just for emancipation from one place to a new place but also "*inner* emancipation from the effects of white racism."[71] The reader learns that "Trace" is the last name Joe gives himself when he learns his parents abandoned him without a trace. As he says, "I'm Trace, what they went off without" (124). He further describes himself before meeting Dorcas as a man who had "changed into new seven times" (125) and who had "been a new Negro all . . . [his] life" (129). Into these ruminations about Joe's past, Morrison incorporates the nomenclature of the Harlem Renaissance, also known as the "New Negro Renaissance," to signify that the improvisation that was characteristic of the period was not just cultural but personal.[72] The reader learns that Joe's life narrative, through the space of absence and adjustment to absence, through loss and adjustment to loss, is connected to Violet's and thus illustrates Morrison's geopoetics as a way to represent Black subjectivity, longing, and belonging.

So, in a novel that is ostensibly about the Great Migration, the Harlem Renaissance, and the lure of the city that gave Black people a new way to read themselves and the opportunities available to them in the North that had not been available in the South are the "unspeakable things unspoken" that account for their obsessions, longings, and desires in a new place. These interrelated backstories begin to explain how and why Joe and Violet are attracted to one another, how the North becomes a place of refuge and new beginning, and how their unresolved grieving drives them into alienation from one another. None of these backstories justify Joe's killing of Dorcas, but they do explain the forces at work for these two individuals who arrive in New York City full of anticipation, who get lost in its horrors and possibilities, and who ultimately must come to terms with the melancholia at the center of their souls before they can reconnect and rekindle their love. Indeed, the novel ends with their reconciliation. They appear to relinquish their mutual obsession with Dorcas and turn, instead, to one another:

> A lot of time, though, they stay home figuring things out, telling each other those little personal stories they like to hear again and again, or fussing with the bird Violet bought. . . . They played poker just the two of them until it was time to go to bed under the quilt. . . . Joe . . . wants to slip under it and hold on to her. . . . He wants to imagine, as he lies with her in the dark, the shapes their bodies make the blue stuff do. (223–224)

Reflecting on the metamorphosis of their marriage, the narrator says, "It's nice when grown people whisper to each other under the covers. Their ecstasy is more leaf-sigh than bray and the body is the vehicle, not the point. . . . They are inward toward the other, bound and joined" (228). This poetic description represents the inner emancipation each has been seeking, an emancipation born of their individual and collective memories, experiences, and reimagined readings of themselves. But the final pages point to something else that has been at work throughout the narrative entanglements, backstories, history of racial violence, descriptions of the city, and people's reactions to it all—the reading practices of the narrator.

Throughout the novel, the narrator gives hints of her unsteady ability to know and read the very characters she is offering up to the reader. These misgivings about her reading and Morrison's insistence on integrating them into a sometimes unreliable narrator are critical to an assessment of the novel and of Morrison's geopoetics and narrative intentions. Moreover, it could be argued that these references to questioning or second-guessing her own ability to know or understand the characters or their stories is evidence of Morrison using this novel for more than a fictional foray into the Harlem Renaissance and the Black freedom struggle. It can be argued that the novel is also an example of her self-conscious exploration into the art of narrative fiction as an opportunity to reimagine what reading is, how it is connected to our identity, and what truly constitutes belonging. So, the interrogation of spatializing the self in *Jazz* must also include an interrogation of the narrator and her role in Morrison's larger narrative project.

As mentioned earlier, the novel begins with the narrator's knowledge of the protagonist. The words "Sth, I know that woman" align the narrator with a deep, spiritual knowing suggested in the epigraph to the novel from the Gnostic Gospels. Yet, on the second page of the novel, she begins to introduce herself as a less than all-knowing, reliable narrator when she parenthetically begins to describe herself as one who thinks that Violet's plan to punish Joe might not work: "It could have worked, I suppose, but the children of suicides are hard to please and quick to believe no one loves them because they are not really here" (4). Throughout the novel, the narrator vacillates from presupposing to knowing, from knowing to doubting, from guessing to suspecting what someone is doing, thinking, or feeling. She goes from gossiping about whether a woman needs to "straighten her hair" (5) to expressing exhilaration about being in New York when she exclaims "I'm crazy about this City" (7). Slowly but surely, the narrator makes herself a character even as she simultaneously attempts to keep herself in the background of the narrative. Early in the novel, one of the most telling points of metafiction appears in the following words:

> I haven't got any muscles, so I can't really be expected to defend myself. But I do know how to take precaution. Mostly it's making sure no one knows all there is to know about me. Second, I watch everything and everyone and try to figure out their plans, their reasonings, long before they do. You have to understand what it's like taking on a big city. I'm exposed to all sorts of ignorance and criminality. Still, this is the only life for me. I like the way the City makes people think they can do what they want and get away with it. . . . I lived a long time, maybe too much in my own mind. People say I could come out more. (8–9)

Through this narrative device, Morrison not only destabilizes the relationship between the reader and the text; she also places the reader in an interstitial space, where the reader, much like Morrison the artist and the narrator she creates, must navigate between what they know and what they don't know. In fact, near the end of the novel, she says:

> I believed I saw everything important they did, and based on what I saw I could imagine what I didn't: how exotic they were, how driven. Like dangerous children. That's what I wanted to believe. It never occurred to me that they were thinking other thoughts, feeling other feelings, putting their lives together in ways I never dreamed of. (221)

It is the discursive mediation between what the narrator thinks she knows and what she imagines that produces something new that the characters did not know or see prior to the encounter with others and the locations in which they found themselves. Just as the couple finds themselves through such an encounter, the narrator finds herself only by acknowledging what she could not know. The narrator identifies this new place where she finds herself as home in the same language Morrison uses in the essay "Home" and that will appear in her next novel, *Paradise*. She thinks: "I want to be in a place already made for me, both snug and wide open. With a doorway never needing to be closed, a view slanted for light and bright autumn leaves but not rain" (221).

The novel ends, however, with a twist on its metafictional strategies. One way of reading this ending is that the novel is not only about how the characters in *Jazz*, including the narrator, engage in spatializing themselves; it is also about how Morrison the artist is engaged in the same process by reimagining spaces for the reader. Moving beyond the desire to fill in the lacunae of histories of the Harlem Renaissance that ignored the "grounded aesthetics" of folks who were not famous and who had not been historicized in the telling of the Great Migration or the Harlem Renaissance, Morrison affirms her own pleasure, longing, and belonging in capturing the reader's imagination through her literary imagination. The final lines of the novel say it all:

> I can't tell anyone that I have been waiting for this all my life and that being chosen to wait is the reason I can. If I were able I'd say it. Say make me, remake me. You are free to do it and I am free to let you because look, look. Look where your hands are. Now. (229)

As Carmen Gillespie rightly asserts, "the narrator reveals herself to be the book, the narrative itself."[73] The final lines of this novel provide evidence of her pleasure and the narrator's in yet another variation of a third space for the reader—between the pages of a book, with language she has used, with the narrative she has created, all for their enjoyment in the space she has imagined and provided for their reading pleasure. The self-conscious narrator reflects on the self-consciousness of the author, whose geopoetic resources—namely, language, narrative, memory, and her imagination—empower her to reimagine Harlem, the people who migrated there, and the cultural renaissance that occurred in their midst. She takes the reader on a journey into spaces they both recognize, but only partly, and together they discover and improvise on the meanings of Black pain, pleasure, and love in a new way through the power of the word. Moreover, in her comments about the conclusion of the novel, Morrison expresses her intentionality in connecting the reader to the text when she says: "These paragraphs also activate the complicity by calling attention strenuously, aggressively to the act of reading as having public consequences and even public responsibility . . . the novel . . . encourages ways to experience the public—in time with affect, in a communal space."[74]

In *Paradise*, the last book of the trilogy, published in 1998, the power of the word is on full display in public spaces in terms of both human interaction and the consequences of human interpretations of divine utterances—that is, the Word of God. Morrison shifts from a focus on romantic love to a focus on excesses of religious love and to the ways in which that love coupled with excesses of male power, intraracial bigotry, and sexism can be dangerous for women in both private and public spaces. Though she uses a more conventional, reliable narrator than she does in *Jazz*, her geopoetics of creating and representing emancipatory spaces nevertheless enable her to illuminate in some very unconventional ways how four endangered women find refuge in a place called the Convent and by so doing discover a third space of physical and spiritual safety and healing between the danger they knew and the space of the unknown. Yet, though the narrator's voice may seem more conventional in one sense, Morrison again challenges her readers with her meandering narrative strategy of revealing, layering, and intermingling multiple stories within the framework of the novel to offer the reader a more complex way of thinking about place, race, and belonging. With a focus on how the four women outcasts read and navigate the unsafe spaces where they find themselves and the unknown to which they are fleeing, Morrison illustrates what is at stake—not only for their safety but also for the safety of the community of religious leaders from which they have fled. In *Paradise*, Morrison's geopoetics of creating emancipatory space illustrate Kirby's assertion that "it is precisely when the space of the body coincides with the space of ideology that violence can occur."[75] The violence found in the opening sentence—"They shoot the white girl first" (3)—alerts the reader to the intersectional dimensions of the story and again represents Morrison's penchant for beginning a novel *in medias res* and for thereby disrupting reader expectations for narrative signposts as a guide into the novel.

In some respects, Morrison uses *Paradise* to put a different spin on the familiar migration narrative. Rather than solely relaying another story of the migration route from South to North, this novel tells the story of Black freedmen who leave Mississippi to establish Haven, an all-Black town in Oklahoma in 1889, and who leave Haven to form another all-Black town that they name Ruby in honor of the sister of two of the founders. Unlike *Jazz*, where Morrison tells the story of migration motivated partly by racial violence but often by the longing for a new kind of freedom from the Jim Crow South, *Paradise* is about a group of Black families who move after establishing an all-Black town (Haven) and then form a new one (Ruby); they are motivated to do so by intraracial violence that they refer to as the "Disallowing" (189). In other words, place is complicated in these migrations toward the Southwest, not solely by Black/white hostilities but predominantly by dark-skinned Black people who Patricia, the town historian, refers to as "8-rocks" (193), and who are excluded from towns populated by light-skinned Black people. Fully aware of the racial assaults and terrorism on Black communities such as the one in 1921, when "Tulsa was bombed" (108), Morrison is interested in another dimension of racial bigotry—the kind motivated partly by colorism and partly by religious zeal.[76] She does not abandon her interrogation of the intersection of place and race but takes it to another level to interrogate how internalized racism and religious fervor infiltrate a Black community and inspire intraracial and misogynistic hostilities that become the source of its undoing. Three particular places in the novel—the Oven, which is built in Haven, described as the "dreamtown" turned "ghosttown" (5), where it is taken apart and transported to the new all-black town of Ruby; the church, where the wedding and dueling sermons based on diametrically opposed interpretations of the Word (that is, God's word) takes place; and the Convent, where the four women are murdered—provide examples of where Morrison's geopoetics of emancipatory spaces enable her to illustrate how Black subjects read and make meaning where they find themselves.

Morrison situates the Oven as an important symbol in the center of Haven, the town founded by a group of men referred to as the "Old Fathers" (6). Their sons, all WWII veterans, read the Oven as a symbol of their fathers' accomplishment and as a source of pride and inspiration:

> An Oven. Round as a head, deep as desire ... the Old Fathers did that first: put most of their strength into constructing the huge, flawlessly designed Oven that nourished them and monumentalized what they

had done. When it was finished . . . the ironmonger . . . fashioned an iron plate . . . and set it at the base of the Oven's mouth. It is still not clear where the words came from. Something he heard, invented, or something whispered to him. . . . Words that seemed at first to bless them; later to confound them; finally to announce that they had lost. (6–7)

Morrison uses references to the Oven throughout the novel as a symbolic place that connected the identity of the town and its people to their sense of Black subjectivity and community. Initially a gathering spot not unlike the Clearing, where Black people affirmed their identity and their success in creating a Black space where they believed they could enjoy relative freedom from the menace of the white gaze and white bigotry, Haven is described as a place where communal cooking took place and the community gathered to "gossip, complain, roar with laughter and drink walking coffee in the shade of the eaves" (15). Its name—*Haven*—invoked the kind of paradise they envisioned it would be. The descendants of the Old Fathers recall everything "they listened to, imagined and remembered" (16) as they reflect on how the town residents began leaving and began distinguishing where they were from where they wanted to be.

As Haven began to lose its residents and vitality, the descendants began exploring their options for a new location for their families. Morrison intersperses references to the founders of Haven with the concerns of the younger generation to reveal how the white presence prevails as a menacing presence from one generation to the next. She capitalizes "Out There" (16) to describe how what appeared to be vacant places were a threat to Black bodies:

> Ten generations had known what lay Out There: space, once beckoning and free, became unmonitored and seething; became a void where random and organized evil erupted when and where it chose. . . . Out There where your children were sport, your women quarry, and where your very person could be annulled, where congregations carried arms to church and ropes coiled in every saddle. Out There where every cluster of whitemen looked like a posse, being alone was being dead. But lessons had been learned and relearned in the last three generations about how to protect a town. (16)

So the migration to Ruby was partly about creating a new safe space and haven where they could shape a new beginning for themselves and their families. It is described as a place where from the beginning its people were free and protected. A sleepless woman could always rise from her bed, wrap a shawl around her shoulders and sit on the steps in the moonlight. . . . Nothing for ninety miles around . . . or . . . on out beyond the limits of the town . . . thought she was prey. (8–9)

With these two descriptions, Morrison establishes how Ruby was a haven from harm and a kind of paradise for its inhabitants until the women at the Convent made them feel otherwise.

The dispute over the words on the Oven, originally conceived as a unifying symbol, is Morrison's narrative strategy for representing the kind of ideological and generational shift that occurs among the men in Ruby. The Oven is significant because it represents the historical, ideological, religious, and gendered underpinnings of thought that shape the male behavior of two generations—that of the Old Fathers and that of the generation after them. The words that Zechariah Morgan inscribed on the Oven—"Beware the Furrow of His Brow"—created a conundrum that "was not a command to the believers but a threat to those who had disallowed them" (195). Furthermore, the words were conceived "to have multiple meanings: to appear stern, urging obedience to God, but slyly not identifying the understood proper noun or specifying what the Furrow might cause to happen or to whom" (195). First, the fact that there is no consensus as to whether the words were "invented" or stolen suggests that there may be a flawed premise at the onset upon which they attempted to build their idea of a "safe haven" away from racial discrimination. Second, the use of the words *bless them, confound them,* and *announce* when referring to their inability to maintain the identity of the town they worked so hard to create foreshadow for the reader the intergenerational conflict and the confluence of forces that conspire to pit old against young, denomination against denomination, and men against women. While the Old Fathers are convinced that the original words on the Oven were "Beware the Furrow of His Brow," the younger generation advocates for changing the words to "Be the Furrow of His Brow," a reinterpretation that suggests the heart of the ideological perspectives and attitudes toward God that divide them. The inability to agree on the meaning of the words parallels the divergent readings and misreadings of scripture, of history, of the places where they have been, and of how they were treated in those places. As Gillespie rightfully asserts, "the reinterpretation of the Oven offends the elder men of the town because it shakes their confidence about their control of Ruby's central narrative."[77] Near the end of the novel, the reader learns that "the young people had changed its words again. No longer were they calling themselves Be the Furrow of His Brow. The graffiti on the hood of the Oven . . . [finally] reads 'We Are the Furrow of His Brow'" (298), and on the back is a Black power symbol of with a fist of "clenched fingers" (102). Morrison ostensibly maps how a "utility became a shrine" (103). In fact, it is this intergenerational desire for control—not only over the message, the meaning of the words, and the central narrative about Ruby but also over the lives of the people in the community—that points to the Oven as a third space and a metaphor for Ruby as a site of struggle and the crucible of the town's undoing.

Morrison places another dispute over the meaning of words at the center of the novel in the church, which is another third space of sorts between the public and private identity. On one hand, the church serves as a location of culture where Black people gather to reify the very notions of God that had ostensibly brought them safely from sites of racial exclusion and oppression to a site of individual and collective freedom. In other words, it is an emancipatory space. On the other hand, Morrison does not indulge the reader in a facile, familiar representation of the Black church. She interrogates and complicates its multivalent presence in the community as a space that shapes individual and collective subjectivity in positive and negative ways. In the context of this novel and for the purposes of this study, it is critical to separate the church from the Convent, however, not only because Morrison does so, but also because they represent two related but different historical religious institutions. Morrison first hints at this distinction early in the novel, when two of the men who are rummaging through the Convent observe that they are "in a place that once housed Christians—well, Catholics anyway—[and there is] not a cross of Jesus anywhere" (7). The significance of this distinction is not a theological one. Instead, it is a distinction that introduces the Black sacred-secular social continuum as just one of the means by which these men judge the women who reside at the Convent to be outside of the norms they deem acceptable and respectable. The fact that the physical space has had three identities—as an embezzler's mansion, as an actual convent, and finally as a safe haven for women—illustrates Morrison's interest in interrogating and signifying on the church as a historical site of struggle. What plays out at the Convent with the women who reside there, therefore, is in many respects a contemporary manifestation of an old struggle for control over women's bodies. At the intersection of religious ideology and the presence of women who allegedly do not adhere to that ideology is violence done in the name of God. Situating the act of violence that opens the novel at the Convent provides a narrative strategy for Morrison to map how multiple ways of thinking and knowing get called into question.

Morrison uses the church to illustrate that its identity as a sacred space gets called into question by communal and political exigencies. For example, when the community determines that the women at the Convent represent an evil rather than a benign presence as they originally thought, they come together, despite denominational differences, to address what they deem is an emergency and an existential threat from a common enemy:

> Once the emergency was plain, representatives from all three churches met at the Oven because they couldn't agree on which, if any, church should host a meeting to decide on what to do now that the women had ignored all warnings. (11)

Morrison's geopoetics work in the interstitial spaces between the extremes of binary oppositions. On one hand, the church—sometimes referred to in literary and religious studies by such theologians as James Cone as "The Black Church"—is represented in the novel by three separate churches (Methodists, Pentecostals, and Baptists) that operate within the confines of their denominational identities.[78] On the other hand, their differences drop away in the presence of what the church folks believe is a threat against them all. The discursive mediation between the church as a sacred institution for good and the church as a secular policing power that will use violent force to oppose a threat to its identity is one of the both/and features of Morrison's geopoetics that manifests itself in this novel. Though it is ultimately at their peril to have done so, the women reside at the Convent and reimagine it as a safe space. Their understanding of the space they occupy is like what McKittrick describes in *Demonic Grounds: Black Women and the Cartographies of Struggle*:

> Black women's histories, lives, and spaces must be understood as enmeshing with traditional geographic arrangements in order to identify a different way of knowing and writing the social world and to expand how the production of space is achieved across domains of domination.[79]

The church is a third space, therefore, in more than one sense. For the Black community, it represents the spiritual version of what Beth Loffreda and Claudia Rankine refer to as the "racial imaginary," a location of culture that enables a kind of freedom from the white gaze.[80] At the same time, because it is a space dominated by a male, patriarchal perspective, it represents the other side of the racial imaginary that adheres to "lines drawn by power."[81] At the intersection and collision of these two anxieties—one about race and one about gender, both infused with religious fervor—are the women at the Convent, whose identity and presence challenge the orthodoxies of the Black Church.

But Morrison illustrates the church as a third (but conflicted) space in another way. The wedding between KD and Arnette devolves into yet another space for the dueling perspectives on the Oven, on God, and on identity to be interrogated from a wider vantage point. In the chapter titled "Divine," Morrison takes the reader to the crux of the matter. Though ostensibly about the wedding between Arnette and KD, the chapter is ultimately about how the community is a site of struggle over identity in public and private spheres. It begins with the words from Rev. Pulliam, the minister whose thinking is aligned with power and the ways of the old generation. His Old Testament tone and his representation of God as the ultimate judge of human behavior serve as an admonishment to those in attendance with a stern definition of love:

> Let me tell you about love, that silly word you believe is about whether you like somebody or whether somebody likes you or whether you can put up with somebody in order to get something or someplace you want.... Love is not of that.... Love is divine only and difficult always. If you think it is easy you are a fool. If you think it is natural, you are blind. It is a learned application without reason or motive except that it is God.... Love is not a gift. It is a diploma.... God is not interested in you. He is interested in love and the bliss it brings to those who understand and share that interest. (141–142)

This lengthy admonition in the middle of the wedding ceremony causes Anna to wonder whom Pulliam's sermon is really addressed to—"to the young people ... or ... their parents ... ?" (142). The answer is that he is speaking not only to the young couple before him but to the congregation in attendance, including the young people who have come under the persuasive influence of his archrival, Rev. Misner. Using the Black oral tradition of call-and-response to have Misner's sermon respond to Pulliam's is Morrison's narrative strategy for creating another space of meaning in the middle of what ostensibly is just a wedding. In his sermon, Misner offers a counternarrative to Pulliam's definition of love, but even before we hear his words, we read his thoughts in the form of his critique of Pulliam's theological perspective. He views Pulliam's words as an example of

> the damage words spoken from a pulpit could wreak ... over ... men finding it so hard to fight their instincts to control what they could and crunch what they could not; in the hearts of women tirelessly taming the predator, in the faces of children not yet recovered from the blow

to their esteem upon learning that adults would not regard them as humans until they mated.... Pulliam's words were a widening of the war. (145)

In response to Pulliam's sermon, which he views as a defilement of the Christian message, Misner removes the cross from the back wall of the sanctuary and returns to the pulpit to offer an alternative message, a counternarrative of Godly love. In indirect discourse, the reader learns from the narrator that Misner's message describes Christ on the cross as a

solitary black man propped up on these two intersecting lines to which he was attached in a parody of human embrace... being both ordinary and sublime... See how this official murder out of hundreds marked the difference; moved the relationship between God and man from CEO and supplicant to one on one? The cross he held was abstract; the absent body was real, but both combined to pull humans from backstage to the spotlight, from muttering in the wings to the principal role in the story of their lives. This execution made it possible to respect—freely, not in fear—one's self and one another. Which was what love was: unmotivated respect. (146)

Yet, these words are what he would have said if he had not chosen to calmly stand before all assembled and say absolutely nothing. In the space of the silence that interrupts the wedding ceremony, Morrison's omniscient narrator moves through the church, providing access to the thoughts of those in attendance. On one hand, the pregnant pause in the ceremony provides the reader with more insights about those in attendance, their grievances against one another, and their overall disgruntlement with having to sit through a wedding in the midst of a town at war with itself because of past and present internecine conflicts. On the other hand, the wedding itself, and the fact that it was commandeered by the elders to save the groom from being spurned after several liaisons with Grace, one of the Convent women also known as Gigi, is a narrative strategy for connecting the church as a conflicted space produced by human readings and misreadings of one another and God. Though Morrison expresses a personal affinity for the religious stance of Rev. Pulliam, artistically, she presents dueling perspectives to give her reader an opportunity to interrogate the merits of both and the interstices between them.[82]

The Convent is the most significant space in the novel; it is where the men of Ruby enter to rid the town of the women who reside there and is an example of where we can see Morrison's geopoetics at work in representing how Black women create an emancipatory space for their survival and healing. The Convent is a place that has been repurposed three times—first as an embezzler's mansion, then as a residence for Catholic nuns who run a boarding school for Arapaho girls, and finally as the sanctuary that it becomes under Consolata (also referred to as Connie). The rationale for the benefactress to purchase the mansion in the first place as a site for so-called "wayward girls" (227) is explained thusly:

> It was an opportunity to intervene in the heart of the problem: to bring God and language to natives who were assumed to have neither; to alter their diets, their clothes, their minds, to help them despise everything that had once made their lives worthwhile and to offer them instead the privilege of knowing the one and only God and a chance, thereby, for redemption. (227)

Despite its earlier identity for religious indoctrination and subjugation, the Convent becomes a very different space under the auspices of Consolata. The four women come to know the Convent as a safe space for recuperating, remembering, and reimagining that part of themselves that society had attempted to minimize and ignore, if not destroy. It becomes a safe space for belonging.

Morrison gives each woman her own story as she interconnects the stories of the women into the narrative of a community, and by so doing, she structures the novel to illustrate what Chimamanda Ngozi Adichie refers to as "the danger of a single story."[83] The stories of each of the women who arrive at the Convent—from Mavis, the first woman who takes refuge there, to Pallas, who gives birth in distress there—shed light on the vagaries of female subjectivity in connection to male power and male productions and uses of space. Each woman arrives either abused, mistreated, or disrespected to the point of alienation from any genuine knowledge of herself or her value. Morrison does not represent the women as entirely innocent in the narrative of how they arrived at their respective predicaments, but she does illustrate how social and cultural mores have largely contributed to the circumstances that create their need for refuge, even when they do not fully know it for themselves. Mavis, for example, is a fugitive who flees her home after she accidentally kills her twin babies by abandoning them to suffocate in the car. What the journalist who interviews her fails to realize is that her less than satisfactory explanation for why she abandoned her babies is connected to her feeble effort to avoid the threat of physical abuse from her husband. In other words, hers is a flight—not only from the scene of her own crime against her children but also from an unsafe domestic space that had become a routine site of physical violence against her body. Her flight, therefore, though it begins as a kind of mindless escape, becomes a plan as she comes to terms with the life she was leaving. And in the safety that the Convent provides for her, she learns, as Consolata reminds her, that "scary things not always outside. Most scary things is inside" (39). Mavis comes to regard the Convent as the safe space that her home was not.

Morrison represents Grace (known as Gigi) as a promiscuous runaway and pot smoker whose father is on death row and as a woman who simply seems to wander from place to place. Despite the apparent aimlessness of her wanderings and her being haunted by her grandfather's news of racial violence against a young activist back in her hometown of Alcorn, Mississippi, her promiscuity is represented by her obsession with finding the rock formation of two people copulating that her boyfriend had told her was in Wish, Arizona, not far from Ruby. She hitches a ride in a van only to learn, to her dismay, that the vehicle is actually a hearse on its way to the Convent to pick up a body. Though Gigi does not initially realize it is a hearse or that the Convent is not a residence for nuns as she presumed, she reluctantly acquiesces to Consolata's request to stay long enough for her to take a nap. Once she takes up residence at the Convent, her frequent squabbles with Mavis create chaos that only Seneca—"always the peacemaker" (131)—seems to be able to resolve. Described as a woman who "preferred traveling resolutely nowhere, closed off from society, hidden among quiet cargo, no one knowing she was there" (138), Seneca arrives at the Convent as yet another female nomad with no particular place to be or belong. Pallas, the youngest and most well-to-do woman to arrive at the Convent, is pregnant, having run away first from her father's home and then again upon learning that Carlos, the janitor at her school and the father of the child she is pregnant with, has slept with her mother. Before she arrives at the Convent, she is raped, all of which adds insult to injury and makes her yet another candidate for the refuge that the Convent can provide.

What connects these women outcasts are circumstances beyond their control, a lack of desire to deal with their troubled lives according to the norms they have observed or learned, and the lack of a place to belong. In fact, Consolata initially has little respect for them because their "voices told the same tale: disorder, deception and, what Sister Roberta warned the Indian girls against, drift. The three *d's* that paved the road to perdition, and the greatest of these was drift" (221–222). In language that almost parodies 1 Corinthians 13:13, the scripture known as the biblical "love text" that says that the "greatest of these [of the three virtues of faith, hope, and love] is love," Morrison describes the terms that have circumscribed their lives up until their arrival while foreshadowing the virtue that will be critical for their spiritual healing. Though grief-stricken and prone to excesses of alcohol, Consolata first offers them refuge from chaos, pain, and a lack of direction in the judgmental terms of the faith she has learned through the nuns, but over time, Morrison represents the Convent as a place to heal and discover and/or recover the love of themselves on new terms.

But Morrison does not portray Consolata as a flawless savior to the women who arrive at the Convent. Described as an orphan and nine-year-old victim of rape who was rescued from Brazil by Mary Magda, Consolata, after arriving at the Convent, lives a life at the sacred intersection of devotion to God and humanity "as if she had taken the veil herself" (225). After thirty years of celibacy, however, she has a brief but "love-struck" (228) sexual affair with Deacon Morgan, one of founders of Ruby. Morrison describes one of their interludes, which is literally somewhere in the middle of nowhere between Ruby and the Convent, in prose that highlights the pleasure of being in a secret place and indulging in forbidden pleasure:

> Out here where wind was not a help or threat to sunflowers, nor the moon a language of time, of weather, of sowing or harvesting, but a feature of the original world designed for the two of them. . . . Finally he slowed and turned into a barely passable track, where coyote grass scraped the fenders. In the middle of it he braked and would have taken her in his arms except she was already there. On the way back they were speechless again. What had been uttered during their lovemaking leaned toward language, gestured its affiliation, but in fact was un-memora-ble, -controllable or -translatable. (229)

Morrison uses this passage to suggest that they are in an Edenic space, both physically and emotionally, a kind of paradisiacal third space where they can lull themselves out of accountability to her unspoken vows at the Convent and to his marital vows of fidelity. But the affair ends when she not only "bit his lip, but when she hummed over the blood she licked from it" (239) and thus crossed a boundary she did not know existed. For the reader at this point in the text, however, the line is a predictable one of a boundary at the intersection of gender and class. As one of the prominent deacons and leaders in Ruby, Deek could not afford to have his reputation besmirched with a woman from "Out There." Moreover, as a man, he could not afford to have her in a position of power to literally consume him. The end of their affair leads Consolata into a depression that takes her to the altar in the Convent, where she prays: "Dear

Lord, I didn't want to eat him. I just wanted to go home" (240). When Mary Magda admonishes her to "Never speak of him again," she acquires "bat vision"—that is, the ability "to see best in the dark" (241).

It could be argued that drinking blood and acquiring bat vision are heavy-handed as narrative elements in the novel, but for Morrison, the symbolism here is the beginning of affirming alternative ways of seeing, knowing, and experiencing the unique space that they occupy. While Mother Mary Magda's admonishment also signifies the line of demarcation between good and evil, when Consolata discovers that she is gifted with the ability to "step in" to raise the dead, she realizes that Mother Mary's binary opposition between good and evil may no longer be a useful way of seeing or knowing. By the time Mother Mary dies, Consolata has emerged as the new Mother Superior of the Convent. Her journey from the vulnerable spaces of orphan status and rape victim in Brazil to the safety of Mother Magda's care to the vulnerable spaces of her heart in an adulterous affair has prepared her to take on the caretaking role she assumes over the Convent. Her own "nomadic subjectivity" and that of the four women, to use Braidotti's term, has equipped her with new ways of knowing and seeing that enable her to facilitate the healing of the women who have taken up residence at the Convent.[84] She transforms it into a sanctuary by engaging them in a process of spiritual healing that enables them to reimagine a way to be in the world with a new sense of authenticity and belonging. She reassures them by saying "I will teach you what you are hungry for" (262) and thus becomes the ideal parent none of them had had:

> This sweet, unthreatening old lady who seemed to love each of them best; who never criticized, who shared everything but needed little or no care; required no emotional investment; who listened; who locked no doors and accepted each as she was. What is she talking about, this ideal parent, friend, companion in whose company they were safe from harm? What is she thinking, this perfect landlord who charged nothing and welcomed anybody . . . in no time at all they came to see they could not leave the one place they were free to leave. (262)

Under the auspice of Consolata's care, they engage in the ritual that will heal their bodies and their souls and help them to reimagine the very notion of home. As Pallas thinks:

> The whole house felt permeated with a blessed malelessness, like a protected domain, free of hunters but exciting too. As though she might

meet herself here—an unbridled, authentic self, but which she thought of as a "cool" self—in one of this house's many rooms. (177).

Morrison's description of what the Convent becomes for the women is an example of what Kirby refers to as "reforming the spaces of the subject" and thereby restructuring and transforming received boundaries and structures into livable spaces for their authentic female subjectivity.[85]

The process by which they prepare for the ritual of healing is nearly as important as the ritual itself. They transform the space that the Convent has been by giving the floor a thorough cleansing and lining it with candles. No longer merely a space of refuge, it becomes a space for living and belonging. Their cleansing and lighting of it with candles prepare them for the spiritual healing they are about to undertake after she tells them to "undress and lie down" (263). After they lie down, she paints a silhouette around each of their bodies and shares her own story and the story of a woman named Piedade, "who sang but never said a word" (264). The ritual continues as "loud dreaming" as they step into "the dreamer's tale" and listen to one another's life narratives of abandonment, being silenced by men, raped by men, and unloved by mothers. The text explains that the ritual "of loud dreaming, monologue . . . no different from a shriek; accusations directed to the dead and long gone are undone by murmurs of love" (264). Then they take paint and draw templates of their own bodies. They begin to talk to one another "about what they had dreamed and what had been drawn" (265). Over time, Connie realizes that a transformation has occurred that distinguishes them: "Unlike some people in Ruby, the Convent women were no longer haunted. Or hunted either, she might have added. But there she would have been wrong" (266). She is wrong, of course, because by this point in the novel, the reader is aware that despite the warning from Lone, the midwife, the men of Ruby arrive at the Convent to hunt them down like prey.

What is significant about the women at the Convent is that they represent Morrison's geopoetics of creating emancipatory spaces for reimagining Black female subjectivity. The reconfiguration of the space known as the Convent into a safe haven for healing and self-reclamation is indicative of Morrison's desire to create a space that is both "snug and wide open" to explore subjectivity in ways that are in the interstices that race and gender have created. Despite what the self-righteous men of Ruby thought they were doing, Morrison represents the women of the Convent as women who have suffered at the hand of patriarchal, misogynistic logic and misreading. The safe space that they find and create makes them the very prey the men of Ruby had attempted to protect their own women from becoming. Yet, despite the murder of the women,

Morrison gets the last word through her narrator, who describes a ship of "crew and passengers, lost and saved, atremble. . . . Now they will rest before shouldering the endless work they were created to do down here in Paradise" (318). With this elusive ending in a space that the reader cannot definitively identify, Morrison leaves the reader with a new reading of Paradise that suggests it is not elsewhere but in our midst and requires reimagining our relationship to ourselves and to one another.

3

Circling the Subject

The Geopoetics of Narrative Rememory

> Of concern . . . are the ways memory acts in the service of redress rather than an inventory of memory.
> —Saidiya V. Hartman, *Scenes of Subjection*[1]

After the ghost is expelled from the community at the end of *Beloved*, the community's attitude toward the past is expressed in the words "Remembering seemed unwise" (274), but remembering is precisely what Morrison places at the center of the novel and her entire literary project. As for the subject of slavery, however, making it the focus of her fiction had not always been of interest to her. Indeed, on more than one occasion in various interviews, she expressed her own reluctance to write about slavery.[2] Yet, connecting both the spoken and unspoken, the written and the unwritten, through the sieve of her imagination to address what previous accounts had omitted was precisely what Morrison set about doing in the complex narrative structure of the novel that focuses on the horrors of enslavement and its aftermath, especially from the intersectional perspective of Black female subjectivity. It could be argued that the goal of her nuanced, complex uses of memory in narrating the story of Sethe in *Beloved* and in writing the novels that came after it were not only to participate in a form of redress for the silences of the unspeakable things unspoken, as Hartman argues, but also to structure her narratives in ways that imitate the circuitous manner in which the mind remembers, the imagination creates, and the two interact in the interstices of "the quality of being" that Victor W. Turner suggests is "betwixt and between."[3] The meandering ways in which Morrison structures the narrative and draws attention to it aesthetically and stylistically for the reader is what constitutes what I believe is a third geopoetic strategy: *narrative rememory*. Although narrative rememory is introduced in its most intricate form in *Beloved*, this chapter illustrates how it also shows up in *A Mercy* and *Home* and how Morrison uses representations of the apparatus of memory to structure the narrative, illuminate the subjectivity of her characters, and invite the reader to join her in interrogating the unique ways in which Black subjectivity at the intersection of history and memory is constructed. Ultimately, through the geopoetics of narrative rememory, Morrison's art of narrative fiction redresses received historical representations of the Black presence on American soil and in the African diaspora and thereby illuminates how place, race, and belonging shape Black subjectivity.

By shifting from the known horrors of enslavement chronicled in slave narratives, or what Angelyn Mitchell refers to as "emancipatory narratives," to the unrecognized, marginalized, and devalued dimensions of the interior life of the enslaved, Morrison permanently altered how we think about the subject of slavery in American history.[4] Her explanation for why she wrote the novel *Beloved* speaks volumes about what she understood was the need for it:

> There is no place you or I can go, to think about or not think about, to summon the presences of, or recollect the absences of slaves; nothing that reminds us of the ones who made the journey and of those who did not make it. There is no suitable memorial or plaque or wreath or wall or park or skyscraper lobby. There's no 300-foot tower. There's no small bench by the road. . . . And because such a place doesn't exist (that I know of), the book had to. But I didn't know that before or while I wrote it. I can see now what I was doing on the last page. I was finishing the story, transfiguring, and disseminating the haunting with which the book begins. Yes, I was doing that; but I was also doing something more. I think I was pleading for that wall or that bench or that tower or that tree when I wrote the final words.[5]

In her effort to make *Beloved* that place where readers can both think about and visit the subject of enslavement, Morrison transgresses the boundaries of how it has historically been remembered and represented and suggests through her geopoetics that another story must challenge the received narrative if the nation is ever to heal and be made whole. Put another way, as the novel's ending asserts, Paul realizes he must "put his story next to hers" (273). And, as I argue elsewhere, by entering the history of the Black presence through a totally different and unique rendering of it, Morrison challenges her readers to remember and address the gaps in the American narrative about itself that continue to challenge the psychic wholeness of both the enslavers and the enslaved.[6] By so doing, she brings intentionality to her rendering of history and goes back, as Foucault asserts, from statements preserved through time and dispersed in space towards the interior secret that preceded them, left its mark . . . and a subjectivity that lags behind manifest history: and which finds beneath events, another more serious, more secret fundamental history.[7]

In this discussion, the goal is to interrogate how this different rendering constitutes a geopoetic narrative strategy that provides greater insight into Morrison's overall cultural project.

Like many historians and literary critics, I find the terms *enslaved persons* and *enslavement* to be more linguistically and historically accurate than *slaves* or *slavery*.[8] When quoting Morrison, I use the words *slaves* and *slavery* where she does so, though over time, she, like many other historians, educators, authors, and scholars, began to agree that the change in terminology represents a radical, critical, and meaningful effort to acknowledge that the dehumanizing process of enslaving humans was devastating but not totally successful. In other words, the change emphatically suggests that enslaved persons managed to maintain agency that enabled them to resist their oppression, affirm their humanity, and imagine freedom on the other side of the traumatic places and circumstances in which they found themselves.[9] Thus, this matter of language is directly connected to matters of memory, narrative, and subjectivity at the heart of this discussion.

Although it is in the novel *Beloved* that she formally introduces the term *rememory*, Morrison begins to experiment with it as a narrative strategy in her earlier novels. For example, *The Bluest Eye* is told as the narrator's flashback to the tragic memory of the girl who was the scapegoat of an entire community. And even before it narrates the sad story of betrayal of a female friendship, *Sula* introduces the context of a Black community's memory of racial discrimination and gentrification through what Sheila Wise Rowe refers to as "spatial racism . . . when spaces and structures are purposefully designed to divide or change the demographics of communities."[10] *Song of Solomon* invokes historical memories of how the Black community dealt with discrimination, exclusion, and racialized violence as the context for the protagonist's journey into greater self-knowledge. And even *Jazz* is partly structured through narrative tension, not only through the unreliable narrator's recall of the reparation of a marriage after an adulterous affair but also via the memories of Violet and Joe Trace that are interspersed throughout as they recall their individual lives in the South before they moved North to Harlem. It could be argued, however, that in and after *Beloved*, Morrison begins to use the mechanics of memory to structure narrative in a more intentional, nuanced, and apparent manifestation of her geopoetics by constructing what Larkin refers to as the "literary encounter" for describing the reader's relationship with the text.[11] This chapter interrogates where and how the geopoetic strategy of narrative rememory occurs in Morrison's fiction in and after *Beloved*.

Morrison introduces the term *rememory* early in the novel in a mother-daughter conversation between Sethe and Denver in which Sethe attempts to explain her concept of time:

> I was talking about time. It's so hard for me to believe in it. Some things go. Pass on. Some things just stay. I used to think it was my rememory. You know. Some things you forget. Other things you never do. But it's not. Places, places are still there. . . . If a house burns down, it's gone, but the place—the picture of it—stays, and not just in my rememory, but out there, in the world. What I remember is a picture floating around out there outside my head . . . a thought picture. . . . It's when you bump into a rememory that belongs to somebody else . . . it's always going to be there waiting for you. (36)

Rememory is introduced, therefore, as a mnemonic and spatial phenomenon that the mind engages in on its own. In many respects, Morrison illustrates how the manipulation of her own body through spatial and tactile movements mitigates the pain of difficult memories. For example, when the memory that her own mother had been lynched comes to Sethe during another one of her conversations with Denver, the text reads: "She had to do something with her hands because she knew she was remembering something she had forgotten she knew. Something privately shameful that had seeped into a slit in her mind" (61). Morrison represents Sethe with an understanding of her interior life even if she is unable to articulate it and can only engage in behavior to protect herself and her daughter from her thoughts. By so doing, she reveals how her memories are connected to place, subjectivity, and the structures of feeling that are associated with those places and experiences, even experiences that have long been entrenched in the past. For the reader, what Sethe describes as her rememory invokes a phenomenon that Paul Ricoeur describes as "the enigma of memory as presence of the absent encountered previously."[12] In Sethe's description, this enigma of presence and absence, therefore, has a both/and quality. She knows the memory is based on the past but is intimately aware of how she connects with the past in the present and that she is not alone in doing so.

Thus, rememory is represented as a phenomenon that is individual and collective, embodied and disembodied at the same time. Morrison's reference to the "keeping room" as the space to which she retreats to experience her thought life is an ironic, metaphoric reference to her mind as a third space. Indeed, it could be argued that Morrison's geopoetics provide the reader with an example of Sethe engaged in metacognition, recognizing how her brain is functioning in a way that she could not predict or control:

> She worked hard to remember as close to nothing as was safe. Unfortunately her brain was devious. . . . She would be hurrying across a field. . . . Nothing else would be on her mind. . . . The picture of the men coming to nurse her was as lifeless as the nerves in her back where the skin buckled . . . then something rolled itself out before her in shameless beauty. . . . Boys hanging from the most beautiful sycamores in the world. It shamed her—remembering the wonderful soughing trees rather than the boys. Try as she might to make it otherwise, the sycamores beat out the children every time and she could not forgive her memory for that. (6)

Morrison includes this scene early in the novel, just as Paul D arrives, to introduce the reader to a mnemonic pattern that will shape the entire work. In the midst of the traumatic memory of the child she killed and the two sons who left, Sethe attempts to empty her mind of memory only to have the trauma of sexual assault to her own body interrupt her efforts to do so. Her imagination, however, interrupts memory and creates the third space of imagining and recollecting beauty in the midst of remembering public space racism—that is, the horror of seeing lynched Black bodies.[13] As Evelyn Jaffe Schreiber suggests, Sethe's memory is operating precisely as the mind of a woman who has experienced trauma from events (the killing of her child and sexual assault against her body) and from an environment (the plantation, where violence against other Black bodies took place in the form of lynching and other forms) would operate.[14] Thus, Morrison attempts to represent the mind navigating the spaces between events and environments, time and place, through narration. In many respects, she structures the novel as the mind working to navigate the spaces between a network of narratives about a network of memories. Some of the memories belong to Sethe, some belong to the ghost, some belong to Denver, and still others belong to Paul D and the women who help rescue and heal Sethe by exorcising the ghost from her body and the community. Morrison painstakingly structures the novel, however, to focus on Sethe's memory and narrate the unspoken collective story of Black subjectivity during enslavement through the unspoken narrative of Black female subjectivity that is embedded in it. According to the psychology of how the mind remembers,

Avivah Gottlieb Zornberg reminds us that "narrative needs time to do its work, to renegotiate the sense of total presence and fullness that the self craves."[15] Morrison uses narrative rememory to redress the horrors of enslavement by representing the mind's work of "beating back the past" and of dealing with the return of the repressed and "the role of the unconscious, of memory traces."[16]

Morrison's geopoetics of narrative rememory show up in *Beloved* in three ways—her meticulous description of Sethe's memory and metacognition, the narrative strategies she uses to describe how Sethe shares her memories with Paul D, and her structuring of the flow of narrative in the novel itself. When Paul D arrives at her home at 124, Sethe gradually begins to put elements of her thought life that she had not articulated to anyone into language. Her initial resistance to sharing her interior life with him shows up in the following description of her metacognition: "Her brain was not interested in the future. Loaded with the past and hungry for more, it left no room to imagine, let alone plan for, the next day. . . . Other people went crazy, why couldn't she? Other people's brains stopped, turned around and went on to something new, which must have happened to Halle" (70). Morrison illustrates the implications of a thought life torn between a preoccupation with remembering the past and a determination to forget it. Thus, it could be argued that Morrison structures the novel and Sethe's subjectivity to illustrate what Avivah Gottlieb Zornberg refers to as "the paradox of remembering and forgetting."[17] On one hand, Sethe is desperate to forget the infanticide that she deemed an act of love, the haunting of her home by the ghost of the child she killed, and the atrocities of enslavement that robbed her of autonomy over her own body, of her husband, and of a sense of belonging to her community. On the other hand, she learns over time, through various storytelling events with Denver but more so with Paul D, that the path to forgetting and the healing that can accompany it can only be reached through remembering. Morrison uses narrative rememory to delineate the various places and spaces that Sethe—and by extension, the reader—must traverse to come to terms with the past. Sethe's overactive, trauma-induced thought life makes her even attempt to imagine and anticipate what Paul D is thinking:

> He wants to tell me, she thought. He wants me to ask him about what it was like for him—about how offended the tongue is, held down by iron, how the need to spit is so deep you cry for it. She already knew about it, had seen it time after time in the place before Sweet Home. Men, boys, little girls, women. The wildness that shot up into the eye the moment the lips were yanked back. (71)

Morrison thus uses Sethe's thought life and her memories of the atrocities of enslaved life to narrate the story of how she is remembering the details of her own past in the present and also to incorporate elements of the larger history of enslaved persons and the oppressive apparatus of the institution of enslavement, such as the bit that was used to silence the enslaved. *Rememory*, in Morrison's formulation of it through Sethe, is both a noun and a verb—a thing that is produced from the act of recalling the past and the process of engaging in recalling and recollecting moments from the past. Gradually, being with Paul D allows her to experience "trust and rememory . . . the way she believed it could be" (99). Although initially as guarded and self-centered about her memories and experiences about Sweet Home as Paul D is, over time, she begins to regard

> his mind as one that knew her own. Her story was bearable because it was his as well—to tell, to refine and tell again. The things neither knew about the other—the things neither had word-shapes for—well, it would come in time. (99)

With this description of the burgeoning love affair, Morrison illustrates how Sethe's memory life begins to incorporate shared memories of a trauma-inflicted past. Or, as Mitchell argues, memory may be a "repository of trauma," but the one who has experienced the trauma needs an "empathic listener" for the narrative to be a liberatory one of healing.[18] Until Paul D's arrival, Sethe has no such empathic listener. After he arrives, rememory is not a solitary process but a dialogic one that begins to transform her notions of subjectivity over time.

Morrison shifts from the interiority of Sethe's efforts to navigate time and memory in the private space of mind to her efforts to do so in shared physical space as the relationship between her and Paul D develops. This shift from the workings of Sethe's interior life to her efforts to engage in sharing with Paul D in her external life represents the second way that narrative rememory structures this novel. This shift is best represented in the passage that describes Sethe's struggle to get the emotional wherewithal to share more of her story:

> It made him dizzy. At first he thought it was her spinning. Circling him the way she was circling the subject. Round and round, never changing direction, which might have helped his head. . . . Sethe knew that the words she did not understand hadn't any more power than she had to explain. . . . I did it. I got us all out. . . . Me using my own head. But it was more than that. . . . It felt good. Good and right. (161–162)

As she engages in a nervous attempt to share with Paul D tidbits of her personal narrative that he could not have known from their life at Sweet Home or afterward, she continues "circling, circling . . . gnawing something else instead of getting to the point" (162). Her realization that she "knew that the circle she was making around the room, him, the subject, would remain one . . . that she could never close in, pin it down for anybody" (163), is manifested in the strategy she adopts in the external physical space for dealing with the interior space of feelings, emotions, and memories she cannot control. Recognizing her lack of control, she chooses instead to "circle the subject." Morrison's language and choice of words in this passage are reminiscent of what she articulates in her Nobel Prize lecture where she says "language can never 'pin down' slavery. . . . Nor should it yearn for the arrogance to be able to do so. Its force, its felicity, is in its reach toward the ineffable."[19] What Morrison achieves in the storytelling exchanges between Sethe and Paul D, however, is an illustration through the structure of the narrative, and here, even in the circuitous description of the telling itself, of how narrative and memory operate. She structures the interweaving narrative in the description of thoughts but also in the ways her characters navigate space and time to accommodate the vagaries of their interior lives and to shift from avoidance to engagement with their own minds and the memories that reside there in a new way.

The meandering in and out of Sethe's narrative, then Paul D's, and then that of others that they both remember is intentional as a structural device designed to imagine and create a new protocol of reading Black female subjectivity and the narrative about enslavement. In contradistinction to the autobiographical slave narratives that typically begin with the words "I was born" and develop in a chronological linear path from enslavement to freedom, Morrison begins her novel *in medias res* and in a place only identified as "124," a house on Bluestone Road that is haunted with individual and collective memories of enslavement.[20] By beginning and organizing her novel with a place and time out of nowhere but loaded with spaces and histories of somewhere, of what Hartman calls "scenes of subjection," Morrison uses narrative rememory in a third way—to structure the entire novel.[21] Though Morrison is aware the intentional narrative indirection may be off-putting for the reader, her goal is to engage in "disseminating the haunting" throughout the narrative, to circle the subject of enslavement, and to destabilize the narrative in all its private and public contours to illustrate that received dominant narratives about the subject could never do it justice.[22]

Thus, from the narrative circles around the act of infanticide to those immediately affected by it—Sethe's children, her mother-in-law, Baby Suggs, Paul D, and her husband, Halle, whose status as an enslaved man meant he was unable to do anything to interrupt the assault on the body of his wife, Morrison structures the narrative around engagement with and avoidance of the memories that have shaped Sethe's subjectivity. Integrated into the narrative are the stories of how Sethe's mother-in-law ministered to the enslaved in the Clearing and what the vagaries of enslavement were like on two differently run plantations—Sweet Home, where enslaved women and men "were believed and trusted, but most of all . . . listened to" (125), in contradistinction to the plantation run by Schoolteacher, who lined up "human characteristics" on one side of a ledger and "animal ones on the right" (191). The reference to Schoolteacher's ledger is significant to Morrison's geopoetics and narrative project, because despite the ways enslavement was institutionalized and codified by law, Morrison was interested in the reality that, as Hartman says, the "bifurcated existence as both an object of property and a person" remained to be addressed.[23] Or, as Steven Weisenberger explains, the novel suggests that beneath the legal contradictions that were exposed in the court case of Margaret Garner (the actual enslaved woman upon whom the character Sethe is based) about the enslavement of human beings was not only the reality "that slavery . . . constituted a historical trauma whose forgetting . . . put a people's collective sanity in chronic peril" but also the reality that despite "others' obscurely coded stories about her," she was "herself a feeling and thinking subject."[24] In many respects, the novel addresses the bifurcation of being both human and property, subject and object, as the commodification of one's body exposed the untenable nature of the laws invoked to punish Sethe's crime at the same time that the crime of trafficking in human flesh that led to her act is overlooked and normalized. The novel addresses the absurdities of the responses to Sethe's act as well as the absences and the various omitted iterations of the demands enslavement made on Black female subjectivity and agency that Morrison found lacking in her own reading of the slave narratives.

Morrison punctuates the narrative with references to the story of Stamp Paid and his leadership role in the Underground Railroad, with references to the Middle Passage, and with the respective and joint memories of Sethe, Beloved, and Denver, where their subjectivities merge to describe their interior lives through forays into their dialogic intersubjective stream of consciousness. Through an intermingling of the places where the enslaved have had to eke out a life to sustain their physical bodies, to the interior life where their imagination helped them shape a third space of subjectivity, to the ways in which the chorus of women who first wanted the worst to happen to Sethe to punish her for what they perceived as a prideful lack of remorse—they wonder "was her head a bit too high?" (153)—but later join in prayerful song to facilitate her healing, Morrison manages to demonstrate how memory shapes narrative and vice versa. As she says in her Nobel lecture: "Narrative is radical, creating us at the moment it is being created."[25] She takes her reader through what Adrienne Rich calls "a whole new psychic geography" by reentering the narrative of enslavement through Black female subjectivity and the interstices of time, place, and memory.[26] At the end of the novel, when the chorus of women who have exorcised the ghost and facilitated Sethe's healing reflect on what has happened, Morrison writes that they thought "it was not a story to pass on" (274), but, of course, in Morrison's protocols of reading, only by acknowledging the "disremembered and unaccounted for" (274) and engaging in the paradoxical work of remembering and forgetting could a new, more profound understanding of Black subjectivity be possible. Indeed, her geopoetics of narrative rememory created spaces for the reader that enabled a new rendering and telling of the narrative of enslavement.

By way of her geopoetics of narrative rememory, Morrison continues her exploration of the subject of enslavement in the novel *A Mercy*. Published in 2008, it turns to a related but unfamiliar place and time—that of the New World of America in the seventeenth century—before enslavement was institutionalized on the basis of race. The archive or site of memory to which Morrison turns in this novel is therefore the archive of the nation's narrative about its own origins and the geographic locations where the subjugation of Native American and Black bodies along with poor white people obscured their subjectivity. The narrative is indeed what she calls "literary archaeology," where, she says:

> you journey to a site to see what remains were left behind and to reconstruct the world that these remains imply. What makes it fiction is the nature of the imaginative act: my reliance on the image—on the remains—in addition to recollection.[27]

Morrison seeks to imagine a way of telling the story of how racial logic surpassed the other methods of structuring social space and community in the period before the Declaration of Independence, the Constitution, and other early historical documents. She turns to the 1676 story of Bacon's Rebellion, loosely referenced in the novel with the description of the place in Virginia, where Jacob Vaark, a Dutch trader, finds himself before he capitulates to participating in the slave-trading business. Morrison describes the landscape as follows:

> In this territory he could not be sure of friend or foe. Half a dozen years ago an army of blacks, natives, whites, mulattoes—freedmen, slaves

and indentured—had waged war against local gentry led by members of that very class. When that "people's war" lost its hope to the hangman, the work it had done—which included the slaughter of opposing tribes and running the Carolinas off their land—spawned a thicket of new laws authorizing chaos in defense of order. By eliminating manumission, gatherings, travel and bearing arms for black people only; by granting license to any white to kill any black for any reason; by compensating owner for a slave's maiming or death, they separated and protected all whites from all others forever.... In short, 1682 and Virginia was still a mess. (11–12)

Through narrative rememory, Morrison recollects and reassembles early moments in America's founding story to interrogate how place, race, and belonging shape the subjectivity not only of Florens, the Black female orphan protagonist, but also of Vaark, the white trader who purchased her for his wife, Rebekka, the indigenous young woman, Lina, from a nonspecified Native American community, the two white male workers on the property, and the Black male blacksmith, who Florens sets out to find to help heal Rebekka from smallpox. As is characteristic of Morrison, the novel begins *in medias res*, but in this novel, the reader has even fewer narrative guideposts into the story, the character who opens it in the first person, or the circumstances that shape her telling of her story. In many respects, the narrative rememory that structures this novel is one that requires that Morrison imagine the people and the events that took place prior to Bacon's Rebellion to narrate the story of how the seeds of the nation's undoing were embedded in its beginning. By alternating Floren's story with that of the other characters, Morrison circles the subject of the nation's story of its origins and simultaneously deconstructs and reconstructs it by imagining the stories through the memories of those whose voices were excluded or marginalized as insignificant to the hegemonic narrative of the nation.

She signals that the narrative will venture into unchartered territory in the opening words of the text when Florens says:

Don't be afraid. My telling can't hurt you in spite of what I have done and I promise to lie quietly in the dark—weeping perhaps or occasionally seeing the blood once more.... You can think what I tell you a confession if you like, but one full of curiosities familiar only in dreams ... stranger things happen all the time everywhere.... One question is who is responsible? Another is can you read? Other signs need more time to understand. Often there are too many signs, or a bright omen clouds up too fast. I sort them and try to recall, yet I know I am missing much, like not reading.... Let me start with what I know for certain. (3–4)

With these words on the opening page of the novel, Morrison sets the reader up with more questions than answers but leads the reader to be interested in what she was interested in—the ability to return to a story you believe you know only to learn how much has been left unsaid, untold. As the Nobel lecture suggests, she decides to "make up a story," to fill in the gaps and spaces of time and history by returning to a historical place and time despite the difficulties of doing so.[28]

But the reader has very little to go on about the geographical location, who Florens, the first-person narrator, is, or why either matters. The reader has few narrative guideposts aside from the reference to the year 1690 and the general location of "Mary's Land"—that is, Maryland (7)—and references to Virginia. The reader has no idea, for example, that Florens is addressing her words to the blacksmith, the African she has been instructed to find, as he allegedly knows how to heal smallpox, the disease that has caused Vaark's death and is threatening to kill his widow, Rebekka. The reader learns that Florens is on a mission to find the blacksmith for not only Rebekka but also for herself, since he is the object of her affection. The fact that Florens speaks in the historical present and has learned quickly how to "write from memory" (6) and that the voice of her—referred to only as Minha Mae, which is Portuguese for "my mother"—ends the novel are Morrison's way of structuring the novel through the Black female subjectivity that she seeks to foreground as she did in *Beloved*. But what distinguishes this work is that she uses narrative rememory of the other characters, interspersed between those of Florens, to flesh out the novel with the perspectives of the white slave trader, the Native American Lina, Vaark's widow, Rebekka, the pregnant enslaved woman, appropriately named Sorrow, and the two white indentured servants, Willard and Scully. Moreover, she intersperses these perspectives, ruminations, and memories of these characters with descriptions of the fraught nature of the designs that the European invaders have for the place and the people they find there and who they import and enslave to live there.

Where this group of human subjects find themselves and how they regard their place among one another are critical to Morrison's narrative strategy for destabilizing the reading experience. Through narrative rememory, Morrison makes it possible for the reader to navigate their way through the landscape and the spatial arrangements that European gentry imposed on the land to represent the third space of subjectivity. As Kirby explains, attitudes toward geography and land were "directly instrumental in making the new land a commodity and subduing the native people."[29] Morrison illustrates in this novel how both processes were interconnected in ways that created a need to tell a different story. At one point in Lina's ruminations about who she is and those who are part of the Vaark household, she thinks: "As long as Sir was alive it was easy to veil the truth: that they were not family—not even a like-minded group. They were orphans, each and all" (69). It is in the reflections of Willard and Scully that we get another perspective on the vicariousness of time and circumstance that have brought them together:

> They once thought they were a kind of family because together they had carved companionship out of isolation. But the family they imagined they had become was false. Whatever each one loved, sought or escaped, their futures were separate and anyone's guess. . . . Nevertheless, remembering how the curate described what existed before Creation, Scully saw dark matter out there, thick, unknowable, aching to be made into a world. . . . Perhaps their wages were not as much as the blacksmith's, but . . . it was enough to imagine a future. (183)

Morrison structures the narrative to enable the reader to imagine the nation's originary moment of being and the peoples who found themselves together before racial hierarchies began, all of whom in one way or another were orphans suffering from "mother hunger" (73) and who were at the mercy of those who had their own interests in mind at every turn.

Yet, embedded in the chapters of each narrative, from Florens to Lina and those who occupy the landscape with her, are Morrison's intermittent critiques of the exploitation, greed, and subjugation that transformed the Native American soil into what Europeans began to claim as their own. She circles the subject of enslavement by introducing various components of the landscape, the nature of the preracist enslavement that created a social network among the Native Americans, poor whites, and Africans based on class and religious differences, and the apparatus of colonialism, capitalism, and racism that Europeans gradually depended on to construct the nation's economy, laws, and way of being. For example, Vaark is introduced early in the novel as "a ratty orphan become landowner, making a place out of no place" (13), trying to make his way on American soil but vowing that "flesh was not his commodity" (25). His thoughts about those who think otherwise are represented in the following passage:

Access to a fleet of free labor made D'Ortega's leisurely life possible. Without a shipload of enslaved Angolans he would not be merely in debt; he would be eating from his palm instead of porcelain and sleeping in the bush of Africa rather than a four-post bed. Jacob sneered at wealth dependent on a captured workforce that required more force to maintain. Thin as they were, the dregs of his kind of Protestantism recoiled at whips, chains and armed overseers. He was determined to prove that his own industry could amass the fortune, the station, D'Ortega claimed without trading his conscience for coin. (32)

However, after touring the estate of D'Ortega, the slaveowner who ironically had once fallen on hard times but who impresses Vaark with his large house and lavish living from trafficking in human flesh taken from the African diaspora, Vaark is gradually lured into buying Florens and Sorrow to help Rebekka around the house and to keep her company in the wake of their child's death. He begins to fantasize about the life he could have and the house he could build in what he privately thinks is a "most wretched business" (30) and about how he had managed to go "head to head with rich gentry" (31) as an equal. He assuages his conscience by thinking that having "a remote labor force in Barbados" (40) would be much better than have the "intimacy of slave bodies" closer to him on American soil. Eventually, after their lives begin to change, Rebekka works up the courage to question him about the source of their newfound wealth, to which he responds: "New arrangements" (103). "New arrangements" is an understatement for the subject that Morrison is encircling to tell this early American story. Through her narrative rememory, the space becomes three-dimensional in the ways that McKittrick describes because Morrison focuses on the very "subjectivities, imaginations, and stories" of those whose lives were regarded as if they did not matter.[30] Ironically, before the larger house that his engagement in the slave trade has made possible is even furnished, he dies from smallpox. The reader learns, therefore, in the first three chapters of the novel, that Vaark, the architect of the life Rebekka and her household are inhabiting, has gone from shunning the enslavement of Africans to a wholesale embrace of it, only to die before he can enjoy it. Through Morrison's geopoetics, the reader comes to understand how the "production of space" and the social arrangements and hierarchies constructed in those spaces have implications for Black female subjectivity and the subjectivity of others.[31]

As a narrative strategy, therefore, Vaark's death enables Morrison to circle the subject of slavery on American soil in multiple ways. She gives the setting a time and place from history, she problematizes that history by shifting it from a lush place with "the air of a world so new" (13) and "shorelines beautiful enough to bring tears" (13), and then she meticulously shares, from the various viewpoints of her characters, how the landscape becomes a space haunted by trafficking in the purchase and sale of human beings. Morrison uses the memories of those bought and hired to attend to their mistress, Vaark's widow, as a strategy for fleshing out their subjectivity both as spectators—that is, people living in the household and reading astutely what is going on there—and actors with agency in their own lives. Two examples of Morrison representing these characters simultaneously as spectators and actors are Lina and Sorrow. Morrison gives Lina thoughts and memories as a Native American woman who observed how Vaark killed trees but was unable to fully enjoy living in the "profane monument" (51) that he regarded it to be. She ruminates on who her people had been, how the "Europes" (51)—her name for Europeans—first "terrified . . . then rescued her" (51), and how they attempted to use their religion to make her relinquish her own. Morrison gives her agency to resist the absolute takeover of her subjectivity with this description:

> She decided to fortify herself by piecing together scraps of what her mother had taught her before dying. . . . Relying on memory and her own resources, she cobbled together neglected rites, merged European medicine with native, scripture with lore, and recalled or invited the hidden meaning of things. Found, in other words, a way to be in the world. There was no comfort or place for her in the village. (56–57)

Likewise, Sorrow, the apparently mixed-race young girl described at one point as "mongrelized" (142) and given to hallucinations, gains a new sense of agency when she gives birth. After her baby is born, she feels "convinced that this time she had done something, something important, by herself" (157). Moreover, Morrison describes how the death of Vaark and the absence of Florens change the dynamics of the household in a substantive way:

> There had always been tangled strings among them. Now they were cut. Each woman embargoed herself; spun her own web of thoughts unavailable to anyone else. It was as though, with or without Florens, they were falling away from one another. (158)

It is precisely at this juncture, however, of giving birth and recognizing that she cannot count on the other women to be her social network that she gains a sense of agency as a mother and says to her infant daughter, "I am your mother. . . . My name is Complete" (158). Representing her as a Black female subject who relinquishes the name given to her and assumes a new name that she gives herself, Morrison foreshadows the role Florens has in the novel.

Given the way Morrison circumnavigates Florens's story, it is easy to forget that her identity is that of not only an enslaved young woman in the Vaark household but also of an enslaved subject who has access to literacy—that is, she can read and write and is described as "lettered" (4), though she does not know the content of the letter she is to deliver from the mistress to the Blacksmith. Morrison punctuates the role that Christianity has in the occupation of the new geographical landscape with the reference to the "Reverend Father," the priest who both teaches her to read and simultaneously enables her to realize that "priests are unlove here" (8). She does not understand why her mother has sent her away, though the reader learns at the end that it was an act of mercy to spare her from the harsh life of enslavement in Barbados. By representing Florens as the protagonist with the literacy to write her own story on the walls of the house Vaark built, Morrison empowers her with agency to read all that has occurred and to record it for her lover, the Blacksmith, or anyone else:

> In the beginning when I come to this room I am certain the telling will give me the tears I never have. I am wrong. Eyes dry, I stop telling only when the lamp burns down. Then I sleep among my words. The telling goes on without dream and when I wake it takes time to pull away, leave this room and do chores. (185)

Although she remembers that the Blacksmith cannot read and will never know what she has written on the walls unless he learns, Morrison gives her the agency and the sense of subjectivity that comes from literacy, from telling her own story her own way, when Florens writes,

> If you never read this, no one will. These careful words, closed up and wide open, will talk to themselves. Round and round, side to side, bottom to top, top to bottom all across the room. Or. Or perhaps no. Perhaps these words need air that is out in the world. Need to fly up then fall.... You are correct.... I am become wilderness but I am also Florens. In full. Unforgiven. Unforgiving.... Slave. Free. I last. (188–189)

Through the character of Florens, Morrison circles the subject of slavery a different way, using the geopoetics of narrative rememory to expose the vagaries of enslavement on the minds and bodies of the enslaved, the hypocrisy of the enslavers despite their professions of Christian faith, and the multiple ways the nation's originary narrative has always been incomplete. Claiming the very identity that the Blacksmith and others had used against her—"you are nothing but wilderness" (166)—Florens subverts his authority over her body, her heart, and her mind by claiming the sanctity and freedom of her own soul and becoming the subject of her own story.

In the novel *Home*, published in 2012, Morrison returns to another site of memory in American history to interrogate how Black subjects read and move through places and spaces that converge on their subjectivity and sense of self. She focuses on the reverse migration journey of a Black male protagonist, Frank Money, but it could be argued that a Black female story—that of his sister, Cee—is the catalyst for his journey and in many respects the subject at the center of the narrative. Morrison's geopoetics of narrative rememory circle around the subject of two historical realities in American history—the reality of cognitive dissonance that Black soldiers experienced after the Korean War upon returning to both acute and subtle forms of racism back home in the United States and the reality of the medical abuse perpetrated against Black women's bodies during and after the period associated with the Eugenics Movement.[32] Whether the focus is the journey back to the South across multiple geographical landscapes or the journey to the space inside the four walls of the office where a medical doctor engaged in the pseudoscience designed to use Black female bodies as objects for experimentation, Morrison circles the subject of racism on American soil and how it shapes place, subjectivity, and belonging at a more recent time in American history. Despite the memories that made Frank want to forget the South and all that it represented, his sister's cry for help inspires his rememories, and his return takes the reader to sites of memory that represent the intersection of race, gender, and class in American life and culture.

Frank Money, the protagonist, is a Korean War veteran who returns to the states traumatized by the violence he witnessed and engaged in and grieving over the loss of his two "homeboys," who died in the war he survived. Convinced that he does not want to return to the South, he receives a letter summoning him to return to Lotus, Georgia, to see about his sister, Cee, and indicating that he should get there as soon as possible or she would be dead, prompting him to have a change of heart. The novel maps his journey from Korea to the United States at the same time that it maps his return to the South from Seattle and Portland. It takes the reader through his memories of the South and his reading of the present, both of which are colored with the experience of war and the effects of its aftermath on his psyche. Through her geopoetics of narrative rememory, Morrison's rendering of Frank's interior life and the juxtaposition between the America he remembers and the one to which he returns offer her readers a rich engagement with reimagining the meanings of home. Moreover, Morrison uses Frank's arrival in Lotus and his reunion with Cee to represent how a space of healing emerges from the circle of women who care for her, the connections between the individual and the community that cares for them, and the need to confront the very aspects of the past he wanted to forget or may have been tempted to deny or reject.

Reading Morrison's fiction through a framework of geopoetics enables us to discern that the movement through time and space, or what Michele M. Wright refers to as "spacetime," requires that we remain open to the "art of indirection" that governs her work.[33] The reader must develop comfort not only with the discomfort of moving from one place to another but also with Morrison's representation of the influx of memories that occur in whatever order the psyche demands at any given time. As Woolf once said, the work of the novelist requires that they "record the atoms as they fall upon the mind in the order in which they fall . . . trace the pattern, however disconnected and incoherent in appearance, which each sight or incident scores upon the consciousness."[34] In *Beloved*, Morrison's geopoetics of narrative rememory and purposeful indirection enable us to bear witness to the complex consciousness and interior life of a grieving mother. Through a similar act of intentional and purposeful indirection, she moves through time and space in ways that disorient but also invite the reader in *Home* into the interior life of Frank Money. Resisting the linear path of history that one might encounter in the literary narrative genre of the bildungsroman (that she loosely invokes in structuring the narrative of *Song of Solomon*, for example), she strategically deploys an Odysseus-like narrative to represent the circuitous routes of Frank's inner life in the same way that the mind remembers, processes information, and understands cognition.[35] In the character of Frank Money, it could be argued that instead of a grieving mother, we have a grieving man. Through Morrison's geopoetics of narrative rememory, of disorientation, dislocation, and the search for belonging, we bear witness to Frank's return from Korea to Lotus and learn through his journey the vagaries of home from both a global and domestic or local perspective.

The novel begins *in medias res* at a time and place for which the reader has no orientation, other than the name of the town—Lotus—and the fact that there are two young people who "shouldn't have been anywhere near that place" (3) where we first see them. All the reader learns initially is that there are two children, a brother and sister, who bear witness in the span of a few minutes to something awesome (horses that "rose up like men") at the same time that they bear witness to something horrific (men burying a body that they had dragged out of a wheelbarrow and thrown "into a hole already waiting") (4).

By the time the reader gets to the third page of the opening section, which is entirely in italics, the first-person narrator speaks back directly to the author with words of caution and chastisement:

> *Since you're set on telling my story, whatever you think and whatever you write down, know this: I really forgot about the burial. I only remembered the horses. They were so beautiful. So brutal. And they stood like men.* (5)

The narrator admonishes the author, and by extension the reader, at the onset of the novel to relinquish assumptions and presuppositions and to bring instead an inquisitiveness and curiosity that might better serve their navigation through the text. Why did the narrator insist that he forgot about the burial? Considering that the scene is clearly not only one of horses standing like men but of men, presumably white men, unceremoniously burying a Black body that has just been lynched, what does the narrator achieve with this disavowal? Is the disavowal connected to a distinction between how a child reads versus how an adult reads and/or reflects on a moment in retrospect? Is it to distinguish the behavior of the horses from that of the men engaged in burying a Black body after participating in a dehumanizing act of racial violence? What is Morrison as the author acknowledging or achieving through this first-person italicized metanarrative at the beginning of the novel? How does this preemptive beginning shape the narrative of the third-person omniscient narrator or the reader's response to the narrative? While these two sentences may be read as the familiar form of metafictional device that Morrison used in *Jazz* to challenge the reader about relying on the narrator, I believe Morrison introduces this part of the text with italics and metanarrative to express gaps in her own knowledge of how to tell the story of a Korean veteran who is returning to the home in the 1950s to which he said he would never return. In other words, the metafictional pause becomes a literary device in the novel that enables her to begin with a kernel of a story along with an admission of her own authorial humility and limitations. Morrison uses italics this way in this novel seven additional times—in chapters 3, 5, 7, 9, 11, 14, and 17. She is also, by means of this narrative device, inviting the reader to bring the requisite level of humility and curiosity to avoid presumptions and presuppositions about the character or his story. As in other texts, her narrative poetics demand that she withhold certain cues and signposts from the reader so that they remain open to what the text can teach them about the subject and themselves that they may not already know. As she has shared on more than one occasion in discussing her process as a writer and her goal of leaving spaces for the reader, she seeks simultaneously to engage and estrange the reader from the familiar by mystifying it.³⁶ Considering what story the opening scene does and does not tell, Morrison wants the reader to release those presuppositions so that she can map out new spaces on a journey that challenges the very meanings of home they may have brought to the text. She uses these italicized interludes throughout the text to remind readers that they cannot possibly know the complexity of home or war as the protagonist Frank Money has experienced it or what it will mean to return to a place where he never felt he truly belonged. Moreover, this metanarrative device is a strategy to prepare readers for the vagaries of memory that inform Morrison's ongoing use of narrative rememory to navigate the spaces between the past and the present in her fiction.

In some respects, it is ironic that the title of the novel is *Home* and not *War*. Morrison shared on more than one occasion that she actually wanted to give *Paradise* the title of *War*, but her editor talked her out of it.³⁷ Considering that war seems to be a wholly appropriate and apt metaphor for what happens first between Black people fleeing from white people to form all-Black towns and then Black men slaughtering women for simply being different, the level of contention that occurs in that novel is indeed warlike, violent, and deadly. Yet, in a novel that actually includes a soldier returning from literal combat in an actual war—the Korean War, although it was known historically as a "police action"—Morrison chooses instead to connect the story to a word that invokes familiar if not universal feelings of shelter, security, and safety.³⁸ By so doing, she uses her geopoetics to map a circuitous route into the spaces and places where the meanings of war and home get unpacked, destabilized, questioned, and redefined in ways that correspond to the ways in which Black subjects, this time particularly male subjects, navigate the journey from a foreign land back to the Deep South. In her essay "Wartalk," Morrison writes: "The language of war has historically been noble, summoning the elevating quality of warrior discourse; the eloquence of grief for the dead; courage and the honor of vengeance."³⁹ It could be argued that Morrison uses a "reverse migration" narrative of a sort, therefore, to unpack and interrogate the complexities and vagaries of war for Black people. In other words, unlike the Great Migration narratives of going from South to North, as discussed in the previous chapter about the period that preceded the Harlem Renaissance, in *Home*, Morrison's character returns to the South on a journey that is somewhat reminiscent of— though very different from—Milkman Dead's journey from the North to the South on a search for heritage and a sense of identity. Frank Money is a man on a very different kind of mission. His return to the South is more reluctant but also more focused and urgent. His return is not so much about home as it is about family and community and the need to rescue his sister from acute assault and distress, and he is represented through Morrison's prose as a man whose life experiences reveal the less than noble dimensions of war. Even though she includes veterans and references to the aftermath of war in *Sula* and in *Paradise*, she does not focus on war, per se, in those works. In this novel, however, the euphemisms of war come undone through the narrative of one who survived one war but came home to a new battlefield that also had not been named for what it was or how it was being experienced by Black people on American soil.

At the center of Morrison's novels have been her female subjects and the challenges they faced with navigating the spaces of their lives. The first major exception to this pattern was in *Song of Solomon*, where the protagonist is a male, Milkman Dead, who chooses to leave home to undertake a migration to the South, where he is initiated into the truth of his family heritage and a more mature understanding of manhood. By the time we get to Morrison's tenth novel, *Home*, published in 2012, she has already secured her identity as a writer whose understanding of the racial imaginary is as complex, nuanced, and intersectional as the lived lives of Black subjects, especially in the United States. As this study argues, her fiction involves returns to and interrogations of sites of memory, not simply to counter previous narratives of domination and exclusion but more so to uncover the unsaid, untold, discredited forms of knowledge that are revealed from such interrogations. What emerges from the spaces between the official narratives and the narratives that the people themselves have created about their own lives is a liminal third space of disassociation that Frank is experiencing when we first meet him in a mental institution. Although he may not know where he wants to be in the moment, what he does know is he needs to escape from the institution where he has enough sanity, despite the fact that war has traumatized him, to know he does not want to remain in the custody of those retraumatizing him in the psychiatric ward. He even uses familiar wartime strategies from Korea to attempt to outmaneuver the hospital attendants:

> The trick of imitating semi-coma, like playing dead facedown in a muddy battlefield, was to concentrate on a single neutral object. Something that would smother any random hint of life. . . . He would need something that stirred no feelings, encouraged no memory—sweet or shameful. Just searching for an item was agitating. Everything reminded him of something loaded with pain. (7–8)

But in the midst of reverting to a wartime strategy to survive, he remembered the letter he had received from home summoning him to return in language that got his attention: "Come fast. She be dead if you tarry" (8). The word *tarry* communicates with almost biblical significance that he does not have much time if he plans to rescue his sister from danger.

The reason he has been hospitalized in the first place is worthy of note. In the words of the narrative, his crime was "vagrancy." He ruminates on the strangeness of this crime:

> Interesting law, vagrancy, meaning standing outside or walking without clear purpose anywhere. Carrying a book would help, but being barefoot would contradict "purposefulness" and standing still could prompt a complaint of "loitering." Better than most he knew that being outside wasn't necessary for legal or illegal disruption. You could be inside, living in your own house for years, and still, men with or without badges but always with guns could force you, your family, your neighbors to pack up and move—with or without shoes. (9)

In a passage that is reminiscent of the lawlessness of the colonial landscape coupled by the "slave codes" that racialized slavery and policed Black bodies in *A Mercy*, Morrison describes how Frank's ruminations about his predicament invoke a memory from his childhood, when, as a four-year-old, he witnessed neighbors being ordered to leave their own home by members of the Ku Klux Klan—"both hooded and not" (10). By inconspicuously including "and not" to the description of the Klansmen, Morrison ironically calls attention to how white supremacist behavior had infiltrated the community and routinely challenged the sense of belonging that Black people could count on in their own neighborhoods. The one elderly man who refused to leave was beaten to death and "tied to the oldest magnolia tree in the county—the one that grew in his own back yard" (10). The arbitrariness of white violence and the utter cruelty of the eyes of the old man being carved out come back to Frank with haunting clarity, and once again, Morrison circles a subject by narrating the ways in which the past returns and takes residence in the present. Her vivid description of a Black male memory and the awareness of the overarching menacing presence of white supremacy in Black life exposes her mindfulness of what Shabazz describes in *Spatializing Blackness* as "mechanisms . . . of policing, containment, surveillance and the establishment of territory," practices in regard to Black bodies that date back to enslavement, the Civil War, Reconstruction, and Jim Crow.[40] Recognizing from both his memory of home and his memory of war just how precarious Black life in predominantly white spaces could be, Frank understands that escaping from the hospital is literally a matter of life and death. Put another way, in just a few paragraphs into the novel, Morrison illustrates what Brandi Thompson Summers refers to as "the spatial realities of race."⁴¹ These spatial realities explain the overlap between the racial past Frank remembers and the present to which he returns, where Black ownership—whether of one's own body, or of a space bought, paid for, and lived in as home—was precarious and vulnerable to white bigotry. By using the term *vagrancy* to explain why he was stopped by the police, Morrison invokes the reality that Simone Browne so aptly describes in *Dark Matters: On the Surveillance of Blackness*:

> Where public spaces are shaped for and by whiteness, some acts in public are abnormalized by way of racializing surveillance and coded for disciplinary measures that are punitive in effects.⁴²

Moreover, by naming the novel *Home*, Morrison registers her investment in exposing and interrogating the ways in which Black American war veterans returned home to "everyday social spaces of being stopped, frisked, and criminalized through the racist historic machinations of white gazes and racist policies" and routine behaviors that George Yancy argues are from those who believe skin color bestows them with power to dehumanize the racial other.⁴³ In fact, when Frank thinks of home, he remembers that "he hated Lotus. Its unforgiving populations, its isolation, and especially its indifference to the future were tolerable only if his buddies were there with him" (15–16). Returning "home without his 'homeboys'" (15) to such routine acts of surveillance, violence, and disregard was yet another emotional complication to the mental aftermath of war for him.

Embedded in Frank's desperate desire to escape the psych ward of the hospital is a profound knowing that such social spaces constitute another form of incarceration, where Black males are subject to abuse of their minds and their bodies. He is mindful that his breakup with Lily has left him vulnerable to unmanageable anxiety that was filled with "free-floating rage, self-loathing disguised as somebody else's fault" (15), and wandering memories. Yet, these realities do not inspire him to remain inside the strategy of containment that had become a precursor to incarceration for Black men. Instead, he is as acutely aware of his war-induced post-traumatic stress from fighting overseas as he is of the trauma-producing possibilities inside an American hospital psychiatric ward, where whatever sanity he had left would be in grave danger. Morrison subtly insinuates this knowing about spatial realities into the narrative and illustrates another reality of the return home with which Frank must contend. Although we do not get his specific diagnosis, we do learn that his arrest landed him in the psych ward, where "two days' [of] hospital drugging" (16) had left him in and out of sanity but conscious enough to know he needed to escape. Undoubtedly, Morrison was mindful that she was creating the character of Frank Money as an example of how Black veterans returned home to the systemic racism found in both the criminal justice and health-care systems. As Jonathan M. Metzel argues in *The Protest Psychosis: How Schizophrenia Became a Black Disease*, "the intersections of race and mental illness" are so embedded in America's health-care structure that only by historicizing and contextualizing them can we see the confluence of power, racial bias, and public policy at work as they operate to the detriment of Black people.[44] Almost invoking Metzel's analysis of the intersection of race and mental health in America from the twenties through the sixties, Morrison represents Frank's mental health as that dimension of his identity that he chooses to protect from vapid surveillance, prison, and hospitalization. After the trauma of war, the last thing he wants is to be retraumatized in the ways that Black people were historically mistreated in the mental health system. Foucault's argument that "the body is a biopolitical reality; medicine is biopolitical strategy" might not be a conscious reality for Frank, but in his unconscious mind, he reads, knows, and understands that his freedom is at stake.[45] In fact, it could be argued that the novel problematizes how the state is implicated in the fact that criminal justice and health care have been the oxymoronic sites where mitigations against Black well-being have been most acute. Because Frank instinctively doubts that he belongs in the hospital or that he will be safe there, at least in the psych ward, he literally flees from the hospital to save his own life.

Once Frank escapes from the hospital, his first stop is at the AME Zion parsonage that he had observed on his ride in the back seat of the squad car. When he arrives at the parsonage, he is greeted by Rev. John Locke and his wife, Jean, who extend hospitality to him in the form of a meal, a comfortable place to sleep, and even funds to continue his journey to Lotus. They also extend a warning to him not to be misled by the fact that he served in a desegregated army. In the words of Rev. Locke:

> Listen here, you from Georgia and you been in a desegregated army and maybe you think up North is way different from down South. Don't believe it and don't count on it. Custom is just as real as law and can be just as dangerous. (19)

So just a few pages into the novel, Morrison has exposed the global, national, and local conditions of her protagonist but also of Black people as a collective, in social spaces from Seattle, to Portland, to Chicago, to Georgia, and beyond. The fact that Frank's first stop on his journey is at the home of a pastor and his wife shows how the Black church and the community surrounding it have always created a kind of safe haven for Black people. More than a place to eat and rest, the Locke home is also where Frank receives information that is critical to his survival as he navigates the South. In some respects, the Lockes remind him to remember the segregated South that he left, lest his more recent experiences overseas in the army mislead him to believe his homeland has changed more than it has. Through this narrative strategy, Morrison reveals that the novel is not only about Frank as a returning veteran but also about the lived lives of Black people during the 1950s, a period she seeks to deromanticize through narrative rememory just as she deromanticizes America's originary narrative of the New World.

In many respects, the geopoetics of narrative rememory is presented and represented by Morrison's descriptions of Frank's circumstances and mindset and by how he reads and thinks about the logistics of navigating inhospitable spaces. As he continues his journey after the warm hospitality yet stern warning provided by the Lockes, Morrison interrupts the narrative to incorporate Frank's memories—especially those associated with the trauma of war. One of the atrocities he remembers is of a boy attempting to push his entrails back into his body. Another is of a boy calling for his mother "with only the bottom half of his face intact" (21). Yet another is the violence of his encounter with the Korean girl. When he first describes the encounter in italics in Chapter 9, he projects the encounter onto a fellow soldier. In his first description of the incident, Frank interrupts the narrative to share the story of a young girl who routinely came near the soldiers' quarters to scavenge through the garbage for food. On one occasion, she allegedly grabs the crotch of a soldier and says something in Korean that he believes "sounds like 'Yum-yum'" (95), and the soldier "blows her away" (95). Five chapters later, however, Morrison interrupts the narrative again with Frank's italicized first-person commentary, and the reader discovers a startling revision to the earlier version. Frank acknowledges that he is actually the soldier who is sexually aroused by the young girl and who feels compelled to kill her. He makes this confession in words that are rendered on the page as poetry:

> *I shot the Korean girl in the face.*
> *I am the one she touched,*
> *I am the one who saw her smile,*
> *I am the one she said "Yum-yum" to.*
> *I am the one she aroused.*
> *A child. A wee little girl.*
> *I didn't think. I didn't have to.*

Better she should die.
How could I let her live after she took me down to a place I didn't know
   was in
Me? (133–134)

By rendering this intersection of the atrocity of war with sexual violence against a female child, alternating between past- and present-tense verbs, Morrison interrupts the narrative of Frank's return with an example of the propensity to mask the abominations of war in glorified, poetic language. It becomes clear that Morrison's geopoetics of narrative rememory in this novel are about not only Frank's literal return to the South but also his efforts to deny his own complicity in a construction of masculinity that no longer is aligned with the innermost parts of his being. Unpacking and revealing a place within that was previously unknown to the conscious mind and rendering it in its rawest yet most empathic, poetic way is part of the cultural work the novel is doing at its core.

These memories haunt Frank nearly as much as those of his own desperate attempts to step around wounded and dying bodies to keep himself alive as he trekked across white snow covered with red blood do. The only reprieve from nightmares and the haunting memories of war come in the form of his more pleasant recollections of his romantic affair with Lily, a relationship that he was ultimately unable to sustain. Ironically, while Frank's relationship with Lily may seem tangential to the larger narrative, it reveals two other elements of Morrison's geopoetics in the novel. On one hand, it becomes a narrative strategy for representing Frank's personal struggle to come to terms with making human connections and with his received constructions of masculinity on the other side of war. On the other hand, through Lily's personal story of losing her job as an employee at a local theater, Morrison incorporates a historical reference to one of the sites of the so-called Red Scare about communism that took place in Seattle. Morrison includes a reference to a real site of memory, *The Morrison Case* (72), a play that was allegedly banned for its pro-communist leanings, to expand her narrative agenda of removing the romantic veneer of the 1950s that obscured the historical, political, and cultural realities of racism, poverty, and injustice that were part of the American landscape.[46] Moreover, by locating the beginning of the novel in the Pacific Northwest region of the country, Morrison situates the reader outside of the stereotypical locations associated with the Great Migration from South to North to reflect on other places in the North where Black people were located. As Quintard Taylor notes, "the African American migration to Seattle was part of a larger regional transformation stimulated by the growth of World War II defense industries."⁴⁷ By expanding her fictive landscape to a different location from her other novels, she invites the reader to reflect on other dimensions of the racial imaginary that her protagonist is navigating as he returns to the states and begins his reluctant return to the South.

When he resumes his journey to get to Lotus, he arrives in Portland at the home of a second pastor, Rev. Maynard, who gives him a very different and less hospitable kind of reception. Yet, Rev. Maynard does not totally withhold help from Frank; instead, as the text explains: "From Green's travelers' book he copied out some addresses and names of rooming houses, hotels where he would not be turned away" (22–23). The reference to *The Green Book* provides yet another example of the kind of cultural work the novel *Home* is doing. The actual book, titled *The Negro Motorist Green Book*, a replica of which is now on display as part of the permanent exhibit at the African American Museum in Washington, D.C., is a collection of places and spaces where Black people could safely eat, lodge, and enjoy various forms of entertainment free of racial discrimination and/or violence as they traveled from North to South or vice versa, especially during the period of 1937–1966.⁴⁸ The book is a return to an archival site of memory that is very similar to what Hartman calls "everyday practices" that became "pedagogical handbooks" for Black people during the transition from slavery to freedom.⁴⁹ However, during the time of this much later transition, *The Green Book* was a sad commentary on the racial climate Black people traversed during the era of the Jim Crow South, decades after the formal years of enslavement. Thus, *The Green Book* represents the resilience and ingenuity Black people developed to navigate the racial discrimination they faced and sustain themselves in the midst of racial hostility. Through the resources *The Green Book* documented, Black people found a way to secure safe spaces and a sense of belonging, even if only for the short term. It was how, as Gates describes it in the language of the Black church, Black people "made a way out of no way."⁵⁰ So, when Rev. Maynard offered Frank *The Green Book*, he was simultaneously sharing the limits of his own hospitality at the same time that he was acknowledging that Frank would need some form of organic, strategic assistance, given the reality of the homeland America had continued to be while he was away at war. In a real sense, the book was both an index to the ways America had not changed while Frank was away at war in a foreign land and a testimony to how his people had navigated inhospitable places and spaces to survive and thrive. Although the Korean War (1950–1953) was about three decades after Du Bois's essay "Returning Soldiers," about the end of World War I (1914–1918), and although the U.S. Army had become integrated by the later war, Frank discovers on his return to America that "this country... despite all its better souls have done and dreamed, is yet a shameful land."⁵¹

As he continues his journey toward Lotus, Frank boards a train to Chicago. The train, a familiar trope in African American travel literature, especially during the Great Migration from South to North, also represents a narrative strategy for spatializing how Black people navigated their lives from one location to another. The story of racial violence that he learns about on the train reminds Frank that he is naïve to expect an uneventful ride to Chicago. For example, when a wife comes out to help her husband who is attacked after merely trying to get a cup of coffee, she is assaulted with "a rock thrown in her face" (25). While other passengers are distraught over this incident of racial assault on the couple, Frank speculates about an intersectional dimension of the incident that he presumes is yet to come:

> He will beat her when they get home, thought Frank. And who wouldn't? It's one thing to be publicly humiliated. A man could move on from that. What was intolerable was the witness of a woman, a wife, who not only saw it, but had dared to try to rescue—rescue—him. He couldn't protect himself and he couldn't protect her either, as the rock in her face proved. She would have to pay for that broken nose. Over and over again. (26)

This train incident adds another dimension to the meanings of home—an intersectional dimension—where home for a woman could be domestic space under siege from within and without. Frank's understanding of this intersectional reality is reflected in his thoughts about the couple. Frank is convinced that, having endured racial assault outside of their home, the wife will most likely endure physical assault to her body inside her home. Exposing and challenging constructions of masculinity and representing domestic space as a site that can be unsafe are not new to Morrison. In fact, it could be argued that she is always interrogating domestic space from an inside and outside perspective in much of her work. So, in what is ostensibly a novel that centers on a male narrative, her geopoetics demand a multivalent, intersectional reading of the places and spaces where Black women and men attempt to establish a sense of belonging. For the reader, this scene offers a reading of the construction of masculinity that Frank is being forced to rethink.

In one sense, the scene that occurs after this train incident returns the reader to another dimension of the mental landscape of Frank's mind as he observes scenery outside his train window. As he rides by the scenery, he "tried to redecorate it, mind-painting giant slashes of purple and X's of gold on hills, dripping yellow and green on barren wheat fields. Hours of trying and failing to recolor the western landscape agitated him, but by the time he stepped off the train he was calm enough" (27). Morrison's description of Frank's mind at work is indicative of yet another survival technique after the trauma of war. Though his efforts to "recolor" the landscape agitate him, they nevertheless represent one of the ways he copes with yet another form of circumstances beyond his control. When he arrives at Booker's, one of the restaurants that had been recommended, he comes upon a place that is "welcoming," with a "down-home friendliness that led Frank to talk freely to the man on the stool next to his" (28). He also enters a familiar gendered space, where men "began to compete with stories of their own deprived life in the thirties" (28). Again, turning to another African American cultural trope—the trope of verbal banter once referred to as *the dozens*—Morrison incorporates one of the strategies that Black men have historically deployed to create safe spaces wherever they found themselves. As she says in *The Black Book*, the collection she edited, *the dozens* was "the term applied to a ritualized verbal battle that black people developed to insult and humiliate each other.... The winner was the one with the cruelest wit who managed to keep cool."[52] In the midst of Frank's traumatic shifts between memories of the past and the unease of the present, this male space provides a familiarity that welcomes him and offers a reprieve as he contemplates the danger that precipitated the urgent request for him to come home to see about Ycidra, known as Cee.

Morrison shifts the narrative from Frank to Cee in Chapter 4 and begins another form of narrative rememory. The reader learns that when Frank and Cee's parents, Ida and Luther, are evicted from their home, Ida ends up giving birth to Cee "in the street" (45), to use the language of her mean maternal grandmother, Lenore. Rather than having compassion for her daughter's situation of being forced to look for housing and work while she was pregnant, Lenore chooses to say she is not like "decent women [who] delivered babies at home, in a bed attended to by good Christian women who knew what to do." (44). She regards her granddaughter, Cee, as a "gutter child" (45) based on the circumstances of her birth and thus deprives her of the sense of belonging her hardworking parents thought she would receive in her care. When Frank and Cee's parents are finally able to secure their own place to rent, Cee longs for more than her meager circumstances in the small town of Lotus can provide, despite having a comfortable sense of belonging. Described as a reader who yearns for more than *"Aesop's Fable's* and a book of Bible passages for young people" (47) could provide and who feels "adrift in the space where her brother had been" (48), she is easily persuaded, after Frank leaves for the army, to take up with Prince, "the first thing she saw wearing belted trousers instead of overalls" (47).

Her relationship with Prince is as unfulfilling as her grandmother had prophesied it would be. He uses her parents' car to run errands but then convinces them to allow him and Cee to drive it to Atlanta; however, her fantasies of the life they would have there never materialize. Instead, Prince abandons Cee, and the space where her brother had been remains empty, almost full of a double kind of longing. Her brother's absence takes her back to memories of how she and Frank, as children, "like some forgotten Hansel and Gretel, locked hands as they navigated the silence and tried to imagine a future" (53). As she thinks about how Prince abandoned her first emotionally and then physically with the very car her family had made possible for them to have and that he has in turn left her with nothing, she feels "broken. Not broken up but broken down, down into her separate parts" (54). As often is the case with Morrison's female characters, it is in the company of other women that she discovers alternative ways of being, surviving, and imagining her life. When she moves into a cheaper, more affordable room after Prince leaves, the woman who lives in the apartment upstairs from hers befriends Cee, "fusing the friendship with blunt counsel" (51). It is from that space of friendship and wise counsel that she learns about a job offering in the Atlanta suburb of Buckhead, where a doctor is offering both rent-free housing and good pay for an assistant in his home. Even in introducing the home as "a large two-story house, rising above a church-neat lawn" (58), Morrison is simultaneously signifying on two American narratives at once. On one hand, there is the narrative of America's two conflicting stories about itself—the one white people have told and/or believe and the one Black people and indigenous people have lived and witnessed. On the other hand, there is the narrative of how the church has shaped a tidy but equally conflicted foundation for the two-story house that America has been for Black people and white people. The narrative economy of *Home* does not necessitate that Morrison say more, but by signifying on the two stories and on how the exterior belies the truth of the interior, she foreshadows, in just a few words, the profound reality that lies at the heart of this novel.

The reader gets another sense of how the geopoetics of place and race converge in this novel as Morrison unfolds more about the spatial arrangements of Cee's new living quarters and about Dr. Beauregard Scott, known as Dr. Beau, the doctor for whom she will be working. Assigned to quarters below the front porch in a "shallow extension of the house rather than a proper basement" (62), Morrison again signifies on Cee's role as an assistant to the doctor at the same time that she indicates that she is a person of minor status in the larger scheme of his machinations. The larger scheme of things, in one sense, is what is at stake in this novel, though we learn about them through this particularized narrative about this sister-brother relationship. We get Cee's observation of Dr. Beau's seemingly compassionate care for his poor, mostly female patients, his habit of sending patients whose health deteriorated to a "charity hospital in the city" (62), and his donations to cover funeral expenses for patients who died. Morrison's naïve character does not yet know that, as Lipsitz suggests, "the lived experience of race has a spatial dimension, and the lived experience of space has a racial dimension."[53] We instead learn that Cee "loved her work: the beautiful house, the kind doctor, and the wages" (63).

The reader discerns the racist underside of Dr. Beau's compassion when Cee ventures into his office one day before he arrives to work. As she looks more closely at his crowded bookshelves and the mystifying titles of books, the reader gains insight into the evil agenda at work inside the space of the doctor's mind and medical practice. Morrison's notion of geopoetics takes on a new meaning as Cee reads titles that make her reflect "how small, how useless was her schooling" (63) in light of words and meanings that are not available to her. The fact that Dr. Beau's office library contains titles such as *The Passing of the Great Race* and *Heredity, Race and Society* (63) invokes for the reader a sense of how medicine and health care conspired at the intersection of science and race against the interest of women, girls, the poor, and people of color in particular at various points in American history. The fact that Cee realizes she must find more time to read so that she can understand "eugenics" (63) is Morrison's less than subtle way of critiquing and narrativizing the insidiousness of white supremacy into this text by representing its intrusion into the very spaces designed to heal and secure well-being.

Like the violence to his mind that Frank feared would ensue if he had remained in the psych ward of the hospital, the violence against Black bodies inside the space of the doctor's office is alluded to with the word *eugenics*. The reader learns that Cee is unwittingly colluding in the "long and truly terrible story of the medical establishment's use of unconsenting and often unaware black subjects for medical experiments," more recently referred to as "medical apartheid."[54] Morrison's geopoetics are meticulously imaginative in mapping for the reader the ways in which violence is hidden in plain sight behind what appears to be safe, orderly, and even pleasing to the eye. She achieves this aesthetic move by following the word *eugenics* with an exquisite representation of domestic security, normalcy, and beauty when Cee thinks:

> This was a good, safe place, she knew and Sarah [the doctor's wife] had become her family, her friend, and her confidante. They shared every meal and sometimes the cooking. When it was too hot in the kitchen, they ate in the backyard under a canopy, smelling the last of the lilacs and watching tiny lizards flick across the walkway. (65)

Despite the benign façade of this scene, Morrison attempts to make it abundantly clear that Cee is not in a safe space when she and Sarah are together in the kitchen about to cut open one of three melons. Referring to one of the melons as female because of the "tiny indentation at the stem break" (66), Cee comments that the female melons are the "juiciest" (66); then, Sarah "slid a long, sharp knife from a drawer and, with intense anticipation of the pleasure to come, cut the girl in two" (66). We come to understand that this scene is nothing short of a foreboding and a commentary at the same time on the larger system of racial oppression that Black women endured, often with the complicit presence of white women.

The juxtaposition of this kitchen scene with the shift in narrative back to Frank in the next chapter, which is italicized, provides an opportunity for Morrison to develop the character of Frank in terms of his thoughts about gender and relationships with women and his understanding of the construction of masculinity. We learn that other than casual encounters with prostitutes, he has "had only two regular women" and that what he liked regardless of "their personality, smarts or looks . . . [was] something soft [that] lay inside each . . . like a little V" (67). We discover that he is attracted to "the small breakable thing inside each one . . . knowing it was there, hidden from me, was enough" (67). But when he meets Lily, he meets "the third woman who changed everything" (67), because "the little wishbone V took up residence in . . . [his] own chest and made itself at home" (67). This section of the narrative also juxtaposes the feeling that he has arrived at an emotional place he can call home with the jarring memory of an ambulance and a medic holding a girl vomiting water and bleeding from her nose; this brings a sadness over him that leads him to take another drink. Seeing his reflection in a store window helps him realize, however, that he wants to "be something other than a haunted, half-crazy drunk" (69). Morrison then disrupts Frank's thought about his attraction to Lily with another form of metanarrative. He informs the narrator that if she thought he "was just scouting for a home with a bowl of sex in it," she is "dead wrong" (69). Morrison goes a step further and represents Frank's need to counter the narrator even more by disputing that he thought the man on the train beat his wife when he got home. Challenging the narrator's ability to predict or know his thoughts, Frank ends this section by questioning whether the narrator knows "much about love" (69) or even about him. What Morrison achieves in this interstitial space between the narrative she's telling and the story that Frank remembers and experiences emotionally is the creation and affirmation of an ontological space of being that undergirds her narrative geopoetics.

Chapter 7 is another italicized interstitial break in the narrative. It begins with a pronouncement about the home to which Frank is returning: "Lotus,

Georgia... the worst place in the world, worse than any battlefield... no future, just long stretches of killing time" (83). In the next and final interstitial passage in Chapter 11, Frank admonishes the reader to clarify his relationship with his sister, who, once his homeboys are dead, is his "only family" (103):

> *When you write this down, know this: she was a shadow for most of my life, a presence marking its own absence, or maybe mine. Who am I without her—that underfed girl with the sad, waiting eyes! No more people I didn't save. No more watching people close to me die. No more.* (103)

In many respects, by the time the reader gets to this point in the narrative, it is clear that Frank is undergoing a transformation of two dimensions. On one hand, he is returning to the very place he deemed to be the worst. On the other hand, he is rethinking his sense of being and belonging—a reconsideration that has emerged from the trauma of violence and senseless death, some of it by his own hands. But a third thing is also happening; Morrison is shifting the narrative from a focus on absence or spaces in his life to a focus on presence. As in other Morrison novels, most notably *Beloved*, an absence marks a presence and a presence also calls attention to an absence. Her geopoetics call attention to the interplay between these two dimensions of being to illustrate how Black people navigate the spaces of their lives. Frank's challenge to the narrator's perception of who he is, therefore, is yet another narrative strategy—one designed to challenge readers from too hasty a conclusion born of presuppositions about her characters or their motivations. Seemingly aware of how such hasty perceptions perpetuate the very biases and stereotypes she seeks to disrupt, she provides Frank with a new battlefield—the battlefield of the mind—to prepare the reader for his transformation and for his reunion with his sister.

Gradually, the reader learns that what has happened to Cee is criminal. Morrison seems to make an aesthetic decision that less is more, that to fill in the spaces of the narrative of Dr. Beau's crimes with any greater detail would be counterproductive to keeping the locus of the narrative on Cee, the crime against her body, and the trauma that needed attention. Summarizing the goal of his crime with the words "improving the speculum" (113) is Morrison's way of illustrating once and for all that the crime against a Black woman's body was again viewed as merely a means to a white, racist, utilitarian end. Choosing not to romanticize or fetishize the violence of the crime but to shift the focus on the communal process that would address and heal it is Morrison's narrative imperative. The narrator takes the reader through a morass of innuendo and suggestion to reveal that Cee has fallen victim to the racist, violent inhumanity of eugenics perpetrated on Black women. But the economy of language about the crime against Cee's body is quickly overtaken by the communal responses that Frank's actions initiate on behalf of his sister. Despite his thoughts that Lotus is the worst place, he is very much aware of the communal network of women whose grassroots knowledge and spiritual practices would restore his sister to healing. In fact, that communal network is signaled in Sarah's thoughts as soon as Frank comes through the door to rescue Cee:

> Thank God. Exactly the way the old folks said: not when you call Him; not when you want Him; only when you need Him and right on time. (113)

When he gets to Lotus, he senses the communal network of women led by Miss Ethel Fordham will heal Cee and is inspired to reimagine Lotus. His sense of the place is transformed by the colors he sees for the first time—"Crimson, purple, pink and China blue . . . deep deep green" (117)—by the "pleasure of being among those who do not want to degrade or destroy you" (118), and by the "feeling of safety and goodwill" (118).

Accepting that he would need to be excluded from the work of her healing because Miss Ethel and her female network "believed his maleness would worsen her [Cee's] condition" (119), Frank leaves the scene to focus on looking for work and cleaning his parents' home. His new way of reading his home space is balanced against the work of healing Cee begun by Miss Ethel. What he notices about her when he finally sees her is indicative of what Morrison attempts to reveal about the space of healing where Frank left her. She was not only healed; she was also transformed. As Miss Ethel tells her, "The important thing is to get a permanent cure. The kind beyond human power" (124). The narrative explains it this way:

> Cee was different. Two months surrounded by country women who loved mean changed her. The women handled sickness as though it were an affront, an illegal, invading braggart who needed whipping. They didn't waste their time or the patient's with sympathy and they met the tears of the suffering with resigned contempt. (121)

One index of the "mean" love that Miss Ethel and the circle of women deploy for Cee's healing is when she pleads ignorance in terms of knowing Dr. Beau would do her harm. They ask: "Who told you you was trash?" and, as if prepared for an anemic response, they close the conversation by saying, "You good enough for Jesus. Tha's all you need to know" (122). Over time, the women healers approach Cee differently:

> As she healed, the women changed tactics and stopped their berating. Now they brought their embroidery and crocheting, and finally they used Ethel Fordhams's house as their quilting center. Ignoring those who preferred new, soft blankets, they practiced what they had been taught by their mothers during the period that rich people called the Depression and they called life. Surrounded by their comings and goings, listening to their talk, their songs . . . Cee had nothing to do but pay them the attention she had never given them before. . . . Mourning was helpful but God was better and they did not want to meet their Maker and to explain a wasteful life. They knew He would ask each of them one question: "What have you done?" (122–123)

Surrounded by these women who shift their focus from her body to her soul, Cee experiences the power and authority they possess. In addition to their skills as healers of the body, they bring familiarity and proximity to their capacity. Ethel reminds her that she knew her "before she could walk" (125) and, most importantly, informs her that "you back home" (125). Moreover, Ethel adds the language of liberation when she says: "Somewhere inside you is that free person I'm talking about. Locate her and let her do some good in the world" (126). The evidence that Cee's healing is complete is when she responds, "I ain't going nowhere, Miss Ethel. This is where I belong" (126).

Morrison's portrayal of Cee's time in the company of women healers and the lessons learned about life there are critical to her idea of reimagining spaces for the reader. The fact that Cee learns how to quilt and joins the others in quilting represents the healing that has been underway both within and without. Cee's new way of reading her life enables her to reconnect with Frank on her own terms, not his. Once back home with her brother, Cee realizes his presence was "comforting, but she didn't need him as she had before" (131). Instead, she discovers within the sanctity of her own soul that she was "not going to hide from what's true just because it hurts" (131). In a real sense, her quilt becomes a metaphor for the pieces of her life that she has learned to connect into a pattern that is meaningful to the life she has lived with all of its complexity. Put another way, she discovers what Morrison describes in these words:

> We are subjects of our own narrative, witnesses to and participants in our own experience, and in no way coincidentally, in the experience

of those with whom we have come in contact. We are not, in fact ,"Other." We are choices.[55]

Once she and her brother are reunited—Frank with a new way of reading the spaces of home and Cee with a new way of reading the interior space of her soul—they are ready to take on the difficult work together of confronting the evil they had observed as children. They are prepared to make the shift from innocent spectators to engaged readers of the narratives of their own lives from an informed, historical context.

It is in the company of men and "the gatherings that made men comfortable" (137) that Frank learns the story behind the horses he remembered from his childhood. The men who gather around his grandfather to play checkers and chess recount the narrative of the racial violence that led to a father and son being pitted against one another with switchblades. With this knowledge, Frank learns the truth about the childhood memory. Armed with this new information, he convinces Cee to bring her newly made quilt with him to the site where the body of the slain son had been unceremoniously buried. He places the bones in the quilt, and the "bone-filled quilt" becomes "first a shroud, now a coffin" (144). What Morrison achieves in this narrative is the transformation of a place remembered for its lack into a space of healing, where its abundance could be recaptured both in memory and in meaningful labor to connect head and heart, body and soul. When the final italicized page of the novel ends with a poem in Cee's words—"Let's go home" (147)—Morrison is signaling a narrative space of healing for not only Frank and his sister but also the reader. As Griffin says of Morrison's late fiction, it "imagines worlds that were, and in so doing, provides a template for what might be."[56] Through the geopoetic strategy of narrative rememory, however, she demonstrates for the reader the necessity of coming to terms with the past, its manifestations in the present, the way both shape subjectivity, and how one navigates the interstices between time and space.

4

A Matter of Be/longing

Geopoetic Interrogations of Home

> When historical visibility has faded, when the present tense of testimony loses its power to arrest, then the displacements of memory and the indirections of art offer us the image of our psychic survival. To live in the unhomely world, to find its ambivalences and ambiguities enacted in the house of fiction, or its sundering and splitting performed in the work of art, is also to affirm a profound desire for social solidarity.
> —Homi K. Bhabha, *The Location of Culture*[1]

As this study has revealed in the previous chapters, most of Morrison's work has been concerned with interrogating Black subjectivity in the context of the various places and spaces where Black subjects have found themselves. From her first novel to her last, her writing has always evinced a profound sense of knowing how the disruptions and dislocations of enslavement and other assaults on Black bodies have shaped Black subjectivity and mitigated the ways in which Black subjects experience various spaces, especially the places they identified as "homespaces," to use Harris's term.[2] To demonstrate the effects that the vagaries of homelessness have had on Black subjectivity, she has consistently chosen narrative strategies that locate subjectivity as a third space between binaries of containment and freedom, that represent how Black subjects have historically read the spaces where they find themselves, and that privilege the value of indirection for circling the subjects that expose the forces designed to marginalize Black subjectivity. Moreover, Morrison's writing reveals that she understood, as Wright suggests in *The Physics of Blackness: Beyond the Middle Passage Epistemology*, that the understanding of Black subjectivity requires more than understanding the history of the Transatlantic Slave Trade, the Middle Passage, or enslavement.[3] Through her representations of Black subjectivity, Morrison's readers learn that she is concerned not only with the legacy of displacement and enslavement but also with diverse ways of knowing, being, and belonging that shape Black subjectivity that cannot be contained and/or accounted for solely in references to enslavement or entirely in relation to the racial imaginary of the past. She is also concerned with how Black subjects read and experience the various intersections at which they find themselves in the present, how they read and remember such intersections from their more immediate past, and how they imagine themselves outside of the white gaze as a sole point of reference. Her narrative strategies and geopoetics are designed, therefore, to represent these more complex ways of thinking about Black life and culture.

It could be argued that the very elusiveness of home—from the way she represents it in a childhood primer, through the lens of poverty and fear of being kicked "outdoors" in *The Bluest Eye*, to the vagaries of living in a haunted house in *Beloved* in the wake of the grief and traumas of enslavement at a place called "Sweet Home," through the chaos that ensues at the newly built mansion on the Vaark plantation, to the loss of belonging that colorism perpetuates in *God Help the Child*—is the subject of the house of fiction Morrison created over the nearly fifty-year span of her career as a novelist. And over time, she becomes more convinced, as she explains in her essay "Home," that her fictional project evolved into a focused interrogation of how race simultaneously matters and does not matter as Black subjects navigate various so-called home spaces to make sense simultaneously of their humanity and the nature of their belonging.[4] Although she does not assert as hooks does that "home is the only place where there is no race," Morrison is clearly invested in imagining home as a third space of sanctuary that is not defined by the workings of white supremacy and anti-Black strategies of containment but is experienced instead as a space of freedom that "maximizes well-being," the imagination, and belonging.[5] This chapter explores how Morrison's interrogations of home in the essay and novel by the same name, in her last novel, *God Help the Child*, and in her 2002 essay "The Foreigner's Home" constitute a fourth example of her geopoetics. This chapter concludes with a discussion of the exhibit that Morrison organized as guest curator in 2006 at the Louvre under the same title—*The Foreigner's Home*—to illustrate how her ongoing ruminations and interrogations about home are both local and global, domestic and foreign, personal and public. The exhibit was in many ways a multi-genre articulation of her interest in how we might reeducate ourselves and reimagine how we read and think about the meaning of home.

Morrison's essay "Home," in the collection of essays titled *The House That Race Built*, was originally delivered as the opening lecture of the "Race Matters Conference" at Princeton University in 1994. In the essay, she makes one of her most extensive statements about how interrogations of home shape her artistic and intellectual desire to "reconceive the racial house without forfeiting a home" of her own and "how to be both free and situated; how to convert a racist house into a race-specific yet nonracist home."[6] In articulating what she refers to as her "house/home antagonism" and her desire to move outside of clichéd metaphors of house and home, she adds that:

> what seems to lie about in discourses on race concerns legitimacy, authenticity, community, belonging. In no small way, these discourses are about home: an intellectual home; a spiritual home; family and community as home; forced and displaced labor in the destruction of home; dislocation of and alienation with the ancestral home; creative responses to exile, the devastations, pleasures, and imperatives of homelessness as it is manifested in discussions on feminism, globalism, the diaspora, migrations, hybridity, contingency, interventions, assimilations, exclusions. The estranged body, the legislated body, the violated, rejected, deprived body—the body as consummate home. In virtually all of these formations, whatever the terrain, race magnifies the matter that matters.[7]

At the time that she gave this lecture, she was working on the novel *Paradise*, which she describes as a project to interrogate "whether or not race-specific, race-free language is both possible and meaningful in narration . . . where race both matters and is rendered impotent; a place 'already made for me, both snug and wide open.'"[8] The phrase *snug and wide open* is not only a conceptualization of place characterized through binary polar opposites as experiential descriptions of place—snug on one hand, wide open on the other—but also the articulation of a desire for spaces of being and belonging in the interstices between the two extremes.

After opening *Paradise* with the words "They shoot the white girl first," Morrison goes on to interrogate how the inhabitants of Ruby seek to make a new home where race does not matter yet fail to notice that they had internalized the racism and the sexism that accompanied patriarchy and thereby undermined the safety of the home they attempted to create for themselves.[9] Morrison takes the reader on a journey to discover how the safety the patriarchs craved for themselves, first in Haven and then in Ruby, but were not willing to extend to the women at the convent is an example of "how matters of race and matters of home" are interconnected priorities in her work.[10] Thus, *Paradise* is an example of both how Morrison spatializes the subjectivities of the women who find safety from being regarded as "prey" only at the Convent in the community of women they create among themselves and her geopoetic strategy of interrogating the meanings of home from multiple perspectives. In Morrison's intersectional rendering of home, she exposes what Caren Kaplan refers to as "sites of racism, sexism, and other damaging social practices" from which her characters must extricate themselves, despite them being the very spaces they regarded as home.[11] The community the women create inside the Convent is one characterized by their efforts to make it a third space that is both "snug and wide open," where the telling of their stories to one another creates a new narrative architecture for the subjectivity of each woman in the shared space they regarded as a sanctuary, a safe haven, and a home. Indeed, it was such a space until the men who considered them a threat murdered them. In a sense, Morrison continues the racial experiment she began in *Paradise* in her next novel, *Love*, which she situates in what is ostensibly a Black space of an African American hotel and resort community but nevertheless unravels under the weight of racial politics, gender politics, memories of family trauma, and multiple unresolved conflicts. These conflicts mitigate the efforts of Black subjects to experience the safety and belonging associated with home at a space they attempt to create away from home, as Beavers and Schreiber point out in their respective discussions of the novel.[12]

Morrison's geopoetics of interrogating home show up in her fiction and nonfiction in three ways. Her interrogations of home are most obvious in her representations of domestic space at the intersection of race, gender, and class. They are also evident in her interrogations of the nation as the space of home, represented by historical and current vestiges of the racial imaginary. And her interrogations of home show up in her representations of global notions of home, where divisions of humanity designed and utilized to police, displace, and relocate those deemed to be "other" mitigate their ability to locate "social space that is psychically and physically safe."[13] What she describes as the "anxiety of belonging" colors these representations and shows up clearly in *A Mercy*, for example, where the household of enslaved and indentured Africans, poor whites, and indigenous peoples is transformed from a farm into a racialized house after Vaark decides to enter the slave trade to enhance his social status by building a bigger house. Morrison structures the narrative to enable the reader to witness this transformation and the vicariousness of the colonialist home space with its racialized hierarchies after the death of the architect who built it. Her geopoetics meticulously illustrate through the interior thoughts and memories of each member of the Vaark household how a racialized logic unravels the "imagined community" they presumed they had created, to use Benedict Anderson's term, and exposes the sense of agency the enslaved women exercise by retreating to the third space of their hard-earned interiority to create new terms of belonging.[14]

In *Home*, her penultimate novel, written fifteen years after she first articulated her preoccupation with notions of home, Morrison explicitly engages in discursive mediations between how race does and does not matter. Based on his memories of home, Frank Money has no desire to return to the South and its politics of race. In the narrative device of the interstices between the chapters, Morrison interrupts to inform the reader why Frank's return is less than desirable—because of both what he remembers and what he experiences with his return to the United States after war. In other words, from a racialized reading of home as nation and home as the South, he views both as scenes of subjection where his subjectivity is constantly in jeopardy. His thoughts are an example of what Morrison describes as an awareness that "W.E.B. Du Bois's observation about double-consciousness is a strategy" that he must rely on to navigate his homeland.[15] The double-consciousness, however, is about both a racialized reading of the space between knowing how to perceive his surroundings and knowing how he is perceived by others and disinvesting in his strictly masculinist mode of reading to incorporate women's ways of knowing and doing into his reading of the spaces he entered on his return to Lotus.

Thus, Morrison integrates a gendered interrogation of home in a novel that is ostensibly written from a Black male perspective. Frank's desire to go to war is not solely based on a desire to leave the racial politics of the South but also on a desire to engage in a kind of rite of masculinity we associate with the bildungsroman. As Massey suggests:

> How frequently the characterization of place as home comes from those who have left, and it would be fascinating to explore how often this characterization is framed around those who—perforce—stayed behind; and how often the former was male, setting out to discover and change the world, and the latter female . . . personifying a place which did not change.[16]

By the time readers complete the novel, they have a perspective on both—the male who left home and the female who never left. Reading the novel through Morrison's geopoetics of narrative rememory and interrogations of home engages the reader in rethinking and reimagining subjectivity in the spaces between the binaries of male and female, global and local, North and South, Black and white, past and present, public and private. The task for the reader is to discern how the changes Frank experiences in returning home to Lotus from Korea are connected to the experiences of his sister, Cee, whose trauma derives from the fact that racism against Black people and upon Black women's bodies has not changed in the home where they were born and raised. Ultimately, the goal for Morrison is not only to discern the precise nature of the trauma her characters experience but also to illustrate how Black subjectivity is constructed at scenes of subjection against Black bodies located at the intersection of power and violence that have exiled Black people from the spaces they identified as home.

One example of how house and home are interrogated from a gendered perspective in *Home* is in the characterization of Lily, the woman with whom Frank has an affair when he returns to the States. Desiring to purchase a "house of her own" (72), she discovers a property that was a bit of a distance from the cleaners where she worked but close to the kind of neighborhood where she wanted to live. In an oblique reference to the racialized politics of respectability that inspire her to be "neatly dressed" and to have perfect "straightened hair," she is unprepared for the rental agent to say the home is unavailable because of "restrictions" (73). The restricted codes that the agent shares with Lily read as follows:

> No part of said property hereby conveyed shall ever be used or occupied by any Hebrew or by any person of the Ethiopian, Malay or Asiatic race excepting only employees in domestic service. (73)

As Ta-Nehisi Coates documents so well in his famous 2014 article "The Case for Reparations," the 1930–1960s were a time when "Black people across the country were largely cut out of the legitimate home mortgage market" and confined to less than desirable places and spaces for living.[17] The reference to the reality of housing discrimination in the novel reiterates Morrison's geopoetic intentions to frame Black desire both inside and outside the constraints of white supremacy as it manifested itself in the housing industry.[18] The passage from the rental codes illustrates her ongoing interest in representing how Black subjects read official language, deconstruct it for what it does and does not say, and govern their responses based on their reading. Her interrogation of home in the novel, therefore, includes the vagaries of homeownership during the 1950s in ways that represent the lived lives of those back at home while others were away at war. The rejection did not end Lily's desire for the house she wanted to buy. Instead, "into that restlessness stepped a tall man with a bundle of army-issue clothes for 'same-day' service" (74). Although Lily and Frank quickly settled into "becoming a couple" (75), over time, her yearning for a home and his haunting from war made it inevitable that their relationship would not be the third space of belonging that each was seeking.

As suggested earlier, the novel concludes with a new understanding of home based on multiple interrogations of it from Frank's memories and experiences in real time. Coming to terms with home as a sense of belonging and community rather than the rugged, masculinist, individualistic notion of it that the racism of the South and the violence of war had taught him, Frank begins to integrate past and present with a "feeling of safety and goodwill" (118) and wonderment. In fact, after he witnesses the community of women who help to heal his sister, he realizes that "he could not believe how much he had once hated this place" (132). Morrison uses her interrogations of home to represent not only how his return was critical to his sister's healing but also how his own healing was connected to her reading of home and her understanding of home in the context of community.

In Morrison's last novel, *God Help the Child*, published in 2015, she continues her interrogation of home through the perspective of childhood—a perspective, ironically, that shows up in most of her novels in one way or another. By the time many readers get to *God Help the Child*, they discover that she has come full circle with her literary goal of mapping "a critical geography . . . to open . . . space for discovery, intellectual adventure, and close exploration."[19] Though she expressed this goal in a lecture on "whiteness and the literary imagination" in 1990, she was already exploring the contours of it in "Recitatif," her one and only short story, published in 1983, about the effects of the racial imaginary on the Black female child.[20] And, as early as *The Bluest Eye* (1970), Morrison foregrounds the elementary school primer through which children are literally first introduced to the skill of reading, the ways in which her protagonist reads her culture, and how the reader reads the narrative of both.

Morrison carries these complexities of identity, belonging, and reading into *God Help the Child* by interrogating how a child internalizes the racialized thinking and colorism that have infected her mother and others in her family. The novel also interrogates how that child's efforts to resist such readings of her identity create a complex third space for being and belonging. Using Kirby's approach to subjectivity by drawing on "psychic, discursive, and social" dimensions of space as a multidimensional concept, this chapter argues that Morrison's geopoetics seek to illuminate the complexity of Black subjectivity beyond the sole focus on the Black body.[21] In other words, to regard Black subjects primarily as Black bodies only, especially when framed solely by the racial imaginary left in the wake of enslavement, is to overlook and marginalize the existential dimensions of Black being that concern her. In text after text, Morrison takes on these very existential dimensions of her characters by representing their interior lives, their desires to belong, and their efforts to connect with others in meaningful ways despite the traumas of their lives. Her writing reflects an abiding interest in the implications of racism on the Black girl child. Her representations of Black female childhood are designed to foreground those consequences for children as readers of themselves and of the adults in their lives who are responsible for their care. The geopoetics of place, race, and belonging from the early part of her career to the latter reveal that Morrison was always seeking to push readers back to how they read a text, why they read it that way, and what the consequences of their reading are for themselves and others.

In *God Help the Child*, we have another example of the contested emotional landscape at the intersection of the mother-daughter relationship. The novel squarely fixates on the racial imaginary—namely colorism—and how it manifests itself in home spaces in the Black community and, more specifically, in the psyche and interior life of a mother, Sweetness, and her very dark-skinned daughter, Lula Ann, who renames herself Bride. The narrative economy of the novel is frightfully deceiving. Though it is a relatively short novel, Morrison illustrates the deleterious ways in which the racial imaginary infiltrates and shapes the consciousness of Sweetness, Bride, and Bride's lover, Booker, among others. The novel is thus another example of Morrison's geopoetics of race, place, and belonging that provide more insight into her project of interrogating what she calls the "discourses of race."[22] In developing the novel from the consequences of colorism, or what can also be described as internalized racism, on both the victimizer (Sweetness) and the victim (her daughter, Bride), Morrison offers her readers an opportunity to return to an old trope in a new way. That is, though we may recall how the mother-daughter relationship between Pecola Breedlove and her mother precipitated Pecola's eventual demise, in this last novel, Morrison offers a very different, more nuanced conclusion for her protagonist. Bride navigates the pain and trauma of her mother's rejection and the vagaries of the racial imaginary and its effect on her psyche to the best of her ability and offers the reader an altogether new way of imagining the "house that race built."[23] Through her geopoetics, Morrison shifts the reader's attention beyond the particularities of the mother-daughter relationship to how the vagaries of the racial imaginary have affected relationships outside of the domestic space of the family home, in the domestic space of the nation as home.

On one level, *God Help the Child* is a novel about a very dark-skinned child whose skin color is represented as the basis for her mother's disdain, her father's abandonment, and her community's ridicule of her "blue-black" (5) skin. On another level, the novel tells the story of how this same child transforms the negative obsession with her color into a fetishization of her beauty and success in the cosmetic industry as an adult. Unlike Pecola in *The Bluest Eye*, who desires to look like the racial other, Bride takes pride in her physical beauty and participates in its commodification, aware of the sex appeal it garners. On yet another level, however, the novel is about rejection and the loss of a sense of belonging that she experiences when her lover, Booker, rejects her. That rejection catapults her into a state of emotional disarray and into a journey to understand how his rejection was based on her not being, to quote him, "the woman [he] thought she was" (32). And finally, the novel is about multiple forms of physical, emotional, and spiritual assault on children that force them to navigate physical and interior spaces in ways that reflect on the adults and the culture that gave birth to them. In many respects, the novel is an indictment, a form of prophetic lament, and an interrogation by way of discursive mediation into how the imagination creates spaces of belonging despite the forces that mitigate such belonging. Embedding all these levels of physical and spiritual rejection into a love story is how Morrison redeems the Black racial imaginary as a narrative of healing and belonging. Bride converts the rejection of her mother into a narrative of the reclamation of the self—what hooks calls a new "way of inhabiting space, a particular location, a way of looking and becoming."[24] But the narrative journey to healing is complex and fraught with cultural, political, and spiritual realities that Morrison maps for the reader through her geopoetics of narrative rememory and interrogations of home.

The novel begins with a chapter titled "Sweetness," the so-called "safer" name that the mother prefers "instead of 'Mother' or 'Mama,'" maternal designations she chose because, she reasoned, "being that black and having what . . . are too thick lips . . . would confuse people" (6). "Sweetness" is also the title of a later chapter in Part I, and the last chapter of the book in Part IV goes by that name as well. As it so happens, the three chapters that now appear in the novel were originally published as a short story in *The New Yorker* with no mention that the story was actually an excerpt from the forthcoming novel.[25] While excerpting the "Sweetness" sections from the context of the novel foregrounds the conflicted, racialized thinking of a mother infected with the colorism of internalized racism, it is not the most important point for Morrison. Instead, by incorporating the mother's perspective into the larger context of the novel through the first-person narrative of the daughter, Morrison continues her literary project of interrogating the impact of racism, both internalized and otherwise, on a Black female child, the most vulnerable member of the family and community. In other words, beyond the memories of the mother, we get the effects on the daughter and how her memories shape her sense of subjectivity both in and outside the confines of home. As Wilkerson explains in *Caste: The Origins of Our Discontents*, racialized anxieties along the color line *within* the African-American community stem from the desire to be "closer . . . to the dominant caste in skin color and in hair and facial features."²⁶ The novel interrogates, therefore, what happens when these racialized anxieties are recalcitrant and resistant to change inside the space of home.

The reader needs the narrative of Lula Ann—that is, of Bride—to fully appreciate the implications of the racial imaginary for this mother-daughter relationship, the daughter's relationship with herself, and Bride's relationship with her lover. Viewing Sweetness as the "site of memory," to use Morrison's expression, this time to describe the archive that is the site of the psychic trauma that Bride endures, is the best way to read the liminal space that Bride occupies because of a mother (and father) who do not know how to love her with her very dark skin.²⁷ As Morrison says in her essay "Peril":

> Certain kinds of trauma visited on peoples are so deep, so cruel, that unlike money, unlike vengeance, even unlike justice, or rights, or the goodwill of others, only writers can translate such trauma and turn sorrow into meaning, sharpening the moral imagination.²⁸

In many respects, Morrison represents the mother-child relationship as the site of memory to which each woman must return. As suggested in Hartman's reference to the archive in *Lose Your Mother*, Morrison represents home as an archive of relationships that must be remembered and revisited because it "dictates what can be said about the past and the kind of stories that can be told."²⁹ The epigraph to the novel, taken from the Bible—"Suffer the little children to come unto me, and forbid them not" (Luke 18:16)—invokes another third space, the protected sacred space within the spiritual self, as the ultimate witness to the tale of woe that is about to be told. The epigraph also foreshadows a kind of *metanoia*, the Greek word for a sorrowful change of heart that anticipates the kind of afterthought articulated in the implied regret of the opening words of the novel: "It's not my fault" (3). Like the words "Quiet as it's kept" in *The Bluest Eye*, which foreshadow an unspeakable thing that has not been kept quiet or secret after all, the opening words to *God Help the Child* prepare the reader to learn exactly how the speaker's disavowal is not to be trusted, accepted, or believed.

Indeed, beginning the novel with this disclaimer suggests, like the line from Hamlet, that "The lady doth protest too much."³⁰ As a narrative strategy, beginning with these words sets the reader up to discover the nature of the matter for which the mother is denying culpability. At the same time, however, the words entice the reader to discover just how she might indeed be at fault. Many people of color—women of color, in particular—immediately recognize on the first page of the novel that the sin of colorism is at the center of the very crime of which she is claiming to be innocent:

> It's not my fault. So you can't blame me. I didn't do it and have no idea how it happened. It didn't take more than an hour after they pulled her out from between my legs to realize something was wrong. Really wrong. She was so black she scared me. Midnight black, Sudanese black. I'm light-skinned with good hair, what we call high yellow and so is Lula Ann's father. Ain't nobody in my family anywhere near that color. Tar is the closest I can think of yet her hair don't go with the skin. (3)

One way of understanding colorism requires that we go to the very time and space where the novel begins, at the moment of birth, where the innocence of a child is sullied by the way the adults—in this case her mother and father—read color on the skin of her body and attach meaning to it. It is easy to go directly and quickly to the colorism of this passage itself, but going first to the birth canal, to the site of birth at "the space between the legs," to quote Philip, is to return to the site that has been exploited historically by regimes of power that the Black woman did not control—enslavement and sexism, to name two—and to read that same site through a geopoetics lens.[31] In other words, the reader might also pause to consider how the mother who has just given birth is now complicit, as the thoughts of her interior life reveal, in devaluing the Black body of her own baby girl, Lula Ann. By the time we get to *God Help the Child*, we have moved far beyond the geopoetics of *Beloved*, a text set in the nineteenth-century historical moment, to a contemporary, late twentieth-, early twenty-first-century narrative that invites the reader to consider the psychic remnants of internalized racism at the site of childhood. By structuring the novel through a series of call-and-response first-person narratives, Morrison enables the reader to decipher for themselves who or what is at fault and, more importantly, to discover how colorism and the racism that gave birth to it undermine Black subjectivity. It can be argued that although Sweetness opens and closes the novel with her memories, Morrison is attempting to capture the imagination of the reader through Bride's account of how she constructs a counternarrative of her subjectivity to resist the trauma that is nearly the source of her undoing, despite her mother's disclaimers.

Yet, before we get to Bride's response to her mother's rejection, Morrison historicizes the rejection that Sweetness engages in by disclosing how colorism had already infected the family psyche. We learn of a grandmother who was able to pass, like "almost all mulatto types and quadroons did . . . back in the day" (3), and of Sweetness's own mother, Lula Mae, who "could have passed easy, but chose not to" and admitted "the price she paid for that decision" (3–4). The price came in the form of how Jim Crow segregation operated and from the cost it exacted from Black subjectivity. For example, when Lula Mae and her husband-to-be went to the courthouse to marry, "there were two Bibles and they had to put their hands on the one reserved for Negroes. The other one was for white people's hands. The Bible! Can you beat it?" (4). When Sweetness considers the irony of her parents not being able to touch the "white" Bible, even though those same white people ate food her mother cooked and allowed her mother to touch their bodies by bathing them, she shifts from reflecting on the indignity of this behavior to noting how Black people managed to "hold on to a little dignity" (4) by creating spaces to reaffirm their humanity:

> Some of you probably think it's a bad thing to group ourselves according to skin color—the lighter, the better—in social clubs, neighborhoods, churches, sororities, even colored schools. But how else could we hold on to a little dignity? How else to avoid being spit on . . . all the name-calling . . . and much, much more. (4)

With this representation of racial memory, Morrison provides an uneasy rationale for the resentments Sweetness harbors toward her newborn child. These thoughts historicize her attitudes by offering reflections on how Black people who could pass navigated public and private spaces. In fact, it could be argued that the resentment toward her baby is because of the indignities she experienced in public spaces in the presence of the racial other:

> I hate to say it, but from the beginning in the maternity ward the baby, Lula Ann embarrassed me. Her birth skin was pale like all babies', even African ones, but it changed fast. I thought I was going crazy when she turned blue-black right before my eyes. . . . I wished she hadn't been born with that terrible color. I even though of giving her away to an orphanage someplace. (5)

Even the intimate act of nursing her newborn child is compromised by the racial imaginary, because rather than seeing the act of breastfeeding as a moment of mother-baby bonding, she is resentful, as indicated by her thoughts that "nursing her was like having a pickaninny sucking my teat. I went to bottle-feeding soon as I got home" (5).

The rationalizations continue when Sweetness blames her baby's skin color on her husband's rejection, first of the baby and then ultimately of their marriage. His first reaction to his newborn daughter—"Goddam! What the hell is this?"—was a preamble to what "broke [their] marriage into pieces" (5). Sweetness then shares that the end of her marriage precipitates her need to move to more affordable housing. Remembering his abandonment of her and her baby, she explains:

> That's when it got worse, so bad he just up and left and I had to look for another, cheaper place to live. I knew enough not to take her with me when I applied to landlords so I left her with a teenage cousin to babysit.... It was hard enough just being a colored woman—even a high-yellow one—trying to rent in a decent part of the city. Back in the nineties when Lula Ann was born, the law was against discriminating in who you could rent to, but not many landlords paid attention to it. They made up reasons to keep you out. (6)

Threaded throughout this narrative rooted in colorism is the other dimension of the racial imaginary—the blatant forms of racism that Black people were forced to contend with and that shaped the contours of their lives in public and private spaces on a daily basis. Even as Sweetness deals with the angst of her attitudes toward her daughter, she also has to deal with the realities of racism and discrimination in the housing industry. Her decision to leave Bride behind with a babysitter to maximize her chances of finding a desirable place to live is reminiscent of poet Toi Derricotte's account in her memoir, *The Black Notebooks*, about house hunting in an exclusive upscale neighborhood as a light-skinned Black woman who could pass by leaving her husband at home.[32] Derricotte's retrospective look at her decision to deploy her skin color as a commodity that she could leverage with a racist real estate industry is a narrative of guilt and shame on one level, but on a deeper level, it is an interrogation of the damage done to the interior spaces of the self. In her words, she returns to the archive of her interior life to break "the silence that exists about internalized racism."[33] It could be argued that Morrison is attempting, in this novel, to break those same complicated silences, or what she calls "unspeakable things unspoken," about the interior spaces of Black subjectivity, as she simultaneously interrogates the multigenerational dimension of the racial imaginary and the domestic space of home.[34] The novel opens with an image of a mother who has abdicated herself from any culpability. Instead, she believes that her "blue-black" daughter's "color is a cross she will always carry" (7).

The immediate consequences of carrying the cross of skin color is articulated in the first lines of the next chapter, narrated in Bride's thoughts: "I'm scared. Something bad is happening to me. I feel like I'm melting away" (8). Bride then recalls the words that ended her love affair—"You not the woman I want"—and her angry retort, "Neither am I" (8), providing an example of Morrison's geopoetics of narrative rememory at once. Her protagonist's memory of feeling scared takes place at the end of her affair as an adult, but her response is a reflection not only on the moment but on her past. Morrison allows her to think "I don't know why I said that" (8), but as readers, we can already read into her retort a presupposition that her childhood is somehow implicated. The remainder of the novel fills in the details of the narrative in typical circuitous fashion, just as the mind remembers by returning "to a site to see what remains were left behind and to reconstruct the world that these remains imply. . . . Therefore, the crucial distinction for me is not the difference between fact and fiction, but the distinction between fact and truth. . . . Recollection . . . moves from the image to the text."[35] Bride's recollection provides readers with pieces of her own narrative that explain why the breakup is not the issue, nor is her success as a cosmetics mogul in the beauty industry. As owner of Sylvia Inc., her own company, and her own cosmetic line, "YOU GIRL: Cosmetics for Your Personal Millennium . . . for girls and women of all complexions from ebony to lemonade to milk" (10), she has located herself in public spaces where she capitalizes on her owning everything about her company—"the idea, the brand, the campaign" (10). What is significant is what precipitated her lover's determination that she was different than he thought. When he learns she is planning to take a gift to the newly released parolee she once falsely accused of child molestation, he decides to end their relationship and leaves. What the reader learns from that point on in the narrative is the backstory that illustrates a truth of Morrison's thinking as an artist:

> We are the subjects of our own narrative, witnesses to and participants in our own experience, and in no way coincidentally, in the experience of those with whom we have come in contact. We are not, in fact, "Other." We are choices.[36]

The reader learns of the choices Bride makes as a child to earn the affection and approval of her mother and a sense of belonging. Those choices take up more space in her interior life than she could have anticipated or understood when she made them as an eight-year-old child. But as Morrison explains in *The Origin of Others*, she is particularly interested in asking, "What is the nature of Othering's comfort, its allure, its power (social, psychological, or economical)? Is it the thrill of belonging—which implies being part of something bigger than one's solo self, and therefore stronger?"[37]

The consequences of her adult choice, however—to visit Sofia Huxley at the Decagon Women's Correctional Center on the day of her release—catapult her into a downward spiral in the space between "the harm of racial self-loathing," as Morrison names it, and a confrontation with a life-altering childhood decision that emerged from longing to be loved and accepted.[38] With an intention of presenting Sofia Huxley with a promotional gift box of her YOU GIRL cosmetics, "five thousand dollars in cash . . . and . . . a three-thousand-dollar Continental Airlines gift certificate" (12), Bride arrogantly hopes to assuage her own guilt by attempting to "comfort her . . . help forget and take the edge off bad luck, hopelessness and boredom" (12). Morrison's geopoetics here takes liberty with what the reader does not yet know about how Sofia got imprisoned or what Bride's role was in her imprisonment. In her prideful arrogance about her own guilt, Bride has no comprehension of the prison for "evil women" (13) or the politics of state financing that provides a workforce for "adding wing after wing to house the increasing flood of violent, sinful women committing bloody female crimes. Lucky for the state, crime does pay" (13). The reader learns that Bride, in her ignorance, has imagined what the space of containment is like but has no idea, only childhood notions. The correctional center and its residents, like Bride's idea of Sofia, are similar to what Anderson would describe as an "imagined community."[39] Short of any real-life experience with Sofia or the facility from which she is to be released, Bride is left to her own imagination and misreading of both. What she could not anticipate because of her own presuppositions is the utter physical beating she would get at the hands of Sofia.

Building on the ways in which one retreat from the truth leads to another, Morrison introduces Brooklyn, Bride's white best friend, as the one to hear the lie of how a "would-be rapist" (25) is the one who has beaten her. Although Brooklyn doesn't know the details of the truth, she knows her friend is lying and chooses simply to get her home. As if to summarize the novel itself, in the next sequence of narrative from Bride, she thinks, "Memory is the worst thing about healing" (29). Yet, it is through narrative rememory that she must travel to reconcile with the truth of her being outside of the harm her mother's parenting has done. In the next few pages, the reader learns the sequence of events connecting her and Sofia. As an eight-year-old girl on the stand in a courtroom where white adults were on trial for child molestation, she was one of five juvenile accusers. The racial imaginary manifests itself in the way in which "the worker and psychologist who coached" (30) the children embrace the other children but only "smiled" at Bride and in her mother's response. Indeed, her mother's response is pivotal:

> I glanced at Sweetness; she was smiling like I've never seen her smile before—with mouth and eyes. Best of all was Sweetness. As we walked down the courthouse steps she held my hand, my hand. She never did that before and it surprised me as much as it pleased me because I

always knew she didn't like touching me. I could tell. Distaste was all over her face when I was little and she had to bathe me. Rinse me, actually, after a half-hearted rub with a soapy washcloth. I used to pray she would slap my face or spank me just to feel her touch. I made little mistakes deliberately, but she had ways to punish me without touching the skin she hated—bed without supper, lock me in my room—but her screaming at me was the worst. . . . Frightened as I was to appear in court, I did what teacher-psychologists expected of me. Brilliantly, I know, because after the trial Sweetness was kind of motherlike. (31–32)

The word choice of *motherlike* suggests that Bride's subconscious awareness of what it took to get this approximation of mothering and belonging is significant. Morrison engages here in a complex level of what she calls "literary archaeology."[40] On one hand, Bride performs childhood by being "behaved and behaved and behaved" (32) to earn her mother's acknowledgment and maternal affection in public. On the other hand, the fact that Bride's sense of belonging in public spaces comes after years of humiliation and detachment in the private spaces of their home is the narrative Morrison is foregrounding through her geopoetics. The irony of this hard-won sense of belonging, however, is that it is based on a lie that cost a white woman fifteen years of freedom. Based on Morrison's careful but sparse narrative scaffolding of knowledge and information, the reader does not learn the lie until later, however, so with the racial imaginary of the Black-white binary, justice appears to be what brings Sweetness and Bride into a right mother-daughter relationship.

As suggested earlier, this novel is not only about the destructive force of colorism or the "color fetish"; it is also about the destructive force of racism and the haunting it causes in the interior space of the psyche and the soul. Bride is aware that she sold her "elegant blackness to all those childhood ghosts" (57) that haunted her. Moreover, those childhood ghosts are a matter of not just how her mother treated her but also what she observed and held in silence. She shares with Booker the trauma of enduring name-calling and bullying because of her color and of watching the landlord molest a child in the neighborhood, only to have her mother insist on silence even though he called her "a little nigger cunt!" (55). The silence at school was to prevent being "suspended or even expelled" (56), and the silence over Mr. Leigh's child molestation and racist slur was about avoiding eviction. Her mother knew "it would be hard finding a location in another safe, meaning mixed, neighborhood" (54). The theme of the harm done to children by adults continues with the narrative of Booker's childhood, but before we learn about it in any detail, Morrison takes the reader on Bride's intricate journey to find him. She learns when she goes to pick up whatever he has left at the pawn shop that he has moved to a place called Whiskey, California. She pays for the item, which happens to be his trumpet, and then heads for Whiskey in her Jaguar. Stopping at a diner with a Confederate flag on the wall and "that redneck version of digestible food" (81), Bride continues her journey to find Booker to both return his trumpet and force him to come to terms with abandoning her. When she looks in the mirror, she observes that she is no longer the embodiment of beauty by which she knows herself. Instead, she notices she is losing pubic hair, which she refers to as her "hairless pudenda" (80), her clothes are no longer fitting, and she has a "scary memory of altered earlobes" that are adding to the "alterations to her body" (81). In a scene reminiscent of Milkman's trip to the South in *Song of Solomon*, Bride ends up in the middle of nowhere, far from the comforts of home and her privileged life, when she crashes into a tree and totals her car.[41] A husband and wife, Steve and Evelyn, come to her rescue along with their adopted daughter, Raisin, who they name "Rain," because that is where they found her.

Neither this couple nor Rain are terribly significant, in and of themselves, but in Morrison's geopoetics, they represent a space where Bride is made to feel at home by perfect strangers. Moreover, the fact that they "found" Rain continues the theme of children who are abandoned emotionally, spiritually, or physically at the hands of adults. Bride realizes, at one point, however, that these people are different: "Here she was among people living the barest life, putting themselves out for her without hesitation, asking nothing in return . . . the kind of care they offered—free, without judgment or even passing interest in who she was or where she was going" (90). When she learns that Evelyn and Steve are content with this kind of bohemian life, living out in the middle of nowhere, with "no money, no television . . . no washing machine, no fridge, no bathroom, no money!" (91), she says nothing, realizing she knew nothing "about good for its own sake, or love without things" (92). And even in the midst of this education in the wilderness with no place to call home, she discovers after six weeks with them that she has had enough. Still preoccupied with her body and her vanishing good looks and vanishing flesh, "she discovered her chest was flat . . . completely flat, with only the nipples to prove it was not her back" (92). Although she assumes she is "sick" or "dying" (93), she finally realizes that her "shrinking body" (93) and "body changes began not simply after he left, but because he left" (94). The very body that she had commodified and fetishized to protect herself from childhood trauma was now abandoning her because of the man who had abandoned her. The realization makes her more determined to find him.

Morrison's geopoetics of narrative rememory involve telling and withholding, delay and circuitousness, because she is determined to unfold the pieces of her characters' lives in all their complexity—not for the ease of her readers but for her distinction between fact and truth. Facts may govern the outer spaces of her characters' lives, but truth governs the interior spaces of their lives and is sometimes hidden even from the characters themselves until a life-altering moment frees them from whatever trauma has them bound. For Sofia, it was the brutal confrontation with Bride that freed her from the bondage—not of the physical prison but of the one in her mind. It is not until she is abandoned that Rain is found and loved unconditionally by Evelyn and Steve. And it is not until Part III of the novel that we learn Booker's story of house and home, racial terror, and loss depriving him of a sense of belonging. The reader does not learn immediately that the loss of Bride matters to him at all, because Morrison wants the reader to learn what forces have shaped who he is. As an undergraduate student, he observes a child molester on the playground and punches him. Although he returns to class, his mind wanders during the lecture to the man he punched:

> Bald. Normal-looking. Probably an otherwise nice man—they always were. The "nicest man in the world," the neighbors always said. "He wouldn't hurt a fly." Where did that cliché come from? Why not hurt a fly? Did it mean he was too tender to take the life of a disease-carrying insect but could happily ax the life of a child? (111)

We learn that he is unimpressed by such clichés because, as a well-read man, he has already learned to question and unpack what he is told. In his African American Studies classes, he observes that though his professors are brilliant, they "could not answer to his satisfaction any question beginning with 'Why'" (110). Not content as the narrator is in *The Bluest Eye*, who says "since *why* is difficult to handle, one must take refuge in *how*," Booker "suspected that most of the real answers concerning slavery, lynching, forced labor, sharecropping, racism, Reconstruction, Jim Crow, prison labor, migration, civil rights and Black revolution movements were all about money. Money withheld, money stolen, money as power, as war."[42]

Booker's personal narrative is delayed with further information about how he reads the world. While this might seem superfluous narrative material, it extends Morrison's larger interrogation of how race operates on a global scale:

> Where was the lecture on how slavery alone catapulted the whole country from agriculture into the industrial age in two decades? White folks'

hatred, their violence, was the gasoline that kept the profit motors running. So as a graduate student he turned to economics—its history, its theories—to learn how money shaped every single oppression in the world and created the empires, nations, colonies with God and His enemies employed to reap, then veil, the riches. He habitually contrasted the beaten, penniless, half-naked King of the Jews screaming betrayal on a cross with a bejeweled, glamorously dressed pope whispering homilies about the Vatican's vault. *The Cross and the Vault* by Booker Starbern . . . would be the title of his book. (111)

So, the image of him as student is that of a man who thinks about the geopolitical economy in terms of life in the United States and in the world. His critique of the state and the church suggests not only that he is well-read but also that he has lived the realities of racial history and oppression that have convinced him he is right.

Morrison describes Booker as a man "raised in a large, tight family with no television in sight." He viewed mass communication with suspicion that it was "loaded with entertainment but mostly free of insight or knowledge" (112). His home life is described as one where he "had been shaped by talk in the flesh and text on paper. Every Saturday morning first thing before breakfast, his parents held conferences with their children requiring them to answer two questions put to them: 1. What have you learned that is true (and how do you know)? 2. What problem do you have?" (112). These "Saturday morning conferences" (113), as he called them, coupled with "the highlight of the weekend—his mother's huge breakfast feasts" (113), portray him as a man who grew up in a home space where he was loved, educated, and inculcated with a sense of belonging. Born a twin whose brother died in childbirth, he was very close to his brother Adam. When Adam was found dead in a culvert, a victim of racial violence at the hand of a pedophile and child molester, Booker begins to regard himself as an abandoned man, first by his twin and then by his brother who had taken his place. The abandonment turns to anger, however, when he begins to feel his family did far too little to follow up on the murder of his brother. After he goes home to celebrate the completion of his master's degree, his grieving family does not understand his rage. He turns to playing his trumpet and to writing "unpunctuated sentences into musical language" (123), and going to the room he once shared with Adam causes him to pick a fight with his sister. When his father tells him that he must be civil or leave their house, he chooses to leave, as his father does not seem to understand that their failure to act ends Booker's sense of belonging. Wounded by racism and his family's response to it, he moves in and out of employment.

When he meets Bride, he is "dumbstruck by her beauty" and her "blue-black skin" (130). Their relationship is intense, and they appear similar at the time of their meeting, with no family ties. Six months into the affair, which develops into "the bliss of edible sex, free-style music, challenging books, and the company of an easy undemanding Bride, the fairy-tale collapsed into the mud and sand on which its vanity was built. And Booker ran away" (135). Her search for him eventually takes her to Queen, his aunt. When she sees Bride, she says, "You look like something a raccoon found and refused to eat" (144), an assessment that reminds Bride of how far she has come—not just from home but also from the glamorous life she had created for herself. She realizes she is no longer the "exotic," "gorgeous" woman who had built her reputation in the cosmetics industry (144). Instead, she has become, once again, "the ugly, too-black girl in her mother's house" (144). Living out in the middle of nowhere—this time in the California town of Whiskey—Queen is reminiscent of other Morrison elders, like Pilate in *Song of Solomon*, Baby Suggs in *Beloved*, and Consolata in *Paradise*, who represent the author's notion of "rooted" women, whose wisdom is instructive for the homeless, the lost, and those who have been marginalized as if they do not belong. What Bride learns from her intimate talk with Queen is the depth of grief Booker has been carrying, the anger he harbored toward his family, and the love he had written of in his poems about her. When Queen shares his poetry, written without punctuation, Bride learns that the words affirm a subjectivity she had not yet embraced. In the second person, he writes "you do belong finally to the planet you were born on and can now join the out-there world in the deep peace of a cello" (149). Another poem speaks of "a grief so deep it would break not the heart but the mind that knows the oboe's shriek and the way it tears into rags of silence to expose your beauty too dazzling to contain and which turns its melody into the grace of livable space" (150–151). When Queen encourages Bride to go to his quarters, she realizes "she had counted on her looks for so long—how well beauty worked" (151) that she was unsure of herself without it.

Booker's response, however, is not about her looks but about his certainty that he had escaped her and his rage at being wrong. The violent tussle they get into becomes the turning point, and Bride confesses to him that she had lied about the woman in the courtroom just to have the experience of her mother holding her hand and treating her as if she belonged. When Queen convinces Booker that his childhood is haunting him in an unhealthy way as well, we have a Morrisonian elder who, despite her multiple husbands and unsuccessful relationships, becomes the guide who leads them back to one another. They begin planning how they will continue to care for her and find a home that the three of them can share when the fire at her home requires them to care for her, bathe her, and replace her bandages from her burns. After having Queen serve her role in the narrative of the two lovers, Morrison brings Bride full circle to the lines from Booker's poem—she is a person who belonged to the planet and deserved a livable space. Moreover, Booker writes one last poem apologizing to his brother Adam for "enslaving [him] in order to chain [himself] to the illusion of control and the cheap seduction of power. No slaveowner could have done it better" (161). But the care that Booker and Bride provide for Queen as she lay dying is another kind of full circle. They go from being two self-absorbed adults wounded from childhood, racism, and a loss of home and belonging to becoming two caring human beings invested in the well-being of another:

> Neither one spoke during those ablutions and, except for Bride's occasional humming, the quiet served as the balm they both needed. They worked together like a true couple, thinking not of themselves, but of helping somebody else. (167)

Although she appears to recover from her burns, Queen dies, and Bride realizes "their focus was on a third person they both loved" (173). Indeed, in Morrison's geopoetics, Queen becomes the third space needed to step outside of themselves to consider the space of community they could create. When Bride reveals to Booker that she is pregnant, however, and that the baby is his, he responds, "No. . . . It's ours" (174). They "each begin to imagine what the future would be. . . . A child. New life. . . . All goodness. Minus wrath. So they believe" (175).

The fact that Morrison does not end the novel with the reconciliation of Bride and Booker is instructive to the reader. Despite the fact that she appears to give the novel a romantic ending, she allows Sweetness to have the final word. Although she is in an assisted-living facility and suffers from a bone disease that she came down with at the young age of sixty-three, she is receiving good care and is apparently grateful to receive the news that Lula Ann is pregnant. She acknowledges that she does not pay the name Bride any attention, and she begins to wonder if the father is "as black as she is. If so, she needn't worry like I did. Things have changed a mite from when I was young. Blue blacks are all over TV, in fashion magazines, commercials, even starring in movies" (176). Convinced because there is no return address that Bride still hates her, Sweetness goes into her self-consoling rationales about skin color, though she thinks to herself, "I forgot about her color" (177). She acknowledges, however, that underneath all her disclaimers "is regret" (177). The tone of the ending, however, undermines the sincerity of the regret in the mind of the reader. She ends on a note of certainty when she thinks, "You are about to find out what it takes, how the world is, how it works and how it changes when you are a parent. Good luck and God help the child" (178). What her sarcastic tone and attitude at the end of the novel reveal is that Sweetness does not know that Bride has recovered from the colorism and commodification of her body that once defined her sense of value and selfhood. Though she is momentarily relieved that her body had returned to its earlier beauty, what the novel reveals is the journey to healing of the interior spaces of the self, where she and Booker begin to reimagine their lives through the lens of belonging and defining life and home on their own terms instead of the other way around.

By imagining a way to connect history with what was possible in spite of that history in her late fiction, Morrison reconsiders notions of home spaces that have always been implicated but never fully articulated in her earlier fiction. It is no surprise, therefore, that in the collection of nonfiction she published before her death, the first section of twenty essays would be curated under the heading "The Foreigner's Home."[43] By so naming the first set of essays, she signals her desire to focus on another set of "unspeakable things unspoken"— that is, on the binary of home and not home. That binary appeared in her nonfiction as early as the 1993 Nobel Prize lecture, where the young interlocutors ask the old woman at the center of the narrative to

> tell us what it is to be a woman so that we may know what it is to be a man. What moves at the margin. What it is to have no home in this place. To be set adrift from the one you knew. What it is to live at the edge of towns that cannot bear your company.[44]

As early as this lecture, she was interested in the implications of being adrift, of being displaced, of finding oneself in a liminal space between home and not home. In the essay "Home," from the Princeton lecture at the "Race Matters" conference in 1994, Morrison explicitly shares her misgivings about representing home when she is so acutely aware that the word is fraught with the "anxiety of belonging [that] is entombed within the central metaphors in the discourse on globalism, transnationalism, nationalism," and so on.[45] Pointing out how the "world-as-home . . . [is] already described in the raced house as waste," Morrison signals her desire to join other scholars in taking on what had not yet been fully interrogated in her own work or that of others at that point. This first section of *The Source of Self-Regard*, therefore, represents a desire to reflect on the binaries of home and not home, race mattering and not mattering beyond the boundaries of the nation. The title essay, "The Foreigner's Home," is a lecture she delivered in Canada in 2002; in it, she catalogues the various forms of atrocities that homelessness can create:

> The flight of war refugees, the relocation and transplantation of the management and diplomatic class to globalization's outposts . . . [and] . . . the spectacle of mass movement draws attention inevitably to the borders, the porous place, the vulnerable points where one's concept of home is seen as being menaced by foreigners.[46]

By shifting to insights beyond American borders, Morrison begins to interrogate the language and politics of othering on a global scale and moves toward what Bhabha refers to as "spaces of intervention in the here and now" and "contingent 'in-between' space that innovates and interrupts the performance of the present."[47] In shifting from the geopoetics of her fiction to the geopolitics of the transnational reality, Morrison relocates her reader to a new space of how to read and reimagine the ways in which notions of home and community have been permanently transformed into a "third space."[48]

It could be argued that Morrison literally enters this third space through the exhibit at the Louvre, where she served as guest curator in 2006. Shifting her attention from "how writers invented and dealt with their notion of who belonged and who did not" for a course she was about to teach at Princeton to instead focus on Theodore Gericault's *The Raft of the Medusa* (1819), one of the most iconic paintings in the Louvre collection, she literally and artistically enters a new aesthetic space that is beyond her own customary art form of words on the page. The installation that she curates includes a collage of programs (i.e., lectures, films, concerts, dance, spoken word poetry) that enable her "to look at wordless forms like painting and choreography as journeying somewhere that I'd never thought of."[49] Morrison included readings from Michael Onadaatje, Edwidge Danticat, and Assia Djebar in the nearly month-long exhibit because, as she says, they are authors who "are writing in places where they were not born or writing about being demonized in their own home."[50] It is likely that a similar motive inspired her to include spoken-word artists from around Paris, many of whom had never been inside the Louvre prior to her invitation to include them. According to one American newspaper account of the opening, many of the "slam poets" were from the "troubled Paris suburbs," where their anger "about discrimination and alienation among French teenagers of immigrant origin, many of them of Muslim North African and African descent," was precisely part of the story of "national identity, exile and belonging" that was of interest to Morrison.[51] The Louvre becomes a space, therefore, where Morrison's geopoetics connects three narratives at once—that of her own oeuvre as an African American writer, that of Gericault's painting and its controversial foregrounding of France's racial politics of the seventeenth century, and that of the Black French population of young immigrants whose contemporary lives were connected to her interrogation of home.

In a real sense, the exhibit was a destabilizing agent of change and resistance to the forces of exclusion and racialized displacement that inspired the spoken-word artists. Though she acknowledged that she had to have translators to understand their lyrics when she went to visit them in their suburban homes, she said it was important to hear them because their work represents a phenomenon in which "what you think you know about U.S. culture . . . much of it, its roots are from African-Americans. We made modernity in that country."[52] She argues that she was convinced that the young people in Paris would likewise use the disadvantages and the energy that comes from their lives to create "a new thing that has never been seen before."[53] In this regard, Morrison was a catalyst for their art to receive an audience beyond the spaces in which it was created and for their spoken-word poetry to simultaneously disrupt the very spaces that were part of the destabilization of their lives and join that larger network of artists of color who have always used their art to resist and reimagine a better world in the interstices where they found themselves.

Though she foregrounds various artistic forms with this exhibit, she connects them all thematically and geopoetically through the apostrophe or the grammar of identity in the title—"The Foreigner's Home." On one hand, there is the simple matter of possession—the space that the foreigner identifies as home or the home of the foreigner. On the other hand, the apostrophe can signal the omission of the letter *i* in the word *is* for the "foreigner is home," with the verb representing a state of being and defiance in spite of circumstances to the contrary. But then there is a third reading of the apostrophe in the name of the exhibit; it can represent the marking of plurality—several foreigners, even though customarily, the apostrophe would follow the *s* for more than one. Regardless of how the reader reads the apostrophe, there is a space for interpretation that is generative and leads to the larger question Morrison is interrogating: Who is the foreigner anyway? Or, to put it another way, how do we determine who is home and who is not at home and therefore the foreigner? Well aware of the transnational history of enslavement, Morrison is intentionally and geopoetically implicating all of these interpretations of this grammar and punctuation of identity. All the meanings are at play because all the histories are implicated in one another if we consider how notions of home have been complicated by systems of oppression, subjugation, violence, and displacement. The very notion of the African diaspora comes into play in the prestigious, privileged space of the Louvre, and Morrison stands at the intersection of race, gender, and class, directing our readings of it all but dramatically standing back, almost as an absent presence, to see what she and the spectators/readers of the exhibit will discover about the subject and object of the art created.

Although "The Foreigner's Home" exhibit took place in France in 2006, six years before she published *Home*, by the time she returned to her fiction, she had been on so-called foreign soil, much like Frank Money, and she was ready to continue her interrogation of the conflicted notions of home on American soil. Unlike Baldwin, who writes in "The Discovery of What It Means to Be an American" that white Americans were "no more at home in Europe than [he] was," Morrison had already begun interrogating the paradoxes of American identity in one novel after another and was able, in her later fiction and in the exhibit at the Louvre, to reimagine ways of reading home spaces in new places to expose the forms of resistance and resilience in spite of the traumatic destabilizing forces of war and racial oppression.[54] Ultimately, her geopoetics enable her to see, like Baldwin, that the "interior life is a real life" and "intangible dreams have a tangible effect on the world."[55] Morrison's geopoetics—especially through narrative interrogations of home—reveal to the reader that the local and the global are interconnected in ways that enable us to reimagine our subjectivities as inclusive of our embodiment of them and in ways that are beyond the borders designed to contain us or our own presuppositions of how we are and are not connected to one another.

Conclusion

Toni Morrison's Spaces for Readers

The Geopoetics of the Dancing Mind

> The dream is no outward thing... It lives in the inward parts, it is deep within, where the issues of life and death are ultimately determined.
> —Howard Thurman, *Strange Freedom*[1]

By the time many of her readers get to Toni Morrison's last novel, *God Help the Child* (2015), they discover that she has come full circle with her literary goal of mapping "a critical geography... to open... space for discovery, intellectual adventure, and close exploration."[2] Though she expressed this goal in a lecture on "whiteness and the literary imagination" in 1990, she was already exploring the contours of it in 1983 in "Recitatif," her one and only short story, again about the effects of the racial imaginary on the Black female child.[3] Even in her first novel, *The Bluest Eye* (1970), Morrison foregrounds the elementary school primer through which children are literally first introduced to the skill of reading, the ways in which her protagonist reads her culture, and how the reader interprets the narrative of both. Given her preoccupation with the role of the reader and her self-conscious intentional desire to destabilize the reading process to reimagine issues of place, race, and belonging and their role in shaping subjectivity, any discussion of Morrison's oeuvre would do well to consider how these preoccupations show up in this unique story. By concluding this study of her geopoetics with a reference to this story, I seek to consider how her preoccupation with the reading-writing process remained central to her work, even as she deepened and expanded her interrogations into Black subjectivity through her novel and nonfiction about what is at stake in the reading-writing process for her as an artist and for her readers.[4]

"Recitatif" contains many of the aesthetic, political, and geopoetic hallmarks that prophetically foreshadow the persistent concerns, themes, and motifs of Morrison's fiction and nonfiction and have been the focus of this study.[5] In this short story, Morrison foregrounds the effects of racism on Black female subjectivity and on the domestic space of home as a site of memory where both identity formation and destabilization can occur and the implications for how Black subjects, especially female children, read, mediate, remember, and resist the discourses that surround and implicate them. She strategically and intentionally withholds racial markers in "Recitatif," thereby forcing the reader to engage in discursive mediation—reading themselves in between the spaces of the text even as they read her characters. In fact, it could be argued that by playing with the relationship between the absence and presence of such markers, she forces the reader to engage in a kind of racial metacognition, even as they attend to other features of the narrative and the characters in the story. Morrison discloses that the "modes of interaction," as Kirby refers to them, between the text and the reader that shape the "space of subjectivity" of her readers, just as the characters are developed through their relationship with one another.[6] As the reader works to read the text, the text works on the reader. Thus, by withholding racial markers, Morrison situates readers in such a way that they are left to fall back on their own ways of reading and belonging.[7] By so doing, readers betray and implicate themselves in what Shanna Benjamin refers to as "the racial conundrum" in the story as well as in the same conundrum that is so indicative of the American racial imaginary that Morrison interrogates throughout her literary career.[8] More importantly, however, through the geopoetics of discursive mediation, narrative rememory, emancipatory space-making, and the interrogations of home that structure the story, Morrison invites the reader into the third space that has been the focus of this study—the interior archive that reveals the prism and parameters of subjectivity through the racial imaginary.

From beginning to end, "Recitatif" foregrounds the notion of belonging. How two girls end up in an orphanage and therefore simultaneously belong to their absent mothers and to the state is the first way in which belonging is represented in the story. How the girls begin as strangers, become roommates, become estranged, and then become friends again is a process that invites the reader into an interrogation of what forces mitigate belonging and community in a nation that fixates on race, socioeconomic class status, and other forms of difference to make meaning in society.[9] How these forms of difference, with race being primary, affect the friendship between the two girls and their memory of their time in the orphanage is central to understanding what is at stake in the story. Moreover, how the notion of belonging works in both ways—in the reader's efforts to determine the racial identity of both girls at the orphanage and in Morrison's narrative geopoetics for exposing the reader's need for such a determination—is the real ethical/moral dilemma of the narrative.

Morrison carries these complexities of identity, belonging, and reading into her last novel, *God Help the Child*, by interrogating how a child internalizes the racialized thinking and colorism that have infected her family and her relationship with her mother. The novel also interrogates how that child's efforts to resist such readings of her identity create a complex third space for being and belonging. Like Kirby's approach to subjectivity that draws on "psychic, discursive, and social" dimensions of space as a multidimensional concept, this book has argued that Morrison's geopoetics seek to illuminate the complexity of Black identity beyond the focus on the Black body.[10] In other words, to regard Black subjects primarily as Black bodies only, framed solely by the racial imaginary left in the wake of enslavement, is to overlook and marginalize the ontological dimensions of Black being. In text after text, Morrison takes on these very existential dimensions of her characters by representing their interior lives, their desires to belong, and their efforts to resist marginalization and connect with others in meaningful ways despite the traumas of their lives. This chapter examines how Morrison's writing reflects an abiding interest in the implications of racism on the Black female child and on the adults in their lives who are responsible for their care. The geopoetics of place, race, and belonging from the early part of her career to the latter reveal that Morrison was always seeking to push the reader to interrogate how they read a text, why they read it that way, and what the consequences of their reading are for themselves, others, and the culture in which they reside.

"Recitatif" is the story of two eight-year-old girls—Twyla Benson and Roberta Norton—who first meet one another in the orphanage where they had been placed as roommates. By setting this story in St. Bonaventure, an orphanage in New York City referred to as St. Bonny's, Morrison purposely situates the girls in a liminal space—that is, a place in between their literal homes from which they have been taken and the institutional "home" at the orphanage that the state established for children whose parents have been deemed unfit. When we meet them, they have already been displaced from the space they know as home and relocated to what is ostensibly a temporary home until a permanent place of belonging can be determined. As readers, we do not get the specific details of what necessitated the state to step into their homes and to deem their mothers unfit, but we do learn from the very first sentence of the story that Twyla's "mother danced all night" and that "Roberta's was sick."[11] Thus, their mothers and the state are implicated in their homelessness. As early as the second paragraph of the story, the reader learns Twyla's thoughts about race as well as her mother's:

It was one thing to be taken out of your bed early in the morning—it was something else to be stuck in a strange place with a girl from a whole other race. And Mary, that's my mother, she was right. Every now and then she would stop dancing long enough to tell me something important and one of the things she said was they never washed their hair and they smelled funny.[12]

Thus, when the girls first meet one another, the first sign of their "reading" one another is represented in Twyla's thoughts and in Roberta's query "Is your mother sick too?"[13]

From that auspicious beginning, the narrative develops through a series of encounters—between the two girls themselves, between them and the other girls who are residents at St. Bonny's, and between them and their mothers. Through Twyla's early observations of the place where they find themselves, we learn that "for the moment it didn't matter that [they] looked like salt and pepper . . . that's what the other girls called [them] sometimes," nor did it matter that they "didn't like each other that much at first."[14] Unlike the other girls, who were "real" orphans, Twyla and Roberta were not there because they had "beautiful dead parents in the sky"; instead, they were there because they "were dumped."[15] Early in the story, Morrison manages to do several forms of cultural work at once. She simultaneously foregrounds racial difference while managing to minimize it by withholding the specificity of which girl is Black and which is white. She also foregrounds the diversity among the orphans and provides a kind of global description of how they came to be at St. Bonny's: "They were put-out girls, scared runaways most of them. Poor little girls who fought their uncles off, but looked tough to us, and mean."[16] The reference to the girls as "put-out" girls is reminiscent of the ideas expressed by the narrator in *The Bluest Eye*, Claudia McTeer, who observes:

Outdoors, we knew, was the real terror of life. The threat of being outdoors surfaced frequently in those days. . . . There is a difference between being put out and being put out*doors*. If you are put out, you go somewhere else; if you are outdoors, there is no place to go. The distinction was subtle but final. Outdoors was the end of something, an irrevocable, physical fact, defining and complementing our metaphysical condition. Being a minority in both caste and class, we moved about anyway on the hem of life, struggling to consolidate our weaknesses and hang on, or to creep singly up into the major folds of the garment. (17)

In "Recitatif," Twyla, Roberta, and the other girls know that the identity that binds them beyond race is their socioeconomic class status of simultaneously being outdoors and being put out, of being in a place that is designated as their home even as they recognize they have no home to which they can return. The one space besides the orphanage that binds them is the apple orchard, the open space outdoors where all the girls gather to play and make fun of one another and of Maggie, the kitchen woman. As the readers move through the story, they discover that Morrison deploys this space as a third space that is replete, like the biblical Garden of Eden, with references to innocence and guilt that will both delight and haunt these two protagonists.

By the third page of the short story, Morrison introduces Maggie and her disability as another layer of intersectional difference. She is introduced through Twyla's memory of her as the kitchen woman and is described as old, deaf, and mute, with "legs like parentheses"; she "fell down there [in the orchard] once."[17] The orchard is considered an insignificant space where "nothing really happened," yet Twyla admits that she dreamt about the orchard all the time and remembers it as the place where Maggie fell.[18] With these words, the story unobtrusively introduces the central scene of the respective yet shared memory of living at the orphanage. Morrison develops the narrative by introducing four separate encounters that the girls have over the next twenty years after they leave the orphanage. Each encounter reveals new ways that they have read, misread, or misremembered the incident with Maggie. And, as Benjamin argues, the very scene that appears insignificant creates an interstitial space for analyzing "familiar recollections and repressed emotions" that reveal that Maggie's presence in their shared recollection is not ancillary but central to the story in the way it "punctuates America's grammar of race."[19] While Benjamin argues that Maggie's place in the narrative points to her as a mother figure on whom the two girls project the grief and trauma of their childhoods that precipitated their placement in the orphanage, there is another way to read her place in Morrison's geopoetics. She represents that space between the racial binary where being is not only a function of the body and the physical spaces one inhabits but also a function of one's interior life and how one understands, remembers, and imagines oneself in the neglected spaces of one's subjectivity. What appears merely parenthetical is actually more significant, or, as Morrison says in *Jazz*, "something else you have to figure in before you can figure it out."[20]

In their first encounter after they become adults, which takes place at the Howard Johnson diner in a working-class neighborhood in the New York suburb of Newburgh, where Twyla works, the two women are cordial yet almost dismissive as they appear to size up their class distinctions and ask about their mothers in a perfunctory kind of way. The second encounter, at a grocery store, is when they move beyond niceties and begin "behaving like sisters" and falling into "recollection like veterans."[21] The second meeting is also when it becomes clear that they have two very different recollections of what happened to Maggie. Twyla, the narrator, recalls that Maggie fell and that the other girls, who they referred to as the "gar girls," laughed. Roberta, however, insists that "Maggie didn't fall . . . those girls pushed her down and tore her clothes. In the orchard."[22] Between the second and third encounter, the narrative shifts to the historical context of "racial strife" that is engulfing the nation in the aftermath of school desegregation orders.[23] The third encounter places them among other mothers on opposing sides of a school busing order. At the point where they both think the same thought—"I wonder what made me think you were different"—the reader gets an insight into how Morrison is simultaneously structuring sameness and difference in this story to illustrate the destabilizing effects of the racial imaginary. They carry two different signs at the protest—"MOTHERS HAVE RIGHTS TOO!" and "AND SO DO CHILDREN!"—which devolves from being "dignified" to "name calling and finger gestures."[24] Twyla realizes her protest sign "didn't make sense without Roberta's."[25] Morrison scaffolds the narrative in this story to illustrate this very point—that the racial imaginary, referring to the ways in which the mind structures the meanings of race, has created this space of interconnection, interdependence, and intersubjectivity, despite denials to the contrary. She places the women literally at an intersection that mirrors the intersection of race and education where the nation has remained stuck.

It could be argued that another dimension of this seemingly parenthetical yet critical detail of the narrative is not only whether Maggie fell or was pushed but also whether she was Black or white. Whereas Roberta remembers Maggie as "a poor old black lady," Twyla realizes she "couldn't be certain."[26] Thus, Morrison structures the narrative so that the reader is unable to determine the racial identity of the two protagonists and the protagonists are unable to determine the race of an ostensibly minor character in their own lives. Morrison uses this kind of doubling to further illustrate that what the reader brings to the encounter with a text, whether the text of a short story or the text of an encounter on the street at a protest rally, is critical for how they make meaning of place, race, and belonging. The reality of this doubling of the complication of reading is most apparent in the final encounter between Twyla and Roberta, which takes place on Christmas Eve. When they meet on this occasion, Roberta not only apologizes for insisting that Maggie was Black but also acknowledges that she cannot be sure whether she was Black or not. She also acknowledges that although she knows the "gar girls" are the ones who pushed and kicked Maggie she wanted to do so as well. She admits that "wanting to is doing it."[27] In that admission is a space of not only intimacy and vulnerability but also belonging. In the third space of belonging, outside of their respective family histories, racial backgrounds (which we are never able to determine), and shared memory of being orphaned and abandoned by their mothers, we bear witness to the social space of intimacy. When Roberta raises her hands at the end of the story and cries out, "Oh shit, Twyla. Shit, shit, shit. What the hell happened to Maggie?" the story concludes on an interrogative note of what has been at stake all along. Morrison constructs the story to illustrate how fixating on race has obscured the deeper, more meaningful dimensions of intimacy and belonging that the girls were denied by their mothers, even if they had managed to create it between themselves. With the focus on what happened to Maggie rather than on trying to determine her race, the two women create a third space characterized by intersubjective connection to one another based on a shared memory and empathic concern for someone other than themselves. Their surrender to this shared memory represents a shift in the narrative that illustrates what Benjamin describes as the "intersubjective mental space" characterized by "freedom from any intent to control."[28]

Only when they arrive at this third space do they see both their own humanity and Maggie's. Taking into consideration that the word *recitatif* is a French version of the word *recitative*, which refers to a style of delivery in the space between song and ordinary speech that intermittently advances the narrative inside of opera, Morrison uses two forms of interstices in this short story.[29] On one hand, she names the story with a form of interstices. On the other hand, she places an interstitial occurrence involving Maggie, the old, deaf kitchen woman whose legs resemble parentheses, at the center of their story. Thus, the understood dialogic refrain of the story is really an ethical, existential one of how meaning is constructed, remembered, and imagined beyond the racial imaginary, even as race and gender are constitutive of that meaning. The parenthetical third space of belonging is paradoxically the very space where the women reconnect, even if the mystery that brought them together ultimately remains unsolved. Like the "interstitial narrative housed within the parenthetical space," to use Benjamin's conceptualization, Twyla's narration and Maggie's presence both choreograph and orchestrate the reader's response to the text, even as they ultimately abandon the reader with the question only the reader can answer.[30] As this study has shown, what Morrison's orchestration of the narrative has done is abandon readers to their own protocols of reading. She has attempted to create in each of her literary encounters, as Larkin names them, spaces to destabilize and interrupt old protocols of reading "to teach new ways of reading" and to inspire, in an age where literacy itself is in danger, the pleasure that can come between the pages of a book when one experiences "one's own mind dancing with another."[31] With "Recitatif," Morrison stages the reading encounter to delineate the artistic challenges that color her entire career. As she says in the essay "Invisible Ink: Reading the Writing and Writing the Reading":

> What I could not clearly articulate was the way in which a reader participates in the text—not how she interprets it, but how she helps to write it. (Very like singing: there are the lyrics, the score, and then the performance—which is the individual's contribution to the piece.)[32]

Although she includes the specificity of race in most of her novels in one way or another, her geopoetics of place, race, and belonging inspired her to withhold it on more than one occasion so that her readers, like Twyla and Roberta, must wrestle with the consequences of their own reading as they navigate the spaces between the presences and absences in the text.

This study of Morrison is an attempt to connect her narrative aesthetics and cultural politics in an interdisciplinary, intersectional way. The path to that connection came from her own expressed writerly desire to "leave spaces for the reader to come into the text," but it was inspired by a readerly and scholarly desire to determine and delineate how she accomplished this task in her fiction. The idea of geopoetics, based on what has been referred to as the *spatial turn* in the humanities, offers a new path into the familiar and unfamiliar spaces of her writing. Unlike some writers who grant few interviews, give few speeches, and make few public appearances, Morrison began her career in public spaces as an editor, shifted to private spaces to focus on her writing, and lived the bulk of her days navigating language in what this study has referred to as discursive mediation between various binaries—private/public, Black/white, female/male, urban/rural, poor/rich, domestic/foreign, mother/child, and so on. She navigated the spaces between these binaries to destabilize our reading, our desire for facile beginnings and endings, and our propensity to think we know more than we do. In her fiction and nonfiction, she navigates the spaces between celebrations of how Black subjectivity is shaped apart from the white gaze and complicates our memories of the history of racism and being stuck in the racial imaginary—not just for its own sake but for the sake of lament. By the time we get to her last novel, we are able to see that she has navigated the binary between celebration and lament through narrative re-memory—a way of remembering what must be remembered, as her characters learned, before healing could begin. Why lament? I invoke the word *lament*—that biblical term that refers to storytelling as a way of "bringing untold stories to light"—because it helps us move beyond the protest tradition of Black literature with which Morrison was very familiar to a new way of giving voice to silences within the narratives of Black subjectivity.[33] The very absences she found in the narratives of enslaved people, the narratives that Mitchell refers to as liberation narratives, are those Morrison wanted to uncover, interrogate, and bring to light. She wanted to see how Black subjects read their own spaces and the resources within those spaces for surviving, thriving, and imagining a new way of being.

She found no better place to begin this interrogation than the space of home, a space that is sometimes regarded as the intersection of the sacred and the secular. She had a project, even there, of not romanticizing home but of bringing it to a new level of scrutiny to explore how it could be both snug and wide open at the same time that it has the capacity to be the space of a crucible that could destroy. The distinction between home and outdoors that she introduced in *The Bluest Eye* appears in each novel to engage readers in navigating familiar spaces and methods of knowing new ways. She achieves this with her characters, of course, but she does something more. Her geopoetics forces her to play with readers, to mess with facile reading practices by resisting linear telling, by sharing one moment and withholding the next, by taking readers to the precipice of remembering and then withdrawing to elucidate how we circle the subject to forget as Sethe does in *Beloved*. Morrison writes with the confidence of the ancestors and elders in her early essay "Rootedness: The Ancestor as Foundation" but with a sense of humility, like the narrator in *Jazz*, because she may not know the answers, motivations, or rationales for her characters' actions after all. But the joy of writing seems to drive her to stay on task and go into difficult places in Black subjectivity to shine light on the resources there—not to explain anything to white people but to remind Black people to remember and understand the healing power of remembering the very places, spaces, and people we might be tempted to forget.

During the last year of her life, the film *The Pieces I Am* was released. The film title quotes the character Paul D from *Beloved*, who speaks of his friend Sixo as the woman who gathers "the pieces I am" and gives "them back . . . in all the right order." The result leads him to conclude how good it is to have "a woman who is a friend of your mind."[34] The meeting between Bride and Booker in her last novel illustrates the spaces one must navigate to get to that level of knowing, intimacy, and appreciation. Through her geopoetic narrative strategies of discursive mediation, the creation of emancipatory spaces, narrative rememory, and interrogations of home, she takes her readers to difficult but critical spaces of knowing and making meaning. After eleven novels, countless speeches, lectures, children's books, and awards, Morrison's writing illustrates all the ways she has attempted to bring readers to her writing to give them a space to acknowledge injustice and celebrate the resources they forgot they had and to challenge them to discover the value of redefining the meaning of belonging in the third spaces of intersubjectivity and community. She shifts her readers from a focus on the exterior of their lives so they may engage in the work of interrogating how they came to know what they know and how that knowing may actually be hiding a deeper sense of knowing, a deeper subjectivity that the forces of the racial imaginary, the gender imaginary, and other ways of constructing subjectivity have hidden from them. With a relentless effort to imagine new ways of reading, knowing, and being, Morrison sought to gather the pieces we were in the hopes that we would appreciate the value of self-regard—not for selfish reasons but to imagine a new future that is snug and wide open for this generation and the ones to follow. In this way, she has been a friend of our mind, and we are the better for it.

Yet, she did not limit herself to the domestic space that America has been. When she wrote *Tar Baby* and *Home* and curated the exhibit "The Foreigner's Home," she imagined a wider canvas for her interrogations into language and narrative and the arts. Moreover, her forays into poetry, music, painting, dance, and theater all come into play in that exhibit. She seems to let her imagination explore new methods of entering old spaces to tell a new story. What she did with her exhibit was literally curate and create spaces for the marginalized, the young, and people of color, some of whom had never been to the Louvre. She made a connection with a global audience that she had not anticipated would gravitate to her work, and the feeling was mutual. For all those in attendance, it was clear that America's first African American Nobel laureate was at home in the world and felt free to enjoy what her influence had inspired not only in her home country but wherever in the world she chose to be.

But she was aware such connections would not always be the case. She challenged racism and racial injustice wherever she found them, but she also challenged their aftereffects—their manifestations in strange places, homes, neighborhoods, communities, and organizations and how they showed up as colorism or what she calls the fetish of colorism and self-loathing. She interrogates how one could get enamored with the racial other and the politics of class, consumerism, and appropriation and lose one's soul. It seems clear from reading her essays and listening to her interviews and lectures in the last years of her life that she had become even more introspective. But, more importantly, it could be argued that the writerly aspirations she had for her characters were connected to the readerly aspirations that she had for herself and her readers. Whether employing metafictional strategies in *Jazz* and *Home* to draw attention to the construction of the text by frustrating the reader with an unreliable narrator or meandering narratives to challenge the reader's ability to follow the story in *Beloved* or *A Mercy*, she remained committed to "destabilizing the text and reorienting the reader," partly for the joy of the dancing mind that was uniquely hers.[35] Her lecture on goodness and the literary imagination offers a way to give her the last word as a reader, artist, teacher, scholar, and public intellectual who was invested in an informed beloved community:

> Allowing goodness its own speech does not annihilate evil but it does allow me to signify my own understanding of goodness: the acquisition of self-knowledge. A satisfactory or good ending for me is when the protagonist learns something vital and morally insightful that she or he did not know at the beginning.[36]

For all the ways in which Morrison's artful prose and piercing intellect continue to bear witness to the power of her writing to transform us by inviting us into the spaces where new knowledge of ourselves and one another can take place and teach us what work remains to be done, we are forever grateful.

Notes

INTRODUCTION

1. Mikhail Bakhtin, "Discourse in the Novel," in *The Dialogic Imagination*, ed. Michael Holquist (Austin: University of Texas Press, 1981), 257. Epigraph Credit: From THE DIALOGIC IMAGINATION: FOUR ESSAYS by M.M. Bakhtin, edited by Michael Holquist, translated by Caryl Emerson and Michael Holquist, Copyright © 1981. By permission of the University of Texas Press.

2. Toni Morrison, "Rootedness: The Ancestor as Foundation," in *Black Women Writers (1950–1980): A Critical Evaluation*, ed. Mari Evans (New York: Anchor Books, 1984), 341.

3. See Marilyn Mobley McKenzie, "Spaces for Readers: The Novels of Toni Morrison," in *Cambridge Companion to the African American Novel*, ed. Maryemma Graham (Cambridge: Cambridge University Press, 2004), 221–232, where my article proposes a different title for this book-length study at an earlier stage in my research.

4. Morrison, "Unspeakable Things Unspoken: The Afro-American Presence in American Literature," *Michigan Quarterly Review* 28, no. 1 (Winter 1989): 33.

5. Morrison, *Nobel Lecture*, 22.

6. See Steven Mailloux, *Interpretive Conventions: The Reader in the Study of American Fiction* (Ithaca, NY: Cornell University Press, 1982); Wolfgang Iser, *The Act of Reading: A Theory of Aesthetic Response* (Baltimore: Johns Hopkins University Press, 1978), and *Prospecting: From Reader Response to Literary Anthropology* (Baltimore: Johns Hopkins University Press, 1989); Stanley Fish, *Is There a Text in This Class? The Authority of Interpretive Communities* (Cambridge, MA: Harvard University Press, 1980); Peter Brooks, *Reading for the Plot: Design and Intention in Narrative* (New York: Vintage, 1985); and Patrocinio P. Schweickart, "Reading Ourselves: Toward a Feminist Theory of Reading," in *Gender and Reading: Essays on Readers, Texts, and Contexts*, ed. Elizabeth A. Flynn and Schweickart (Baltimore: Johns Hopkins University Press, 1986), 31–62, for discussions

of reader-response criticism that have shaped my earlier approach to interpreting Morrison's comments about reading her work. Roland Barthes's essay "The Death of the Author" could be read as a critique on referencing an author's intention as a point of departure, but the geopolitical realities of Black and other marginalized peoples call that perspective into question, especially when the critic shares that identity of being a member of a marginalized community.

7. A member of the audience at the "Race Matters" conference at Princeton University in 1994 asked this question.

8. While I do not know the name of the woman who went up to the Nobel laureate at the conference in Princeton, what is significant is that her public response to the author is one heard more frequently in the later years of her career. The Princeton University conference, entitled "Envisioning Paradise: A Conference on the Art and Imagination of Toni Morrison," was held on February 12–13, 1999. Ironically, since her death, book bans have routinely included her books, but she was familiar with such negative attention and had even edited a book about the "peril" of attempting to police the work of writers. See "Peril" in *Burn This Book*, ed. Morrison (New York: Harper Studio, 2009), 1–4.

9. Morrison, *The Source of Self-Regard: Selected Essays, Speeches, and Meditations* (New York: Knopf, 2019), 7–8.

10. Morrison, "Invisible Ink: Reading the Writing and Writing the Reading," in *The Source of Self-Regard*, 350.

11. Morrison, "Invisible Ink," 348, 349.

12. Morrison, "Unspeakable Things Unspoken," 23. In recognition of its historical, political, and cultural significance, the word *Black* is capitalized throughout this study, except when the person being quoted, Morrison included, has used lower case.

13. Morrison, "The Reader as Artist," *O, Oprah Magazine*, July 2006, https://oprah.com/app/o-magazine.html.

14. Morrison, "Goodbye to All That: Race, Surrogacy, and Farewell," in *The Source of Self-Regard*, 337.

15. Kenneth White, *Geopoetics: Place, Culture, World* (Edinburgh: Alba Publishing, 2004).

16. Morrison, "The Site of Memory," in *The Source of Self-Regard*, 233–245.

17. Trudier Harris, *Depictions of Home in African American Literature* (Lanham, MD: Lexington Books, 2021), 2.

18. Raymond Williams, *The Long Revolution* (Harmondsworth: Penguin, 1961), 65; Morrison, "The Site of Memory," 240.

19. *The Foreigner's Home* and *The Pieces I Am* are two documentaries that offer valuable insights into two different aspects of the author—the exhibit she curated in Paris and a retrospective of her life both before and after she became the celebrated writer.

20. Mae Henderson, "Toni Morrison's *Beloved*: Re-Membering the Body as Historical Text," in *Comparative American Identities: Race, Sex, and Nationalities in the Modern Text*, ed. Hortense J. Spillers (New York: Routledge, 1991), 79.

21. Morrison, "Rootedness," 33–45.

22. Gayatri Spivak, "Reading the World: Literary Studies in the 1980s," in *Writing and Reading Differently: Deconstruction and the Teaching of Composition and Literature*, ed. G. Douglas Atkins and Michael L. Johnson (Lawrence: University Press of Kansas, 1985), 30.

23. See Eve Tavor Bannet, *Postcultural Theory: Critical Theory after the Marxist Paradigm* (New York: Paragon House, 1993), 88–112.

24. Homi K. Bhabha, *The Location of Culture* (New York: Routledge, 1994), 36–39; Edward Soja, *Thirdspace: Journeys to Los Angeles and Other Real-and-Imagined Places* (Malden, MA: Blackwell Publishing, 1996).

25. Edouard Glissant, *Poetics of Relation*, trans. Betsy Wing (Ann Arbor: University of Michigan Press, 1997); Elijah Anderson, *Black in White Space: The Enduring Impact of Color in Everyday Life* (Chicago: University of Chicago Press, 2022).

26. In many respects, the earlier research on the connection between Black studies and cultural studies has enabled my approach to Morrison's work of extending cultural studies to spatial literary studies. See Wahneema Lubiano, "Mapping the Interstices between Afro-American Cultural Discourse and Cultural Studies: A Prolegomenon." *Callaloo* 19, no. 1 (1996): 68–77.

27. See Neil Smith, *Uneven Development: Nature, Capital, and the Production of Space* (Athens: University of Georgia Press, 1984, 1990), 223.

28. One critic who has not ignored this dimension of Morrison's work is Farah Griffin, whose work in progress on textual healing examines how Morrison's *Beloved*, for example, has affected women readers to whom she has taught the novel. Griffin presented an excerpt from this study at "Envisioning Paradise: A Conference on Toni Morrison's Art and Imagination," held at Princeton University, February 12–13, 1999. Also see Carole Taylor, *The Tragedy and Comedy of Resistance: Reading Modernity through Black Women's Fiction* (Philadelphia: University of Pennsylvania Press, 2000), on how revisionist readings of tragedy and comedy offer ways of reading resistance in Morrison and other black women writers.

29. A few years before her death in 2002, I had the pleasure of discussing some of my ideas for this project with the much-respected literary scholar Claudia Tate. I am partially indebted to her for expanding my thinking about Bakhtin's concept of dialogism. See "Discourse in the Novel" in *The Dialogic Imagination: Four Essays by M.M. Bakhtin*, ed. Holquist (Austin: University of Texas Press, 1981), 259–422.

30. The Black Lives Matter movement emerged from a "love letter," #BlackLivesMatter, after the shooting death of Trayvon Martin. The Black Lives Matter Network was founded by Alicia Garza, Patrisse Cullors, and Opal Tometi. When Garza spoke at Case Western Reserve University in the spring of 2017, she explained the movement grew out of using social media to express compassion and concern for grieving mothers who had lost their sons to racial injustice, and it developed over time into a way to mobilize people for the struggle against such racial violence. Morrison's work continues to resonate with evolving iterations of the struggle for social justice, equity, and challenges to hegemonic narratives that exclude the imagination, voices, and perspectives of Black subjects.

31. Foucault, *Archaeology of Knowledge*, 23.

32. See Deborah E. McDowell, "Boundaries: Or Distant Relations and Close Kin—*Sula*," in *"The Changing Same": Black Women's Literature, Criticism, and Theory* (Bloomington: Indiana University Press, 1995), 102–117. McDowell's superb essay remains one of the best applications of reader-response theory to Morrison's *Sula*.

33. See Spillers, "Response," in *Afro-American Literary Study in the 1990s*, ed. Houston A. Baker Jr. and Patricia Redmond (Chicago: University of Chicago Press, 1989), 71–73.

34. Morrison, "The Site of Memory," 238.

35. For a discussion of how the effort to desegregate education in America was undermined and has been replaced over the years with a struggle to stem the consequences of resegregation, see Charles J. Ogletree Jr., *All Deliberate Speed: Reflections on the First Half-Century of Brown v. Board of Education* (New York: W. W. Norton, 2004); and Beverly Daniel Tatum, *Can We Talk about Race? And Other Conversations in an Era of School Resegregation* (Boston: Beacon Press, 2007). For a discussion of how making segregation illegal did not prevent inequality in American education from continuing and reasserting itself in new insidious ways, see Nikole Hannah-Jones, *The 1619 Project* (New York: One World, 2021).

36. See Joe Feagin, "The Continuing Significance of Race: Antiblack Discrimination in Public Places," *American Sociological Review* 56 (February 1991): 101–116. Also see Khalil Gibran Muhammad, *The Condemnation of Blackness: Race, Crime, and the Making of Modern Urban America* (Cambridge, MA: Harvard University Press, 2019), 8.

37. Cornel West, *Race Matters* (Boston: Beacon Press, 1993).

38. See Marilyn Sanders Mobley, "Toni Morrison's *Beloved*: The Scandal that Disturbed Domestic Tranquility," in *Scandalous Fictions: The Twentieth Century Novel in the Public Sphere*, ed. Jago Morrison and Susan Watkins (New York: Palgrave, 2006), 150–171.

39. See Dionne Brand, *A Map to the Door of No Return: Notes to Belonging* (New York: Vintage, 2011), 128.

40. Oprah Winfrey is the most famous of readers who publicly expressed difficulty with reading *Beloved*, even though she proceeded with making her film version of the story. Other examples of reader difficulty with *Beloved* and subsequent Morrison novels are primarily anecdotal, from multiple decades of teaching. More substantial data in this regard is outside the scope of this study and is probably the purview of a scholar with more of a social science background who might study reader responses.

41. See Morrison, *Nobel Lecture*, 22.

42. Morrison, 10.

43. Morrison, 1.

44. Morrison, 9. Morrison says she is adapting her version of the tale from other versions she has heard. She makes the elder a Black, blind old woman and adds new layers of complexity to the tale by doing so.

45. Williams, *The Long Revolution* (Harmondsworth: Penguin, 1961), 65. Quoted in McDowell, *"The Changing Same,"* 140.

46. See Charles Taylor, "The Politics of Recognition," in *Multiculturalism: Examining the Politics of Recognition*, ed. Amy Gutmann (Princeton, NJ: Princeton University Press, 1994), 25–73. For a discussion of *nommo*, see William R. Handley, "The House a Ghost Built: 'Nommo,' Allegory, and the Ethics of Reading in Toni Morrison's *Beloved*," *Contemporary Literature* 36, no. 4 (1995): 676–701.

47. Morrison, *Jazz*, 220.

48. Morrison, 228.

49. See Thadious Davis, *Southscapes: Geographies of Race, Region, and Literature* (Chapel Hill: University of North Carolina Press, 2011), 3.

50. bell hooks, *Belonging: A Culture of Place* (New York: Routledge, 2009), 23.

51. Yi-Fu Tuan, *Space and Place: The Perspective of Experience* (Minneapolis: University of Minnesota Press, 1977).

52. Tuan, *Space and Place*, 6.

53. Doreen Massey, *Space, Place, and Gender* (Minneapolis: University of Minnesota Press, 1994), 4.

54. Morrison, "Introduction: Friday on the Potomac," in *Race-ing Justice, En-gendering Power: Essays on Anita Hill, Clarence Thomas, and the Construction of Social Reality* (New York: Pantheon Books, 1992), xvii.

55. West, "Black Leadership and the Pitfalls of Racial Reasoning," in *Race-ing Justice*.

56. Claudia Rankine, "Introduction" in *The Racial Imaginary: Writers on Race in the Life of the Mind*, ed. Rankine, Beth Loffreda, and Max King Cap (Albany: Fence Books, 2016), 17.

57. Morrison, *Playing in the Dark: Whiteness and the Literary Imagination* (Cambridge, MA: Harvard University Press, 1992), xii.

58. Kimberle Crenshaw, "Mapping the Margins: Intersectionality, Identity Politics, and Violence Against Women of Color," in *Critical Race Theory: The Key Writings That Formed the Movement*, ed. Crenshaw, Neil Gotanda, Gary Peller, and Kendall Thomas (New York: The New Press, 1995), 357–383.

59. Spillers, "'All the Things You Could Be by Now, If Sigmund Freud's Wife Was Your Mother': Psychoanalysis and Race," in *Black, White, and In Color: Essays on American Literature and Culture* (Chicago: University of Chicago Press, 2003), 382.

60. Morrison, "Home," in *The House That Race Built: Original Essays by Toni Morrison, Angela Y. Davis, Cornel West and Others on Black Americans and Politics in America Today*, ed. Lubiano (New York: Vintage, 1998), 9. Also see Claudia Tate, *Psychoanalysis and Black Novels: Desire and the Protocols of Race* (New York: Oxford University Press, 1998).

61. Jessica Benjamin, *The Bonds of Love: Psychoanalysis, Feminism, and the Problem of Domination* (New York: Pantheon, 1988).

62. Morrison, "Home," 9.

63. Elissa Schappell and Claudia Brodsky Lacour, "Toni Morrison, The Art of Fiction No. 134," *Paris Review* 128 (Fall 1993).

64. Morrison, "Invisible Ink," 346–350.

65. Lesley Larkin, *Race and the Literary Encounter: Black Literature from James Weldon Johnson to Percival Everett* (Bloomington: Indiana University Press, 2015).

66. Morrison, "Rootedness," 341.

CHAPTER 1

1. Epigraph from Gaston Bachelard, *The Poetics of Space: The Classic Look at How We Experience Intimate Places* (Boston: Beacon Press, 1994), xxxvi–xxxvii. Epigraph Credit: Introduction by Richard Kearney, copyright © 2014 by Richard Kearney; from THE POETICS OF SPACE by Gaston Bachelard, translated by Maria Jolas. Used by permission of Penguin Classics, an imprint of Penguin Publishing Group, a division of Penguin Random House LLC. All rights reserved.

2. For examples of how reading has been racialized and politicized, see Morrison, ed., *Burn This Book*; and Hannah-Jones, *The 1619 Project*. Reading has been racialized for African Americans since the time of enslavement, when literacy was forbidden and policed. In more recent times, the recurring focus on banning books to police what gets included and excluded from America's racial history has come under greater scrutiny. See

Claire Moses, "The Spread of Book Banning," *New York Times*, July 31, 2022, https://www.nytimes.com/2022/07/31/briefing/book-banning-debate.html?smid=url-share.

3. Anne Anlin Cheng, *The Melancholy of Race: Psychoanalysis Assimilation and Hidden Grief* (New York: Oxford, 2001), 18; James Baldwin, "A Talk to Teachers," *Baldwin: Collected Essays*, ed. Morrison (New York: Library of America, 1998), 685.

4. Morrison, "Home," 4.

5. See Yvette Christiansë, *Toni Morrison: An Ethical Poetics* (New York: Fordham University Press, 1993), 139. Morrison, *The Bluest Eye* (New York: Knopf, 1993), 210.

6. Saidiya V. Hartman, *Scenes of Subjection: Terror, Slavery, and Self-Making in Nineteenth-Century America* (New York: Oxford University Press, 1997), 4.

7. Bhabha, *The Location of Culture*, 148.

8. Davis, *Southscapes*, 21.

9. Spillers, "A Hateful Passion, A Lost Love: Three Women's Fiction," in *Black, White, and In Color*, 96.

10. David Boers, *History of American Education Prime* (New York: Peter Lang, 2007).

11. hooks, *Art on My Mind: Visual Politics* (New York: The New Press, 1995), 147; and Fredric Jameson, "Cognitive Mapping," in *Marxism and the Interpretation of Culture*, ed. Cary Nelson and Lawrence Grossberg (Chicago: University of Illinois Press, 1990), 347–360.

12. For an insightful discussion of Morrison's use of the epigraph, see Christiansë, *Toni Morrison*, 221–222.

13. Morrison, "Unspeakable Things Unspoken," 9.

14. Morrison, "The Site of Memory," 231–245.

15. Michel Foucault, *The Archaeology of Knowledge*, trans. A. M. Sheridan Smith (New York: Pantheon, 1972), 130–131.

16. Bhabha, *The Location of Culture*, 1, 36.

17. Morrison, *The Bluest Eye*, 3.

18. See Fred Moten, *In the Break: The Aesthetics of the Black Radical Tradition* (Minneapolis: University of Minnesota Press, 2003), 92.

19. Morrison, "Unspeakable Things Unspoken," 1.

20. Morrison, "Afterword," in *The Bluest Eye* (New York: Knopf, 1993), 214.

21. As President of the Toni Morrison Society (TMS), I began including references to the "community of readers" to indicate to members and potential members that the TMS welcomed scholars and the public to our organization, programs, and events. During her formal remarks on her seventieth-birthday tribute hosted by TMS at the New York Public Library on Fifth Avenue in New York City in 2001, Morrison explained that her audience changed over time from herself, to readers, to critics, and to the larger community. Her expression "the dancing mind" comes from the lecture she delivered upon receiving the National Book Foundation Medal for Distinguished Contribution to American Letters on November 6, 1996. The publication by the same name beautifully describes the relationship between the reader and the writer. See Morrison, *The Dancing Mind* (New York: Knopf, 1996), 17.

22. Morrison, *The Bluest Eye*, 6.

23. Claudia Brodsky, "Aesthetic Activity," in *Toni Morrison: Memory and Meaning*, ed. Adrienne Lanier Seward and Justine Tally (Jackson: University Press of Mississippi, 2014), 207–217.

24. Erica Carter, James Donald, and Judith Squires, eds., *Space and Place: Theories of Identity and Location* (London: Lawrence & Wishart, 1993), x.

25. See Zora Neale Hurston, "Characteristics of Negro Expression," in *Voices from the Harlem Renaissance*, ed. Nathan Huggins (New York: Oxford University Press, 1976), 224–227.

26. For an earlier discussion of this theme in Morrison's work, see Marilyn S. Mobley, "Skin Deep: Toni Morrison's Interrogation of Beauty from *The Bluest Eye* to *God Help the Child*," *International Review of African American Art* 30, no. 2 (2020): 37–41.

27. For a review of intersectionality, see Brittney Cooper, "Intersectionality," in *The Oxford Review of Feminist Theory*, ed. Lisa Disch and Mary Hawkesworth (New York: Oxford University Press, 2016), 385–406.

28. Patricia J. Williams, "The Ethnic Scarring of American Whiteness," in *The House That Race Built*, ed. Wahneema Lubiano (New York: Vintage, 1996), 253–263.

29. Sigmund Freud, "Mourning and Melancholia," in *The Standard Edition of the Complete Psychological Works of Sigmund Freud*, trans. James Strachey (London: Hogarth Press, 1953).

30. Cheng, *The Melancholy of Race*.

31. See Michael Beschloss, "How an Experiment with Dolls Helped Lead to School Integration," *New York Times*, May 6, 2014.

32. Carmen Gillespie, *Toni Morrison: A Literary Reference to Her Life and Work* (New York: Facts on File, 2008), 5. Also see Evelyn Jaffe Schreiber, *Race, Trauma and Home in the Novels of Toni Morrison* (Baton Rouge: Louisiana State University Press, 2010), 8–15.

33. Tressie McMillan Cottom, "In the Name of Beauty," in *Thick and Other Essays*, ed. Cottom (New York: The New Press, 2019), 37–72.

34. Katherine McKittrick, *Demonic Grounds: Black Women and the Cartographies of Struggle* (Minneapolis: University of Minnesota Press, 2006), xiii.

35. Brodsky, "Aesthetic Activity," 204–217.

36. See Ta-Nehisi Coates, "The Case for Reparations," *The Atlantic*, June 2014.

37. Herman Beavers, *Geography and the Political Imaginary in the Novels of Toni Morrison* (New York: Palgrave, 2018), 26.

38. Christina Sharpe, *In the Wake: On Blackness and Being* (Durham: Duke University Press, 2016), 20–21.

39. Baker, *Blues, Ideology, and Afro-American Literature* (Chicago: University of Chicago Press, 1984), 6.

40. Bachelard, *The Poetics of Space*, xxxviii.

41. See Morrison, "Intimate Things in Place: A Conversation with Toni Morrison," in *Chant of Saints: A Gathering of Afro-American Literature, Art, and Scholarship*, ed. Michael S. Harper and Robert B. Stepto (Urbana: University of Illinois Press, 1979), 213; and George Lipsitz, *How Racism Takes Place* (Philadelphia: Temple University Press, 2011), 249. Also see Rashad Shabazz, *Spatializing Blackness: Architectures of Confinement and Black Masculinity in Chicago* (Urbana: University of Illinois Press, 2015), 114–116.

42. Michel de Certeau, *The Practice of Everyday Life*, trans. Steven F. Rendall (Berkeley: University of California Press, 1984), 118, 119.

43. Gurleen Grewal, *Circles of Sorrow, Lines of Struggle: The Novels of Toni Morrison* (Baton Rouge: Louisiana State University Press, 1998), 45.

44. See Mobley, *Folk Roots and Mythic Wings in Sarah Orne Jewett and Toni Morrison: The Cultural Function of Narrative* (Baton Rouge: Louisiana State University Press, 1991).

This book was one of the first cross-cultural studies on Morrison and represents an early attempt to explore her narrative aesthetics. By shifting to a focus solely on Morrison, this study attempts to go beyond those preliminary understandings of her work to a deeper assessment that is informed by both her fiction and nonfiction over the span of her literary career to describe how she achieves what she achieves in her fiction in a new way from a new perspective.

45. M. H. Abrams, *A Glossary of Literary Terms* (Orlando: Harcourt Brace College Publishers, 1993), 161.

46. Abrams, *A Glossary of Literary Terms*, 161.

47. Brooks, *Reading for the Plot*, 4.

48. For a discussion of how black vernacular language operates in parodic ways to comment on authoritative discourse, see Henry Louis Gates, *The Signifying Monkey: A Theory of Afro-American Literary Criticism* (New York: Oxford University Press, 1988), 105.

49. 1 Corinthians 1:11 (King James Version).

50. Morrison, "Foreword," in *Tar Baby* (1981; repr., New York: Vintage, 2004), xii.

51. See Foucault, *The Order of Things: An Archaeology of Human Sciences* (New York: Vintage, 1994).

52. For how the novel was received in early reviews, see Susan Neal Mayberry, *The Critical Life of Toni Morrison* (Rochester: Camden House, 2021), 93–100.

53. Morrison, "Foreword," *Tar Baby*, xiii.

54. Morrison, xiii.

55. See Mobley, *Folk Roots and Mythic Wings*, 150–153, where I discuss the themes of being a cultural orphan and of rootlessness in *Tar Baby* in more detail.

56. Bhabha, *The Location of Culture*, 3.

CHAPTER 2

1. See McKittrick, *Demonic Grounds*, 24.

2. Shabazz, *Spatializing Blackness*, 46.

3. Kevin Quashie, *Black Aliveness, or a Poetics of Being* (Durham: Duke University Press, 2021), 14.

4. Morrison, *Sula* (1973; repr., New York: Vintage, 2004), 102; Morrison, *Song of Solomon* (New York: Knopf, 1977), 149.

5. See Elizabeth Alexander, *The Black Interior* (Saint Paul: Graywolf Press, 2004), 5.

6. Schappell and Brodsky Lacour, "Toni Morrison, The Art of Fiction No. 134," 8.

7. hooks, "Choosing the Margin as a Space of Radical Openness," in *Yearning: Race, Gender, and Cultural Politics* (Boston: South End Press, 1990), 145–153.

8. Morrison, "The Source of Self-Regard," in *The Source of Self-Regard*, 319–320.

9. Moten, *In the Break*, 175.

10. Morrison, "Foreword," *Sula* (New York: Vintage, 2004), xiii.

11. McDowell, "Boundaries," 104, 110.

12. McDowell, "Boundaries," 112–113.

13. Robert Scholes, *Protocols of Reading* (New Haven: Yale University Press, 1989), 27.

14. Myles Horton and Paulo Freire, *We Make the Road by Walking: Conversations on Education and Social Change* (Philadelphia: Temple University Press, 1990).

15. Rosi Braidotti, "Writing as a Nomadic Subject," *Comparative Critical Studies* 11, no. 2–3 (2014): 163–184.

16. Morrison, "The Site of Memory," 233–254; Hartman, *Lose Your Mother: A Journey along the Atlantic* (New York: Farrar, Straus and Giroux, 2008), 17; and Foucault, *The Archaeology of Knowledge*, 120, 126–131.

17. Morrison, "The Site of Memory," 238–239.

18. See Robin D. G. Kelley, *Freedom Dreams: The Black Radical Imagination* (Boston: Beacon Press, 2002).

19. Charles Baudelaire, "The Temple of Nature," in *The Modern Tradition*, ed. Richard Ellman and Charles Feidelson Jr. (New York: Oxford, 1964), 59–60.

20. Bonnie M. K. Hagerty, Judith Lynch-Sauer, Kathleen L. Patusky, Maria Bouwsema, and Peggy Collier, "Sense of Belonging: A Vital Mental Health Concept," *Archives of Psychiatric Nursing* VI, no. 3 (June 1992): 172–177.

21. John 8:11 (New King James Version).

22. James H. Cone, *God of the Oppressed*, rev. ed. (1975; repr., Maryknoll: Orbis Books, 1997), 55.

23. As quoted by Rev. Angela Ford Nelson in "The Message of the Hush Harbor: History and Theology of African Descent Traditions," in *United Methodist Advocate*, ed. Jessica Brodie, March 1, 2019. For other scholarship on hush harbors, see work by Paul Harvey, Albert Raboteau, and Noel Leo Erskine.

24. Bhabha, *The Location of Culture*, 9.

25. Harriet Jacobs, *Incidents in the Life of a Slave Girl* (New York: Oxford, 2001).

26. See McKittrick, *Demonic Grounds*, 59; and Barbara Christian, "The Race for Theory," in *The Black Feminist Reader*, ed. Joy James and T. Denean Sharpley-Whiting (Oxford: Blackwell, 2000), 11–23.

27. See M. Nourbese Philip, "Dis Place—The Space Between," in *A Genealogy of Resistance and Other Essays* (Toronto: Mercury Press, 1997), 76.

28. For Rev. Dr. Martin Luther King Jr.'s concept of the beloved community, see his sermon "Loving Your Enemies" in *Strength to Love* (New York: Harper Row, 1963), 48.

29. See W.E.B. Du Bois, *The Souls of Black Folk* (1903; repr., New York: First Vintage/The Library of America, 1990).

30. Tricia Rose, *Longing to Tell: Black Women Talk about Sexuality and Intimacy* (New York: Picador, 2003), 390.

31. Marc C. Conner, "From the Sublime to the Beautiful: The Aesthetic Progression of Toni Morrison," in *The Aesthetics of Toni Morrison: Speaking the Unspeakable* (Jackson: University Press of Mississippi, 2000), 73.

32. For a discussion of motherhood in Morrison's work, see Andrea O'Reilly, *Toni Morrison and Motherhood: A Politics of the Heart* (Albany: SUNY Press, 2004). Also see Linda Wagner-Martin, *Toni Morrison and the Maternal: From the Bluest Eye to God Help the Child* (New York: Peter Lang, 2019).

33. See Karla F. C. Holloway, "*Beloved*: A Spiritual"; Ashraf H. A. Rushdy, "Daughters Signifyin(g) History: The Example of Toni Morrison's *Beloved*"; and Linda Krumholz, "The Ghosts of Slavery: Historical Recovery in Toni Morrison's *Beloved*," all in *Toni Morrison's Beloved: A Casebook*, ed. William L. Andrews and Nellie Y. McKay (New York: Oxford, 1999), 67–78, 37–66, 107–125.

34. Bhabha, *The Location of Culture*, 17.

35. Bakhtin, *M. M. Bakhtin: Speech, Genres, and Other Late Essays*, ed. C. Emerson and M. Holquist, trans. V. W. McGee (Austin: University of Texas Press, 1986), 93.

36. Bhabha, *The Location of Culture*, 251.

37. Cheng, *The Melancholy of Race*, 8.
38. Benjamin, *The Bonds of Love*, 192.
39. Quashie, *Black Aliveness*, 14.
40. Du Bois, *The Souls of Black Folk*, 252–267.
41. Holloway, "*Beloved*: A Spiritual," in *Toni Morrison's Beloved: A Casebook*, ed. William L. Andrews and Nellie Y. McKay (New York: Oxford University Press, 1999), 76.
42. See Schreiber, *Race, Trauma, and Home in the Novels of Toni Morrison*.
43. Morrison, "Unspeakable Things Unspoken," 9.
44. Baker, *Modernism and the Harlem Renaissance* (Chicago: University of Chicago Press, 1987), 92.
45. See James Van Der Zee, Owen Dodson, Camille Billops, *The Harlem Book of the Dead* (Dobbs Ferry, NY: Morgan & Morgan, 1978).
46. Sharpe, *In the Wake*, 3.
47. See Van Der Zee, Dodson, and Billops, *The Harlem Book of the Dead*, for foreword by Morrison. Also see Paula Giddings, "The Triumphant Song of Toni Morrison," in *Toni Morrison Conversations*, ed. Carolyn C. Denard (Jackson: University Press of Mississippi, 2008), 13.
48. Hartman, *Lose Your Mother*, 17.
49. Van Der Zee, *The Harlem Book of the Dead*, 84.
50. Sharpe, *In the Wake*, 114–115.
51. Rose Gillian, *Feminism and Geography: The Limits of Geographical Knowledge* (Minneapolis: University of Minnesota Press, 1993), 150, 155.
52. Emily Dickinson, "Tell all the truth but tell it slant," in *The Poems of Emily Dickinson: Reading Edition*, ed. Ralph W. Franklin (Cambridge, MA: Belknap Press of Harvard University, 1998). Poet, literary scholar, and educator Kenyatta Dorey Graves has shared with me that recent research and scholarship on the reading process reveal that the reading process itself is also subject to the meandering navigation between the words on the page and what the mind expects and chooses to remember.
53. Morrison, "Rootedness," 341.
54. See Denard, *Toni Morrison Conversations*, 218–219.
55. The term "protocols of reading" is from Jacques Derrida, *Positions, Translated and Annotated by Alan Bass* (Chicago: University of Chicago Press, 1972), 63. Also see Scholes, *Protocols of Reading*; and Morrison, "The Reader as Artist."
56. See Addison Gayle, *The Black Aesthetic* (New York: Doubleday, 1970).
57. Farah Jasmine Griffin, "*Who Set You Flowin'?*" *The African-American Migration Narrative* (New York: Oxford University Press, 1995), 43.
58. See David Levering Lewis, *When Harlem Was in Vogue* (New York: Oxford University Press, 1981). Also see Alain Locke, ed., *The New Negro: Voices of the Harlem Renaissance* (1925; repr., New York: Touchstone, 1992); and Jeffrey C. Stewart, *The New Negro: The Life of Alain Locke* (New York: Oxford University Press, 2018).
59. Salman Rushdie, "An Interview with Toni Morrison," in *Toni Morrison Conversations*, 51.
60. See Beavers, *Geography and the Political Imaginary in the Novels of Toni Morrison*, 94; and Morrison, "Rootedness," 342.
61. See Isabel Wilkerson, *The Warmth of Other Suns* (New York: Vintage, 2010).
62. Wilkerson, *The Warmth of Other Suns*, 280.

63. Griffin, *"Who Set You Flowin'?"* 3.
64. Griffin, 8.
65. Moten, *In the Break*, 119–120. Also see Baker, *Modernism and the Harlem Renaissance*, 92.
66. Moten, *In the Break*, 26.
67. Gates, *The Signifying Monkey*, 181.
68. For reactions to and assessments of The Harlem Renaissance, see Langston Hughes, *The Big Sea* (New York: Hill and Wang, 1940); James Weldon Johnson, *Black Manhattan* (New York: Arno Press, 1968); and Arnold Shaw, *The Jazz Age: Popular Music in the 1920s* (New York: Oxford University Press, 1987), 57–92. Shaw's assessment focuses more on the music and less on the political realities of Black life from which the music emerged and is thus a somewhat romanticized assessment of the period.
69. Hartman, *Lose Your Mother*, 6–17.
70. See Sharpe, *In the Wake*, 79.
71. See Demetrius Eudell, "Come on Kid, Let's Go Get the Thing: The Sociogenic Principle and the Being of Being Black/Human," in *Sylvia Wynter: On Being Human as Praxis*, ed. McKittrick (Duke University Press: Durham, 2015), 236.
72. See Locke, ed., *The New Negro*.
73. Gillespie, *Toni Morrison*, 77.
74. Morrison, "Literature and Public Life," in *The Source of Self-Regard*, 101.
75. Kathleen M. Kirby, *Indifferent Boundaries: Spatial Concepts of Human Subjectivity* (New York: Guilford Press, 1996), 13.
76. See Scott Ellsworth, *Death in a Promised Land: The Tulsa Race Riot of 1921* (Baton Rouge: LSU Press, 1992).
77. Gillespie, *Toni Morrison*, 138.
78. See James Cone, *For My People: Black Theology and the Black Church* (Maryknoll: Orbis Books, 1984).
79. McKittrick, *Demonic Grounds*, xiv.
80. See Loffreda and Rankine, "Introduction," in *The Racial Imaginary*, 17.
81. Loffreda and Rankine, *The Racial Imaginary*, 17.
82. David Carrasco, "Writing Goodness and Mercy: A 2017 Interview with Toni Morrison," in *Toni Morrison: Goodness and the Literary Imagination*, ed. Carrasco, Stephanie Paulsell, and Mara Willard (Charlottesville: University of Virginia Press, 2019), 218–219.
83. See Chimamanda Ngozi Adichie, "The Danger of a Single Story," TED talk, 2009.
84. For her description of "nomadic consciousness" and how it structures subjectivity, see Braidotti, *Nomadic Subjects: Embodiment and Sexual Difference in Contemporary Feminist Theory* (New York: Columbia University Press, 1994), 25, 99.
85. Kirby, *Indifferent Boundaries*, 35.

CHAPTER 3

1. Hartman, *Scenes of Subjection*, 73.
2. Morrison alludes to this reluctance in the documentary *Toni Morrison: The Pieces I Am*, directed by Timothy Greenfield-Sanders (Magnolia Pictures, 2019).
3. Hartman, *Scenes of Subjection*, 76–77; Victor W. Turner, *Dramas, Fields, and Metaphors: Symbolic Action in Human Society* (Ithaca, NY: Cornell University Press, 1974), 41.

4. Angelyn Mitchell, *The Freedom to Remember: Narrative, Slavery, and Gender in Contemporary Black Women's Fiction* (New Brunswick, NJ: Rutgers University Press, 2002), xii, 4–5.

5. From Morrison, "Acceptance Speech for the Frederic G. Melcher Book Award for the Publication of *Beloved*," *World Magazine*, 1989. Quoted in Helena Woodard, *Slave Sites on Display: Reflecting Slavery's Legacy through Contemporary Flash Moments* (Jackson: University of Mississippi Press, 2019).

6. See Mobley, "A Different Remembering: Memory, History and Meaning in Toni Morrison's *Beloved*," in *Toni Morrison: Modern Critical Views*, ed. Harold Bloom (New York: Chelsea House, 1990), 189–200.

7. Foucault, *Archaeology of Knowledge*, 121.

8. Mitchell, *The Freedom to Remember*, 3–4.

9. See Katy Waldman, "Slave or Enslaved Person? It's Not Just an Academic Debate for Historians of American Slavery," *Slate*, May 19, 2015, https://slate.com/human-interest/2015/05/historians-debate-whether-to-use-the-term-slave-or-enslaved-person.html.

10. Sheila Wise Rowe, *Healing Racial Trauma: The Road to Resilience* (Downers Grove: InterVarsity Press, 2020), 170.

11. For a related analysis of the relationship between the text and the reader, see Larkin, *Race and the Literary Encounter*, 4. I am less interested, however, in what she calls a "hostile readership" that sees itself as "universal or race-free" than I am in the narrative strategies Morrison uses to shape her texts for her readers, regardless of their racial background or identity.

12. Paul Ricoeur, *Memory, History and Forgetting*, trans. Kathleen Blamey and David Pellauer (Chicago: University of Chicago Press, 2004), 39.

13. Rowe, *Healing Racial Trauma*, 169.

14. Schreiber, *Race, Trauma and Home in the Novels of Toni Morrison*, 8–9.

15. Avivah Gottlieb Zornberg, *The Particulars of Rapture: Reflections on Exodus* (New York: Schocken Books, 2001), 6.

16. Zornberg, *The Particulars of Rapture*, 451.

17. Zornberg, 454.

18. Mitchell, *The Freedom to Remember*, 147–148. Mitchell references the work of Dori Laub, "Bearing Witness, or the Vicissitudes of Listening," *Testimony: Crises of Witnessing in Literature, Psychoanalysis, and History*, eds. Shoshana Felman and Laub (New York: Routledge, 1992), 57–74.

19. Morrison, *Nobel Lecture*, 21.

20. See James Olney, "'I Was Born': Slave Narratives, Their Status as Autobiography and as Literature," *Callaloo* 7 (Winter 1984): 46–73. Reprinted in *The Slave's Narrative*, ed. Charles T. Davis and Henry Louis Gates Jr. (New York: Oxford University Press, 1991), 148–175.

21. Hartman, *Scenes of Subjection*, 6.

22. Hartman, 5.

23. Hartman, 5.

24. Steven Weisenberger, *Modern Medea: A Family Story of Slavery and Child-Murder from the Old South* (New York: Hill and Wang, 1998), 10.

25. Morrison, *Nobel Lecture*, 27.

26. See Adrienne Rich, "When We Dead Awaken: Writing as Re-Vision," *College English* 34 (October 1972): 18–26.

27. Morrison, "The Site of Memory," 238.
28. Morrison, *Nobel Lecture*, 27.
29. Kirby, *Indifferent Boundaries*, 54.
30. McKittrick, *Demonic Grounds*, xiii.
31. McKittrick, xv.
32. For a description of the experimentation done on Black women's bodies, see Harriet W. Washington, *Medical Apartheid: The Dark History of Medical Experimentation on Black Americans from Colonial Times to the Present* (New York: Anchor Books, 2008), 189–202.
33. See Michele M. Wright, *Physics of Blackness: Beyond the Middle Passage Epistemology* (Minneapolis: University of Minnesota Press, 2015), 20. Also see Holquist, ed., *The Dialogic Imagination: Four Essays by M.M. Bakhtin*, where Bakhtin uses the term *chronotope* to represent a similar phenomenon related to the collapsing of time and space.
34. See Virginia Woolf, "The Novel of Consciousness," in *The Modern Tradition*, 123–124.
35. See Mobley, *Folk Roots and Mythic Wings*, for my discussion of Morrison's male protagonist, Macon Dead. Also see Mobley, "A Different Remembering," 189–199.
36. See Morrison, "Black Matters," in *Playing in the Dark*, 15.
37. See review from Anna Mulrine, "This Side of 'Paradise': Toni Morrison Defends Herself from Criticism of Her New Novel Paradise," *U.S. News & World Report*, January 19, 1998, 71, where Morrison says *Paradise* was originally going to be called *War*.
38. In an interview about the novel, Morrison notes that the Korean War was referred to as a "police action." It is difficult not to note the irony in her voice in pointing out this distinction. Though she does not elaborate, beneath this observation is an implicit critique of the propensity to use euphemism instead of calling out the violence of war for what it is. PBS NewsHour, "In Toni Morrison's 'Home,' Soldier Fights War, Racism," YouTube video, posted May 29, 2012, https://www.youtube.com/watch?v=lZ5XnjiI0gk&list=PLYyiwknF_3XIG5dBUJaQW-CJEkzeVGIqW&index=9.
39. See Morrison, "Wartalk," in *The Source of Self-Regard*, 23.
40. See Shabazz, *Spatializing Blackness*, 2, 20–26, on the criminalization of Black bodies during and after enslavement to and including the present time.
41. Brandi Thompson Summers, *Black in Place: The Spatial Aesthetics of Race in a Post Chocolate City* (Chapel Hill: University of North Carolina Press, 2019), 13.
42. See Simone Browne, *Dark Matters: On the Surveillance of Blackness* (Durham: Duke University Press, 2015), 17.
43. See George Yancy, *Black Bodies, White Gazes: The Continuing Significance of Race in America*, 2nd ed. (New York: Bowman & Littlefield, 2017), xix–xx.
44. See Jonathan M. Metzel, *The Protest Psychosis: How Schizophrenia Became a Black Disease* (Boston: Beacon Press, 2010), 162, 202.
45. Foucault, *Power: Essential Works of Foucault 1954–1984*, ed. James D. Faubion, trans. Robert Hurley and others (New York: The New Press, 1994), 137.
46. See Talks at Google, "Home: Toni Morrison," YouTube video, posted March 4, 2013, https://www.youtube.com/watch?v=pBDARw5fdrg&t=645s. Also see Albert Wertheim, "The McCarthy Era and the American Theater," *Theater Journal* 34, no. 2 (May 1982): 211–222.
47. Quintard Taylor, "Swing the Door Wide: World War II Wrought a Profound Transformation in Seattle's Black Community," *Columbia Magazine* 9, no. 2 (Summer 1995).

48. See Victor H. Green, pub., *The Negro Motorist Green Book: 1940 Facsimile Edition* (Snowball Publishing: New York, 1918). Also see George Petras and Janet Loehrke, "A Look Inside the Green Book, which guided Black Travelers through a Segregated and Hostile America," *USA Today*, February 21, 2021; and Candacy Taylor, *Overground Railroad: The Green Book and the Roots of Black Travel in America* (New York: Abrams Press, 2020). For a history of the interconnections between Black travel by car and the dangers black people faced as they enjoyed the freedom of mobility, see Gretchen Sorin, *Driving While Black: African American Travel and the Road to Civil Rights* (New York: Liveright, 2020).

49. Hartman, *Scenes of Subjection*, 116.

50. See Gates, *The Black Church: This Is Our Story, This is Our Song* (New York: Penguin, 2021), 109.

51. See Du Bois, "Returning Soldiers," *The Crisis* XVIII (May 1919), 13.

52. See Morrison and Middleton A. Harris, eds., *The Black Book* (1974; repr., New York: Random House, 2009), 180.

53. Lipsitz, "Racialization of Space and the Spacialization of Race: Theorizing the Hidden Architecture of Landscape," *Landscape Journal* 26, no. 1 (2007), 12.

54. Augustus A. White III, *Seeing Patients: Unconscious Bias in Health Care* (Cambridge, MA: Harvard University Press, 2011), 225. Also see Washington, *Medical Apartheid*.

55. Morrison, "Unspeakable Things Unspoken," 9.

56. Griffin, *Read Until You Understand: The Profound Wisdom of Black Life and Literature* (New York: W. W. Norton, 2021), 91.

CHAPTER 4

1. See Bhabha, *The Location of Culture* (Routledge: London and New York: 1994), 18, and Caren Kaplan, "Deterriorializations: The Rewriting of Home and Exile in Western Feminist Discourse," *Cultural Critique* 6 (Spring 1987): 194. Epigraph Credit: From Homi K. Bhabha, *The Location of Culture*, © 1994 Homi K. Bhabha. Reproduced with permission of the Licensor through PLSclear.

2. Harris, *Depictions of Home in African American Literature*, 2.

3. See Wright, *Physics of Blackness*, 1–35.

4. Morrison, "Home," 3.

5. See hooks, *Writing Beyond Race: Living Theory and Practice* (New York: Routledge, 2013), 184, 189.

6. Morrison, "Home," 4–5.

7. Morrison, 5.

8. Morrison, 9.

9. Morrison, *Paradise* (New York: Knopf, 1998), 3.

10. Morrison, "Home," 3.

11. Kaplan, "Deterritorializations," 194.

12. See Beavers, *Geography and the Political Imaginary in the Novels of Toni Morrison*, 129–161; and Schreiber, *Race, Trauma, and Home in the Novels of Toni Morrison*, 138–156.

13. Morrison, "Home," 10.

14. Benedict Anderson, *Imagined Communities* (London: Verso, 1983).

15. Morrison, "Home," 12.

16. Massey, *Space, Place, and Gender*, 166–167.
17. Coates, "The Case for Reparations."
18. Morrison, "Home," 9.
19. Morrison, *Playing in the Dark*, 3.
20. Ironically, three chapters of *God Help the Child* were collected and published as a short story under the title of "Sweetness" in the *New Yorker* in February 2015, but it probably would have been more accurate to identity this narrative as an excerpt from the forthcoming novel, which was published later the same year. The point is she only wrote one short story.
21. Kirby, *Indifferent Boundaries*, 15.
22. Morrison, "Home," 5.
23. The phrase come from the title of the book *The House That Race Built*, ed. Lubiano, which contains Morrison's essay "Home."
24. hooks, *Belonging*, 122.
25. See the February 9, 2015, edition of *The New Yorker*.
26. Wilkerson, *Caste: The Origins of Our Discontents* (New York: Random House, 2020), 238–239.
27. Morrison, "The Site of Memory," 233–245.
28. See "Peril" in *The Source of Self-Regard*, vii–ix.
29. Hartman, *Lose Your Mother*, 17.
30. William Shakespeare, *Hamlet*, act 3, scene 2.
31. Philip, *A Genealogy of Resistance and Other Essays, 91*.
32. Toi Derricotte, *The Black Notebooks: An Interior Journey* (New York: W. W. Norton, 1997), 13.
33. Derricotte, *The Black Notebooks*, 16.
34. Morrison, "Unspeakable Things Unspoken," 1–34.
35. Morrison, "The Site of Memory," 238–239.
36. Morrison, "Unspeakable Things Unspoken," 170.
37. Morrison, *The Origin of Others* (Cambridge, MA: Harvard University Press, 2017), 15.
38. Morrison, 14.
39. Anderson, *Imagined Communities*, 6.
40. Morrison, "Site of Memory," 238.
41. Morrison, *Song of Solomon*.
42. Morrison, *Bluest Eye*, 4.
43. Morrison, *Source of Self-Regard*, 3–126.
44. Morrison, *Nobel Lecture*, 28–29.
45. Morrison, "Home," 10.
46. Morrison, "The Foreigner's Home," in *The Source of Self-Regard*, 5.
47. Bhabha, *Location of Culture*, 7.
48. Morrison, "Home," 12.
49. Rachel Somerstein, "A Novelist's Approach," *Artnews*, August 8, 2019.
50. Somerstein, "A Novelist's Approach."
51. Angela Doland, "Toni Morrison Puts Slam Poetry Into Action at the Louvre," *Seattle Times*, November 9, 2006.
52. Doland, "Toni Morrison Puts Slam Poetry Into Action."
53. Doland.

54. Baldwin, "The Discovery of What It Means to Be an American," in *Nobody Knows My Name* (New York: Vintage, 1961), 4–5.

55. Baldwin, "What It Means to Be an American," 12.

CONCLUSION

1. See Howard Thurman, *A Strange Freedom: The Best of Howard Thurman on Religious Experience and Public Life*, ed. Walter Earl Fluker and Catherine Tumber (Boston: Beacon Press, 1998), 305.

2. Morrison, *Playing in the Dark*, 3.

3. Ironically, three chapters of *God Help the Child* were collected and published as a short story under the title of "Sweetness" in the *New Yorker* in February 2015, but it probably would have been more accurate to identity this narrative as an excerpt from the forthcoming novel, which was published later the same year. The point is she only wrote one short story.

4. For a discussion of how Morrison's comments in her forewords represent a kind of writerly anxiety that detracts from her fiction, see Tessa Roynon, "Lobbying the Reader: Toni Morrison's Recent Foreword to Her Novels," *European Journal of American Culture* 33, no. 2 (2014): 85–96. The focus of this study has been on how her nonfiction statements complement the geopoetics at work in her fiction.

5. Morrison, "Recitatif," in *Confirmation: Anthology of African American Women*, ed. Amiri Baraka and Amina Baraka (New York: William Morrow, 1983), 243–261.

6. See Kirby, *Indifferent Boundaries*, 148.

7. I first made this point in my 2013 TEDx talk on "The Paradox of Diversity," April 30, 2013. See TEDx CLE website, accessed December 7, 2023, http://www.tedxcle.com/dr-marilyn-sanders-mobley/.

8. Shanna Greene Benjamin, "The Space that Race Creates: An Interstitial Analysis of Toni Morrison's 'Recitatif,'" *Studies in American Fiction* 40, no. 1 (Spring 2013): 88.

9. For discussions of how Americans dichotomize race, see Karen E. Rosenblum and Toni-Michelle C. Travis, eds., *The Meaning of Difference: American Constructions of Race and Ethnicity, Sex and Gender, Social Class, Sexuality, and Disability*, 7th ed. (New York: McGraw Hill, 2016), 20–23.

10. Kirby, *Indifferent Boundaries*, 15.

11. Morrison, "Recitatif," 243.

12. Morrison, 243.

13. Morrison, 243.

14. Morrison, 244.

15. Morrison, 244.

16. Morrison, 244.

17. Morrison, 245.

18. Morrison, 244, 245.

19. Benjamin, "The Space that Race Creates," 98, 91.

20. Morrison, *Jazz*, 228.

21. Morrison, "Recitatif," 253.

22. Morrison, 254.

23. Morrison, 257.

24. Morrison, 256, 258.

25. Morrison, 258.
26. Morrison, 259.
27. Morrison, 261.
28. See Benjamin, *Beyond Doer and Done To: Recognition Theory, Intersubjectivity and the Third* (London: Routledge, 2018), 23–24.
29. *Merriam-Webster*, s.v. "recitative."
30. Benjamin, "The Space that Race Creates," 100.
31. Morrison, *The Dancing Mind*, 16.
32. Morrison, "Invisible Ink," 347.
33. Soong-Chan Rah, *Prophetic Lament: A Call for Justice in Troubled Times* (Downers Grove: Intervarsity Press, 2015), 208.
34. Morrison, *Beloved*, 272–273.
35. Patricia Waugh, *Metafiction: The Theory and Practice of Self-Conscious Fiction* (London: Routledge, 1984), 22; Morrison, "Invisible Ink," 350.
36. Morrison, "Goodness: Altruism and the Literary Imagination," in *Toni Morrison: Goodness and the Literary Imagination*, 18–19.

Bibliography

Abrams, M. H. *A Glossary of Literary Terms*. Orlando: Harcourt Brace College Publishers, 1993.
Adichie, Chimamanda Ngozi. "The Danger of a Single Story." TED talk, 2009.
Alexander, Elizabeth. *The Black Interior*. Saint Paul: Graywolf Press, 2004.
Anderson, Benedict. *Imagined Communities*. London: Verso, 1983.
Anderson, Elijah. *Black in White Space: The Enduring Impact of Color in Everyday Life*. Chicago: University of Chicago Press, 2022.
Bachelard, Gaston. *The Poetics of Space: The Classic Look at How We Experience Intimate Places* Boston: Beacon Press, 1994.
Baker, Houston A., Jr. *Blues, Ideology, and Afro-American Literature*. Chicago: University of Chicago Press, 1984.
———. *Modernism and the Harlem Renaissance*. Chicago: University of Chicago Press, 1987.
Bakhtin, Mikhail. *The Dialogic Imagination: Four Essays, Edited by Michael Holquist*. Austin: University of Texas Press, 1981.
———. "Discourse in the Novel." In *The Dialogic Imagination*, edited by Michael Holquist. Austin: University of Texas Press, 1981.
Baldwin, James. "The Discovery of What It Means to Be an American." In *Nobody Knows My Name: More Notes of a Native Son*, 4–5. New York: Vintage, 1961.
———. "A Talk To Teachers." In *Baldwin: Collected Essays*, edited by Toni Morrison, 678–686. New York: Library of America, 1998.
Bannet, Eve Tavor. *Postcultural Theory after the Marxist Paradigm*. New York: Paragon House, 1993.
Baudelaire, Charles. "The Temple of Nature." In *The Modern Tradition*, edited by Richard Ellman and Charles Feidelson Jr., 59–60. New York: Oxford, 1964.
Beavers, Herman. *Geography and the Political Imaginary in the Novels of Toni Morrison*. New York: Palgrave, 2018.

Benjamin, Jessica. *Beyond Doer and Done To: Recognition Theory, Intersubjectivity and The Third*. London: Routledge, 2018.

———. *The Bonds of Love: Psychoanalysis, Feminism and the Problem of Domination*. New York: Pantheon, 1988.

Benjamin, Shanna Greene. "The Space That Race Creates: An Interstitial Analysis of Toni Morrison's 'Recitatif.'" *Studies in American Fiction* 40, no. 1 (Spring 2013): 91–98.

Beschloss, Michael. "How An Experiment with Dolls Helped Lead to School Integration." *New York Times*, May 6, 2014.

Bhabha, Homi. *The Location of Culture*. New York: Routledge, 1994.

Boers, David. *History of American Education Primer*. New York: Peter Lang, 2007.

Braidotti, Rosi. *Nomadic Subjects: Embodiment and Sexual Difference in Contemporary Feminist Theory*. New York: Columbia University Press, 1994.

———. "Writing as a Nomadic Subject." *Comparative Critical Studies* 11, no. 2–3 (2014): 163–184.

Brand, Dionne. *A Map to the Door of No Return: Notes to Belonging*. New York: Vintage, 2011.

Brodsky, Claudia. "Aesthetic Activity." In *Toni Morrison: Memory and Meaning*, edited by Adrienne Lanier Seward and Justine Tally, 207–217. Jackson: University Press of Mississippi, 2014.

Brooks, Peter. *Reading for the Plot: Design and Intention in Narrative*. New York: Vintage, 1985.

Browne, Simone. *Dark Matters: On the Surveillance of Blackness*. Durham: Duke University Press, 2015.

Carrasco, David. "Writing Goodness and Mercy: A 2017 Interview with Toni Morrison." In *Toni Morrison: Goodness and the Literary Imagination*, edited by David Carrasco, Stephanie Paulsell, and Mara Willard, 227–244. Charlottesville: University of Virginia Press, 2019.

Carter, Erica, James Donald, and Judith Squires, eds. *Space and Place: Theories of Identity and Location*. London: Lawrence & Wishart, 1993.

Cheng, Anne Anlin. *The Melancholy of Race: Psychoanalysis, Assimilation, and Hidden Grief*. New York: Oxford, 2001.

Christian, Barbara. "The Race for Theory." In *The Black Feminist Reader*, edited by Joy James and T. Denean Sharpley-Whiting, 11–23. Hoboken: Blackwell, 2000.

Christiansë, Yvette. *Toni Morrison: An Ethical Poetics*. New York: Fordham University Press, 2013.

Coates, Ta-Nehisi. "The Case for Reparations." *The Atlantic*, June 15, 2014.

Cone, James. *For My People: Black Theology and the Black Church*. Albany. Maryknoll: Orbis Books, 1984.

———. *God of the Oppressed*. 1975. Rev. ed., Maryknoll: Orbis Books, 1997.

Conner, Marc C. *The Aesthetics of Toni Morrison: Speaking the Unspeakable*. Jackson: University Press of Mississippi, 2000.

Cooper, Brittney. "Intersectionality." In *The Oxford Review of Feminist Theory*, edited by Lisa Disch and Mary Hawkesworth, 385–406. New York: Oxford University Press, 2016.

Cottom, Tressie McMillan. "In the Name of Beauty." In *Thick and Other Essays*, edited by Tressie McMillan Cottom, 37–72. New York: The New Press, 2019.

Crenshaw, Kimberle. "Mapping the Margins: Inter." In *Critical Race Theory: The Key Writings That Formed the Movement*, edited by Kimberle Crenshaw, Neil Gotand, Gary Peller, and Kendall Thomas, 357–383. New York: The New Press, 1995.

Davis, Thadious. *Southscapes: Geographies of Race, Region, and Literature*. Chapel Hill: University of North Carolina Press, 2011.

De Certeau, Michel. *The Practice of Everyday Life*. Translated by Steven Rendall. Berkeley: University of California Press, 1984.

Denard, Carolyn C. *Toni Morrison: Conversations*. Jackson: University of Mississippi Press, 2008.

Derricotte, Toi. *The Black Notebooks: An Interior Journey*. New York: W. W. Norton, 1997.

Derrida, Jacques. *Positions, Translated and Annotated by Alan Bass*. Chicago: University of Chicago Press, 1972.

Doland, Angela. "Toni Morrison Puts Slam Poetry Into Action at the Louvre." *Seattle Times*, November 9, 2006.

Du Bois, W.E.B. "Returning Soldiers." *The Crisis* 18 (May 1919): 13.

———. *The Souls of Black Folk*. 1903. Repr., New York: Vintage/The Library of America, 1990.

Ellsworth, Scott. *Death in a Promised Land: The Tulsa Race Riot*. Baton Rouge: Louisiana State University Press, 1992.

Emerson, Caryl, and Michael Holquist, eds. *M. M. Bakhtin: Speech, Genres, and Other Late Essays*. Translated by Vern W. McGee. Austin: University of Texas Press, 1986.

Eudell, Demetrius. "Come On Kid, Let's Go Get the Thing: The Sociogenic Principle and the Being of Being Black/Human." In *Sylvia Wynter: On Being Human as Praxis*, edited by Katherick McKittrick, 216–248. Durham: Duke University Press, 2015.

Farnsworth, Elizabeth. "Conversation with Toni Morrison." In *Toni Morrison: Conversations*, edited by Carolyn C. Denard, 155–158. Jackson: University Press of Mississippi, 2008.

Feagin, Joe. "The Continuing Significance of Race: Antiblack Discrimination in Public Places." *American Sociological Review* 56 (February 1991): 101–116.

Fish, Stanley. *Is There a Text in This Class? The Authority of Interpretive Communities*. Cambridge, MA: Harvard University Press, 1980.

Foucault, Michel. *The Archaeology of Knowledge*. New York: Pantheon, 1972.

———. *The Order of Things: An Archaeology of Human Sciences*. Translated by A.M. Sheridan Smith. New York: Vintage, 1994.

———. *Power: Essential Works of Foucault 1954–1984*, edited by James Faubion. Translated by Robert Hurley and Others. New York: The New Press, 1994.

Freud, Sigmund. "Mourning and Melancholia." Translated by James Strachey. In *The Standard Edition of the Complete Psychological Works of Sigmund Freud*. London: Hogarth Press, 1953.

Gates, Henry Louis, Jr. *The Black Church:This Is Our Story, This Is Our Song*. New York: Penguin Press, 2021.

———. *The Signifying Monkey: A Theory of Afro-American Literary Criticism*. New York: Oxford University Press, 1988.

Gayle, Addison. *The Black Aesthetic*. New York: Doubleday, 1970.

Giddings, Paula. "The Triumphant Song of Toni Morrison." In *Toni Morrison Conversations*, edited by Carolyn C. Denard, 10–16. Jackson: Mississippi University Press, 2008.

Gillespie, Carmen. *Toni Morrison: A Literary Reference to Her Life and Work*. New York: Facts on File, 2008.
Gillian, Rose. *Feminism and Geography: The Limits of Geographical Knowledge*. Minneapolis: University of Minnesota Press, 1993.
Glissant, Edouard. *Poetics of Relations*. Translated by Betsy Wing. Ann Arbor: University of Michigan Press, 1997.
Green, Victor H. *The Negro Motorist Green Book*. 1940. Facsimile Edition. New York: Snowball Publishing, 1918.
Greenfield-Sanders, Timothy. Director and producer. *Toni Morrison: The Pieces I Am*. Magnola Home Entertainment, 2019.
Grewal, Gurleen. *Circles of Sorrow, Lines of Struggle: The Novels of Toni Morrison*. Baton Rouge: Louisiana State University Press, 1998.
Griffin, Farah Jasmine. *Read Until You Understand: The Profound Wisdom of Black Life and Literature*. New York: W. W. Norton, 2021.
———. *"Who Set You Flowin'?": The African-American Migration Narrative*. New York: Oxford University Press, 1995.
Hagerty, Bonnie M. K., Judith Lynch-Sauer, Kathleen L. Patusky, Maria Bouwsema, and Peggy Collier. "Sense of Belonging: A Vital Mental Health Concept." *Archives of Psychiatric Nursing* 6, no. 3 (June 1992): 172–177.
Handley, William R. "The House a Ghost Built: 'Nommo,' Allegory, and the Ethics of Reading in Toni Morrison's *Beloved*." *Contemporary Literature* 36, no. 4 (1995): 676–701.
Hannah-Jones, Nikole. *The 1619 Project*. New York: One World, 2021.
Harris, Trudier. *Depictions of Home in African American Literature*. Lanham: Lexington Books, 2021.
Hartman, Saidiya V. *Lose Your Mother: A Journey Along the Atlantic Slave Route*. New York: Farrar, Straus and Giroux, 2007.
———. *Scenes of Subjection: Terror, Slavery, and Self-Making in Nineteenth-Century America*. New York: Oxford University Press, 1997.
Henderson, Mae. "Toni Morrison's *Beloved*: Re-Membering the Body as Historical Text." In *Comparative American Identities: Race, Sex, and Nationalities in the Modern Text*, edited by Hortense J. Spillers, 62–86. New York: Routledge, 1991.
Holloway, Karla F. C. "*Beloved*: A Spiritual." In *Toni Morrison's Beloved: A Casebook*, edited by William L. Andrews and Nellie Y. McKay, 67–78. New York: Oxford, 1999.
hooks, bell. *Art on My Mind: Visual Politics*. New York: The New Press, 1995.
———. *Belonging: A Culture of Place*. New York: Routledge, 2009.
———. "Choosing the Margin as a Space of Radical Openness." In *Yearning: Race, Gender, and Cultural Politics*, 145–153. Boston: South End Press, 1990.
———. *Writing Beyond Race: Living Theory and Practice*. New York: Routledge, 2013.
Horton, Myles, and Paulo Freire. *We Make the Road by Walking: Conversations on Education and Social Change*. Philadelphia: Temple University Press, 1990.
Hughes, Langston. *The Big Sea*. New York: Hill and Wang, 1940.
Hurston, Zora Neale. "Characteristics of Negro Expression." In *Voices from the Harlem Renaissance*, edited by Nathan Huggins, 224–227. New York: Oxford University Press, 1976.
———. *Dust Tracks on a Road*. Urbanna: University of Illinois Press, 1984.

Iser, Wolfgang. *The Act of Reading: A Theory of Aesthetic Response*. Baltimore: Johns Hopkins University Press, 1978.

———. *Prospecting: From Reader Response to Literary Anthropology*. Baltimore: Johns Hopkins University Press, 1989.

Jacobs, Harriet. *Incidents in the Life of a Slave Girl*. New York: Oxford, 2001.

Jameson, Fredric. "Cognitive Mapping." In *Marxism and the Interpretation of Culture*, edited by Cary Nelson and Lawrence Grossberg, 347–360. Chicago: University of Illinois Press, 1990.

Johnson, James Weldon. *Black Manhattan*. New York: Arno Press, 1968.

Kaplan, Caren. "Deterriorializations: The Rewriting of Home and Exile in Western Feminist Discourse." *Cultural Critique* (Spring 1987): 187–198.

Kelley, Robin D. G. *Freedom Dreams: The Black Radical Imagination*. Boston: Beacon Press, 2002.

King, Martin Luther, Jr. *Strength to Love*. New York: Harper Row, 1963.

Kirby, Kathleen M. *Indifferent Boundaries: Spatial Concepts of Human Subjectivity*. New York: Guilford Press, 1996.

Krumholz, Linda. "The Ghosts of Slavery: Historical Recovery in Toni Morrison's Beloved." In *Toni Morrison's Beloved: A Casebook*, edited by Nellie McKay and William L. Andrews, 107–125. New York: Oxford, 1999.

Larkin, Lesley. *Race and the Literary Encounter: Black Literature from James Weldon Johnson to Percival Everett*. Bloomington: Indiana University Press, 2015.

Laub, Dori. *Testimony: Crises of Witnessing in Literature, Psychoanalysis, and History*. Edited by Shoshana Feldman and Dori Laub. New York: Routledge, 1992.

Lewis, David Levering. *When Harlem Was in Vogue*. New York: Oxford University Press, 1981.

Lipsitz, George. *How Racism Takes Place*. Philadelphia: Temple University Press, 2011.

———. "Racialization of Space and Spatialization of Race: Theorizing the Hidden Architecture of Landscape." *Landscape Journal* 26, no. 1 (2007): 1–15.

Locke, Alain, ed. *The New Negro: Voices of the Harlem Renaissance*. 1925. Repr., New York: Touchstone, 1992.

Lubiano, Wahneema. "Mapping the Interstices between Afro-American Cultural Discourse and Cultural Studies." *Callaloo* 19, no. 1 (1996): 68–77.

Mailloux, Steven. *Interpretive Conventions: The Reader in the Study of American Fiction*. Ithaca, NY: Cornell University Press, 1982.

Massey, Doreen. *Space, Place, and Gender*. Minneapolis: University of Minnesota Press, 1994.

Mayberry, Susan Neal. *The Critical Life of Toni Morrison*. Rochester: Camden House, 2021.

McDowell, Deborah E. "Boundaries: Or Distant Relations and Close Kin—*Sula*." In *"The Changing Same": Black Women's Literature, Criticism, and Theory*, 102–117. Bloomington: Indiana University Press, 1995.

McKenzie, Marilyn Mobley. "Spaces for Readers: The Novels of Toni Morrison." In *Cambridge Companion to the African American Novel*, edited by Maryemma Graham, 221–232. Cambridge: Cambridge University Press, 2004.

McKittrick, Katherine. *Demonic Grounds: Black Women and the Cartographies of Struggle*. Minneapolis: University of Minnesota Press, 2006.

Metzel, Jonathan M. *The Protest Psychosis: How Schizophrenia Became a Black Disease.* Boston: Beacon Press, 2010.

Mitchell, Angelyn. *The Freedom to Remember: Narrative, Slavery, and Gender in Contemporary Black Women's Fiction.* New Brunswick, NJ: Rutgers University Press, 2002.

Mobley, Marilyn Sanders. "A Different Remembering: Memory, History, and Meaning in Toni Morrison's Beloved." In *Toni Morrison: Modern Critical Views*, edited by Harold Bloom, 189–200. New York: Chelsea House, 1990.

———. *Folk Roots and Mythic Wings in Sarah Orne Jewett and Toni Morrison: The Cultural Function of Narrative.* Baton Rouge: Louisiana State University Press, 1991.

———. "Skin Deep: Toni Morrison's Interrogation of Beauty from *The Bluest Eye* to *God Help the Child*." *International Review of African American Art* 30, no. 2 (2020): 37–41.

———. "Toni Morrison's Beloved: The Scandal that Disturbed Domestic Tranquility." In *Scandalous Fictions: The Twentieth Century Novel in the Public Sphere*, edited by Jago Morrison and Susan Watkins, 150–171. New York: Palgrave, 2006.

Morrison, Toni. "Acceptance Speech for the Frederic G. Melcher Book Award for the Publication of *Beloved*." *World Magazine*, 1989.

———. "Afterword." In *The Bluest Eye*, 209–216. New York: Knopf, 1993.

———. *A Mercy.* New York: Knopf, 2008.

———. *Beloved.* New York: Knopf, 1987.

———. "Black Matters." In *Playing in the Dark: Whiteness and the Literary Imagination*, edited by Toni Morrison, 1–28. Cambridge: Harvard University Press, 1992.

———. *The Bluest Eye.* 1970. Repr., New York: Knopf, 1993.

———, ed. *Burn This Book: PEN Writers Speak Out on the Power of the Word.* New York: Harper Studio, 2009.

———. *The Dancing Mind.* New York: Knopf, 1996.

———. "The Foreigner's Home." In *The Source of Self-Regard: Selected Essays, Speeches, and Meditations*, 5–13. New York: Knopf, 2019.

———. "Foreword." In *Tar Baby*, xi–xiv. 1981. Repr., New York: Vintage, 2004.

———. *God Help the Child.* New York: Knopf, 2015.

———. "Goodbye to All That: Race, Surrogacy, and Farewell." In *The Source of Self-Regard: Selected Essays, Speeches, and Meditations*, 334–345. New York: Knopf, 2019.

———. "Home." In *The House That Race Built: Original Essays by Toni Morrison, Angela Y. Davis, Cornel West and Others on Black Americans and Politics in America Today*, edited by Wahneema Lubiano, 3–12. New York: Vintage, 1998.

———. *Home.* New York: Knopf, 2012.

———. "Intimate Things in Place: A Conversation with Toni Morrison." In *A Chant of Saints: A Gathering of Afro-American Literature, Art, and Scholarship*, edited by Michael S. Harper and Robert B. Stepto, 213–229. Urbana: University of Illinois Press, 1979.

———. "Introduction: Friday on the Potomac." In *Race-ing Justice, En-gendering Power: Essays on Anita Hill, Clarence Thomas, and the Construction of Social Reality*, vii–xxx. New York: Pantheon Books, 1992.

———. "Invisible Ink: Reading the Writing and Writing the Reading." In *The Source of Self-Regard: Selected Essays, Speeches, and Meditations*, 346–350. New York: Knopf, 2019.

———. *Jazz.* New York: Knopf, 1992.

———. *Love.* New York: Knopf, 2003.
———. *The Nobel Lecture in Literature.* New York: Knopf, 1993.
———. *The Origin of Others.* Cambridge: Harvard University Press, 2017.
———. *Paradise.* New York: Knopf, 1998.
———. "Peril." In *The Source of Self-Regard: Selected Essays, Speeches, and Meditations,* vii–ix. New York: Knopf, 2019.
———. *Playing in the Dark: Whiteness and the Literary Imagination.* Cambridge, MA: Harvard University Press, 1992.
———. "The Reader as Artist." *O, Oprah Magazine,* July 2006. https://oprah.com/app/o-magazine.html.
———. "Recitatif." In *Confirmation: Anthology of African American Women,* edited by Amiri Baraka and Amina Baraka, 243–261. New York: William Morrow, 1983.
———. "Rootedness: The Ancestor as Foundation." In *Black Women Writers 1950–1980: A Critical Evaluation,* edited by Mari Evans, 339–360. New York: Anchor Books, 1984.
———. "The Site of Memory, 1987." In *The Source of Self-Regard: Selected Essays, Speeches, and Meditations,* 233–244. New York: Knopf, 2019.
———. *Song of Solomon.* New York: Knopf, 1977.
———. "The Source of Self-Regard." In *The Source of Self-Regard: Selected Essays, Speeches, and Meditations,* 304–321. New York: Knopf, 2019.
———. *The Source of Self-Regard: Selected Essays, Speeches, and Meditations.* New York: Knopf, 2019.
———. *Sula.* 1973. Repr., New York: Vintage, 2004.
———. *Tar Baby.* New York: Knopf, 1981.
———. "Unspeakable Things Unspoken: The Afro-American Presence in American Literature." *Michigan Quarterly Review* 28, no. 1 (Winter 1989): 1–34.
———. "Wartalk." In *The Source of Self-Regard,* 21–25. New York: Knopf, 2019.
———. "The Writer Before the Page." In *The Source of Self-Regard,* 263–270. New York: Knopf, 2019.
Morrison, Toni, and Middleton A. Harris, eds. *The Black Book.* 1974. Repr., New York: Random House, 2009.
Moses, Claire. "The Spread of Book Banning." *New York Times,* July 31 2022. https://www.nytimes.com/2022/07/31/briefing/book-banning-debate.html?smid=url-share.
Moten, Fred. *In the Break: The Aesthetics of the Black Radical Tradition.* Minneapolis: University of Minnesota Press, 2003.
Muhammad, Khalil Gibran. *The Condemnation of Blackness: Race, Crime and the Making of Modern Urban America.* Cambridge, MA: Harvard University Press, 2019.
Mulrine, Anna. "This Side of 'Paradise': Toni Morrison Defends Herself from Criticism of Her New Novel *Paradise.*" *U.S. News & World Report,* January 19, 1998, 71.
Nelson, Angela Ford. "The Message of the Hush Harbor: History and Theology of African Descent Traditions." In *United Methodist Advocate,* edited by Jessica Brodie. March 1, 2019.
Ogletree, Charles J., Jr. *All Deliberate Speed: Reflections on the First Half Century of Brown v. Board of Education.* New York: W. W. Norton, 2004.
Olney, James. "'I Was Born': Slave Narratives, Their Status as Autobiography and as Literature." In *The Slave's Narrative,* edited by Charles T. Davis and Henry Louis Gates Jr., 148–175. New York: Oxford University Press, 1991.

O'Reilly, Andrea. *Toni Morrison and Motherhood: A Politics of the Heart.* Albany: SUNY Press, 2004.

PBS NewsHour. "In Toni Morrison's 'Home,' Soldier Fights War, Racism." YouTube video, posted May 29, 2012. https://www.youtube.com/watch?v=lZ5XnjiI0gk&list=PLYyiwknF_3XIG5dBUJaQW-CJEkzeVGIqW&index=9.

Petras, George, and Janet Loehrke. "A Look Inside the Green Book." *USA Today*, February 21, 2021.

Philip, M. Nourbese. "Dis Place—The Space Between." In *A Genealogy of Resistance and Other Essays.* Toronto: Mercury Press, 1997.

———. *A Genealogy of Resistance and Other Essays.* Ann Arbor: Mercury Press, 1997.

Quashie, Kevin. *Black Aliveness, or a Poetics of Being.* Durham: Duke University Press, 2021.

Raboteau, Albert. *Slave Religion: The Invisible Institution in the Antebellum South.* New York: Oxford University Press, 2004.

Rah, Soong-Chan. *Prophetic Lament: A Call for Justice in Troubled Times.* Downers Grove: InterVarsity Press, 2015.

Ralph W. Franklin, ed. *The Poems of Emily Dickson: Reading Edition.* Cambridge, MA: Belknap Press of Harvard University, 1998.

Rankine, Claudia, Beth Loffreda, and Max King Cap. *The Racial Imaginary: Writers on Race in the Life of the Mind.* Albany: Fence Books, 2016.

Rich, Adrienne. "When We Dead Awaken: Writing as Re-Vision." *College English* 34 (1972): 18–26.

Ricoeur, Paul. *Memory, History and Forgetting.* Translated by Kathleen Blamey and David Pellauer. Chicago: University of Chicago Press, 2004.

Rose, Tricia. *Longing to Tell: Black Women Talk about Sexuality and Intimacy.* New York: Picador, 2003.

Rosenblum, Karen E., and Toni-Michelle C. Travis, eds. *The Meaning of Difference: American Constructions of Race and Ethnicity, Sex and Gender, Social Class, Sexuality and Disability.* 7th ed. New York: McGraw Hill, 2016.

Rowe, Sheila Wise. *Healing Racial Trauma: The Road to Resilience.* Downers Grove: InterVarsity Press, 2020.

Roynon, Tessa. "Lobbying the Reader: Toni Morrison's Recent Forewords to Her Novels." *European Journal of American Culture* 33, no. 2 (2014): 85–96.

Rushdie, Salman. "An Interview with Toni Morrison." In *Toni Morrison: Conversations*, edited by Carolyn Denard, 51–60. Jackson: University of Mississippi Press, 2008.

Rushdy, Ashraf H. A. "Daughters Signifyin(g) History: The Example of Toni Morrison's Beloved." In *Toni Morrison's Beloved: A Casebook*, edited by William L. Andrews and Nellie Y. McKay, 37–66. New York: Oxford, 1999.

Schappell, Elissa, and Claudia Brodsky Lacour. "Toni Morrison, The Art of Fiction No. 134." *The Paris Review* 128 (Fall 1993): 1–37.

Scholes, Robert. *Protocols of Reading.* New Haven: Yale University Press, 1989.

Schreiber, Evelyn Jaffe. *Race, Trauma, and Home in the Novels of Toni Morrison.* Baton Rouge: Louisiana State University Press, 2010.

Schweickart, Patrocinio P. "Reading Ourselves: Toward a Feminist Theory of Reading." In *Gender and Reading: Essays on Readers, Texts and Contexts*, edited by Elizabeth A. Flynn and Patrocinio P. Schweickart, 31–62. Baltimore: Johns Hopkins University Press, 1986.

Shabazz, Rashad. *Spatializing Blackness: Architectures of Confinement and Black Masculinity in Chicago*. Urbana: University of Illinois Press, 2015.

Shakespeare, William. *Hamlet, Prince of Denmark*. *Literature and Its Writers: An Introduction to Fiction, Poetry, and Drama*. Edited by Ann Charters and Samuel Charters. Boston: Bedford Books, 1997.

Sharpe, Christina. *In the Wake: On Blackness and Being*. Durham: Duke University Press, 2016.

Shaw, Arnold. *The Jazz Age: Popular Music in the 1920s*. New York: Oxford University Press, 1987.

Smith, Neil. *Uneven Development: Nature, Capital, and the Production of Space*. Athens: University of Georgia Press, 1984, 1990.

Soja, Edward. *Thirdspace: Journeys to Los Angeles and Other Real-and-Imagined Places*. Malden, MA: Blackwell Publishing, 1996.

Somerstein, Rachel. "A Novelist's Approach." *Artnews*, August 8, 2019.

Sorin, Gretchen. *Driving While Black: African American Travel and the Road to Civil Rights*. New York: Liveright, 2020.

Spillers, Hortense. "A Hateful Passion, A Lost Love: Three Women's Fiction." In *Black, White, and In Color: Essays on American Literature and Culture*, 93–118. Chicago: University of Chicago Press, 2003.

———. "Response." In *Afro-American Literary Study in the 1990s*, edited by Houston A. Baker, Jr. and Patricia Redmond, 71–73. Chicago: University of Chicago Press, 1989.

Spivak, Gayatri. "Reading the World: Literary Studies in the 1980s." In *Writing and Reading Differently: Deconstruction and the Teaching of Composition and Literature*, edited by G. Douglas Atkins and Michael A. Johnson, 27–37. Lawrence: University Press of Kansas, 1985.

Stewart, Jeffrey C. *The New Negro: The Life of Alain Locke*. New York: Oxford University Press, 2018.

Summers, Brandi Thompson. *Black in Place: The Spatial Aesthetics of Race in a Post Chocolate City*. Chapel Hill: University of North Carolina Press, 2019.

Talks at Google. "Home: Toni Morrison." YouTube video. Posted March 4, 2013. https://www.youtube.com/watch?v=pBDARw5fdrg&t=645s.

Tate, Claudia. *Psychoanalysis and Black Novels: Desire and the Protocols of Race*. New York: Oxford University Press, 1998.

Tatum, Beverly Daniel. *Can We Talk about Race? And Other Conversations in an Era of School Resegregation*. Boston: Beacon Press, 2008.

Taylor, Candacy. *Overgrown Railroad: The Green Book and the Roots of Black Travel in America*. New York: Abrams Press, 2020.

Taylor, Carole. *The Tragedy and Comedy of Resistance: Reading Modernity through Black Women's Fiction*. Philadelphia: University of Pennsylvania Press, 2000.

Taylor, Charles. "The Politics of Recognition." In *Multiculturalism Examining the Politics of Recognition*, edited by Amy Gutmann, 25–73. Princeton, NJ: Princeton University Press, 1994.

Taylor, Quintard. "Swing the Door Wide: World War II Wrought a Profound Transformation in Seattle's Black Community." *Columbia Magazine* 9, no. 2 (Summer 1995).

Thurman, Howard. "Keep Alive the Dream in the Heart." In *A Strange Freedom: The Best of Howard Thurman on Religious Experience and Public Life*, edited by Walter Earl Fluker and Catherine Tumber. Boston: Beacon Press, 1998.

Tuan, Yi-Fu. *Space and Place: The Perspective of Experience*. Minneapolis: University of Minnesota Press, 1977.

Turner, Victor W. *Dramas, Fields, and Metaphors: Symbolic Action in Human Society*. Ithaca: Cornell University Press, 1974.

Van Der Zee, James, Owen Dodson, and Camille Billops. *The Harlem Book of the Dead*. Dobbs Ferry, NY: Morgan & Morgan, 1978.

Wagner-Martin, Linda. *Toni Morrison and the Maternal: From the Bluest Eye to God Help the Child*. New York: Peter Lang, 2019.

Waldman, Katy. "Slave or Enslaved Person? It's Not Just an Academic Debate for Historians of American Slavery." *Slate*, May 19, 2015. https://slate.com/human-interest/2015/05/historians-debate-whether-to-use-the-term-slave-or-enslaved-person.html.

Washington, Harriet A. *Medical Apartheid: The Dark History of Medical Experimentation on Black Americans from Colonial Times to the Present*. New York: Anchor Books, 2008.

Waugh, Patricia. *Metafiction: The Theory and Practice of Self-Conscious Fiction*. London: Routledge, 1984.

Weisenberger, Steven. *Modern Medea: A Family Story of Slavery and Child-Murder from the Old South*. New York: Hill and Wang, 1998.

Wertheim, Albert. "The McCarthy Era and American Theater." *Theater Journal* 34, no. 2 (May 1982): 211–222.

West, Cornel. "Black Leadership and the Pitfalls of Racial Reasoning." In *Race-ing Justice, En-gendering Power: Essays on Anita Hill, Clarence Thomas, and the Construction of Social Reality*, edited by Toni Morrison, 390–401. New York: Pantheon, 1992.

———. *Race Matters*. Boston: Beacon Press, 1993.

White, Augustus A., III. *Seeing Patients: Unconscious Bias in Health Care*. Cambridge, MA: Harvard University Press, 2011.

White, Kenneth. *Geopoetics: Place, Culture, World*. Edinburgh: Alba Publishing, 2004.

Wilkerson, Isabel. *Caste: The Origins of Our Discontents*. New York: Random House, 2020.

———. *The Warmth of Other Suns*. New York: Vintage, 2010.

Williams, Patricia J. "The Ethnic Scarring of American Whiteness." In *The House That Race Built*, edited by Wahneema Lubiano, 253–263. New York: Vintage, 1996.

Williams, Raymond. *The Long Revolution*. Harmondsworth: Penguin, 1961.

———. *Marxism and Literature*. Oxford: Oxford University Press, 1977.

Woodward, Helen. *Slave Sites on Display: Reflecting Slavery's Legacy through Contemporary Flash Moments*. Jackson: University of Mississippi, 2019.

Woolf, Virginia. "The Novel of Consciousness." In *The Modern Tradition*, edited by Richard Ellman and Charles Feidelson Jr., 123–124. New York: Oxford University, 1965.

Wright, Michelle M. *Physics of Blackness: Beyond the Middle Passage*. Minneapolis: University of Minnesota Press, 2015.

Yancy, George. *Black Bodies, White Gazes: The Continuing Significance of Race in America*. 2nd ed. New York: Bowman & Littlefield, 2017.

Zornberg, Avivah Gottlieb. *The Particulars of Rapture: Reflections on Exodus*. New York: Schocken Books, 2001.

Index

Abrams, M. H., 45
absences, 68, 76, 79–80, 86, 112; and healing, 139; presence marked by, 107, 136, 166, 172–173; of racial markers, 166–172
Adichie, Chimamanda Ngozi, 98
aesthetics, 1, 72, 78; of belonging, 4–5, 13–14, 21; counteraesthetics, 6–9; grounded, 89; hegemonic, interrogation of, 24; of jazz, 75; politics, connection with, 3–4, 6; of space, 24. *See also* belonging, aesthetics of; poetics
Alexander, Elizabeth, 59
Anderson, Benedict, 143, 154
Anderson, Elijah, 7
The Archaeology of Knowledge and the Discourse on Language (Foucault), 8
archive: home as, 149; as "paradoxical space," 19, 76; return to, 51, 62; as site of memory, 25, 48, 51, 62, 76, 113, 130, 166; source material, 75–76, 78, 129
authorial intention, 1–2, 9, 18, 26–27, 31, 76–78, 165, 178n6; indirection, 111, 121–123, 140, 153; *in medias res* beginnings, 45, 53, 58–59, 74, 90–91, 114–115, 121; metanarrative, 12, 28, 80, 88–89, 122–123, 135, 174; other-directed toward readers, 27; racial markers withheld, 166–172; self-consciousness of, 89–90. *See also* discursive mediation; emancipatory spaces; home; narrative rememory; reader

Bachelard, Gaston, 22, 38
Bacon's Rebellion, 113–114
Baker, Houston A., Jr., 36, 74, 79
Bakhtin, Mikhail, 1, 8, 70
Baldwin, James, 6, 22, 164
banned books, 22, 178n8, 181n2
Bannet, Eve Tavor, 7
Barthes, Roland, 178n6
Baudelaire, Charles, 62
beauty: categorization of, 36–38; commodification of, 31–32, 34, 37–38; fetishization of, 147–148; and privilege, 54; and reading of space, 36–38; resistance to white notions of, 31–32
Beavers, Herman, 36, 78, 143
belonging, 3, 98; aesthetics of, 4–5, 13–14, 21; expansion of to community, 71–72; and forms of difference, 166–167; imagination of, 148; intimacy as gendered site of, 49; mutual, 71; and reader, 16–17; reimagination of, 11, 15, 18, 19, 88, 101–102, 161, 165; and sacred space, 63; spaces of, 13–14, 17, 72, 145, 148, 171; third spaces of, 13, 72, 145, 171. *See also* home; house and home

Beloved (Morrison), 9–11; aurality/orality in, 28; beauty interrogated in, 27–29; "bluest eye" in the subject position of "I," 36; "circling the subject" in, 10, 173; Clearing as emancipatory space in, 62–69, 72, 92; different rendering of history in, 105–106; difficulty of for readers, 2, 180n40; effect on women readers, 179n28; foreshadowing in, 25; geopoetics in, 10; hate and desire in, 32–33; haunted house as interrogation of home, 141; indirection in, 62, 72, 111, 121; intersubjective, intergenerational dialogue in, 69–71, 112; memory in, 104; metacognition in, 108, 109; Morrison's reasons for writing, 105; multiscale reading of systems in, 27, 29, 35; narrative rememory in, 10, 104–107; origins of, 61; psychic shift from self-loathing to fraudulent love in, 33; rememory introduced as term in, 9–10, 106–107; Shirley Temple icon in, 29, 31–34; Sweet Home plantation interrogated as home, 67, 112, 141; three levels of reading in, 27–28; why and how, distinction between, 1, 28, 157. *See also Jazz* (Morrison); *Paradise* (Morrison)
"beloved community," 66
"*Beloved* trilogy," 59; as "meditation on love," 59
Benjamin, Jessica, 17, 71, 169, 171
Bhabha, Homi, 15, 25, 57, 70, 139, 162; "house of fiction," 23, 51, 140
Bhabha, Homi K., 23
bildungsroman, 34, 45, 121, 144
binary oppositional forces, 7, 17–19, 39–40, 53, 56–59. *See also* both/and spaces
Black church and community, 127–128
Black Liberation Theology, 63
Black Lives Matter, 179n30
The Black Notebooks (Derricotte), 152
Black studies, 2, 6, 14–15
blind woman and bird, intergenerational narrative of, 12–13
blues, the, 36
The Bluest Eye (Morrison), 5, 22–40, 147; afterword to 1993 edition, 18, 30–31; assault, multiple sources of, 38–39; beauty interrogated in, 20–34, 37–40; binary oppositional forces in, 39–40; connection between sense of self and sense of place in, 35–37; doll imagery in, 30, 32–33; geopoetics of discursive mediation in, 24–25; homelessness in, 29–30, 141, 168; interconnectedness of narratives in, 15–16; prenarrative from preschool primer, 1, 18, 22–25, 146, 165; scapegoating by community in, 39, 106; Shirley Temple icon in, 29, 31–32, 38
both/and spaces, 4, 7–8; archive as site of, 76; both "snug and wide open," 17, 89, 102, 142–143, 173–174; either/or frameworks, 7, 17, 57; of jazz aesthetic, 81; memory and enigma of presence and absence, 107; place and space, 15; reader oriented toward, 52; sacred-secular social continuum, 95; "snug and wide open" space, 17, 89, 102, 142–143, 173–174. *See also* binary oppositional forces; discursive mediation; space
Braidotti, Rosi, 61, 101
Brodsky, Claudia, 28, 34
Brooks, Peter, 45–46
Browne, Simone, 125
Brown vs. Board of Education, 33

call-and-response tradition, 7, 95, 150
capitalism, 49, 116; intersection of with race, 23–24
Caribbean, 52, 54–55
Carter, Erica, 29
"The Case for Reparations" (Coates), 35, 145
Caste: The Origins of Our Discontents (Wilkerson), 148–149
Certeau, Michel de, 42
Cheng, Anne Anlin, 22, 33, 71
childhood: abandonment in, 151–152, 156, 158; colorism and Black female children, 146–152
choral subjunctive, 58, 71
Christian, Barbara, 65
Christianity, 119
Christiansë, Yvette, 23
church, Black, 93–96, 133; and sacred-secular social continuum, 93–94
"circling the subject," 10, 110, 116–120, 140, 155, 173
Clark, Kenneth, 33
Clark, Mamie, 33
Clearing, in *Beloved*, 62–69, 72, 92
Coates, Ta-Nehisi, 35, 145
cognitive mapping, 24
colorism, 34, 48, 91, 160; within home, 146–152, 155; as internalized racism, 147, 150, 152

community, Black: "beloved," 66; complicity of in tragedy, 39–40; cultural conflicts, 51–52; cultural logic of, 42; displacement and homelessness in, 28–29; diverse public opinion in 1980s and 1990s, 10–11; naming traditions, 41, 50; privilege and power in, 45–47, 52–54, 156. *See also* women, Black, communal network of
community of readers, 27, 34, 182n21
Cone, James H., 63, 93
Conner, Marc C., 68
counteraesthetics, 6–9
counternarratives, 6–7
Crenshaw, Kimberle, 16
criminalization, 154
Cullors, Patrisse, 179n30
cultural studies, 6, 7, 14

"dancing mind," 27, 182n21, 275
Danticat, Edwidge, 162
Dark Matters: On the Surveillance of Blackness (Browne), 125
Davis, Thadious, 14, 23
Demonic Grounds: Black Women and the Cartographies of Struggle (McKittrick), 65, 95
Derricotte, Toi, 152
destabilization, 6, 163; effects of racial imaginary, 170; of meanings of war, 123–124, 164; of narrative linear sequencing, 45–46, 76, 79, 111, 121, 173; of reading, 3, 46, 88, 115, 171–172, 175; of received hegemonic narratives, 9, 24; of received narratives of home, 17; of self-loathing, 37; of text, 3, 88, 111, 170, 175; of "the race house," 22. *See also* narrative rememory
dialogism, 8–9
diaspora, African, 6–7, 31, 52, 57, 105, 142, 164
"The Discovery of What It Means to Be an American" (Baldwin), 164
"discursive archaeology," 62
discursive mediation: absence of racial markers, 166–172; and belonging, 16–17; binary oppositional forces, 7, 17–19, 39–40, 53, 56–69; in *The Bluest Eye*, 15–16, 23–27, 32–33; between Caribbean and the West, 52; between official narratives and lived narratives, 24–25, 46, 124; practiced by Morrison, 172; psychic shift from self-loathing to fraudulent love, 33; of racial markers, 166–172; and "Recitatif," 166; between redemption and condemnation, 39. *See also* both/and spaces; reader
disorientation, historical sense of, 20
Djebar, Assia, 162
doll study (Clark and Clark), 33
double-consciousness, 144
dozens (the dozens), 132
Du Bois, W.E.B., 66, 72, 130, 144

education, 11, 180n35; primers, 22–26
Ellington, Duke, 79
emancipatory spaces, 7, 17, 19, 73–74, 166, 173; Clearing in as, 62–69, 72, 92; Convent as, 97–99; created by Pilate, 60–61; and desire, 66–67; emancipation experienced and imagined in, 64; emancipatory narrative, 105; imagination as, 59–62; interior, 86, 87; Oven as, 91–92; for reader to consider costs of slavery, 68; self-love in, 64–65. *See also* geopoetics; third spaces
Emanuel AME Church (Charleston), 64
enslaved persons: agency of, 63–64, 66, 68, 70, 106, 118–119, 143–144; bifurcated existence of, 112; larger history of, 110; as spectators, 118
enslavement/slavery, 19; atrocities of, 109–110; in Barbados, 117, 119; bifurcation of being both human and property, 112; experience of enslavement through mother-daughter bond, 71; "literary archaeology" designed to fill in blanks, 62; Morrison's reluctance to write about, 104; move away from slavery as term, 106; preracist, 116; psychic implications of, 10; reminders of in present, 52; shift to interior life of the enslaved, 10, 105–106; in the wake of enslavement, 146, 167. *See also* slavery
Eudell, Demetrius, 86
eugenics, 120, 134, 136–137
exile, space of, 3, 16, 142, 145, 162

feeling, structures of, 4, 13, 17, 107
feminist studies, 6, 14
fiction, Black: "migration narrative," 79; normalized protocols of race in, 72; protest tradition, 173

folklore and myth, African American, 44–45; tar baby, 52, 55–56
The Foreigner's Home (Louvre exhibit), 141, 162–163, 178n19
"The Foreigner's Home" (Morrison), 3, 20, 141, 161–162
Foucault, Michel, 8, 53, 62, 105–106, 127
France, racial politics of, 162–163
Freire, Paulo, 61
friendship, Black female, 42–44, 60, 133

Garner, Margaret, 11, 112
Garvey, Marcus, 82
Garza, Alicia, 179n30
Gates, Henry Louis, 46, 80, 130
gentrification, 41
geography, 4–5; Black women's histories linked with, 95; and imagination, 65, 79; landscape, 41, 58, 114–119; psychic, 113. *See also* home; place; space
geopoetics, 2–3; binary oppositions of space, 39–40; defined, 4–5; home, interrogation of, 20; intersection of past and present, 8, 17, 84, 86, 97, 129, 141, 144, 146; at intersection of race and gender, 58; of "literary encounter," 106–107; of metacognition, 108, 109; of place, race, and belonging, 1, 3, 14–15, 18, 20, 44, 90, 105, 114, 147, 165, 167, 170, 172; politics and aesthetics connected through, 3–4; of self-regard, 32, 35–37, 49, 174; spatial logic of, 85–86; spatial turn in humanities, 7, 14, 172; of white domestic spaces, 36–37. *See also* belonging; both/and space; discursive mediation; emancipatory spaces; home; imagination; interiority; narrative rememory; place; reimagination; space; third spaces
geopolitical economy, 157–158
Gericault, Theodore, 162
Gillespie, Carmen, 89, 92
Glissant, Edouard, 7
God Help the Child (Morrison), 1, 20, 146–161, 165; beauty interrogated in, 29, 147–148; chapters published as "Sweetness" in the *New Yorker*, 148, 191n20, 192n3; colorism in, 34, 147; effects of racial imaginary on Black female children, 146–147, 167; epigraph, 149
God of the Oppressed (Cone), 63
"God's Language" (Morrison), 20

Graves, Kenyatta Dorey, 186n52
Great Migration, 19, 74–75, 79, 123, 129–131; to Seattle, 129–130
Green Book (*The Negro Motorist Green Book*), 130, 190n48
Grewal, Gurleen, 44
Griffin, Farah Jasmine, 77, 79, 139, 179n28

Harlem: from Black perspective, 83; racial history of, 81–82
The Harlem Book of the Dead (Van Der Zee), 74–76
Harlem Renaissance, 74; Great Migration as beginning of, 79, 84; "New Negro" image, 78, 86
Harris, Trudier, 4, 140
Hartman, Saidiya, 6, 15, 23, 62, 75, 86, 104, 111, 130
healing, 161; by communal network of women, 71–72, 97–102, 112–113, 121, 137–139, 146; and memory, 109–110, 154, 172–173; spiritual, 72, 100–101, 137–138; textual, 179n28; by women elders, 63–66
Henderson, Mae, 6
Holloway, Karla F. C., 72
home: as archive, 149; beauty learned in contact of, 31–34; binary of home and not home, 13, 161; Black church as, 127–128; Black homeownership, 29; as "both snug and wide open," 17, 89, 102, 142–143, 173–174; childhood perspective on, 146; colorism within, 146–152; and community context, 28; Convent, interrogation of, 101–103, 142–143; destabilization of, 3, 17, 25–26, 123; domestic relations in, 36–37; gendered interrogations of, 144–146; haunted house in *Beloved* as interrogation of, 69–70, 109, 141; housing discrimination, 35, 145, 152; and interiority, 28–29; interrogations of, 39, 141–164, 166, 173–174; at the intersection of race, gender, and class, 143; Morrison's house of fiction, 141; outdoors distinguished from, 29, 35, 141, 168–169, 173; racial house, 141–142, 161; reading of in new places, 164; reimagining, 20, 41, 101, 121, 137, 141, 161–162; and self-regard, 4, 35–37; as site of transgression, 38, 47–48; as site of trauma, 144–145; Sweet Home plantation, interrogation of, 67, 112, 141; as third space of sanctuary,

141; as unsafe site for women, 131, 133–135, 142, 144–145; Vaark plantation, interrogation of, 113, 116–119, 141, 143
Home (Morrison), 20, 105, 120–139; global, national, and local conditions exposed in, 127; home interrogated in, 123–126, 131–139, 144–146; italics as device in, 122–123, 128, 135–136, 139; masculinity in, 128–129, 131–132; *in medias res* beginning, 121; metanarrative, 122–123, 135; narrative rememory in, 105, 120; quilt metaphor in, 138; as reverse migration narrative, 120, 123; title of, 123, 126
"Home" (Morrison), 20, 89, 141–142, 161
homelessness, 29–30, 140–142, 167–169; on global scale, 162; liminal space of, 168–169; outdoors distinguished from being put out, 29, 35, 141, 168–169, 173
"homespaces," 4, 140
hooks, bell, 14, 24, 59, 141, 148
Horton, Myles, 61
"house of fiction," 23, 51, 140–141
The House That Race Built (collection), 141
Hurston, Zora Neale, 29
hush harbor, 64

imagination, 4, 9, 20–21; belonging created by, 148; beyond official narratives, 61–62; in Black homeownership, 29; as emancipatory space, 59–62; of grace, 62, 65; literary, 89, 146, 165, 175; radical, 62; third space created by, 108. *See also* narrative rememory; reimagination
"imagined community," 143, 154
improvisation, 78, 80, 86
Incidents in the Life of a Slave Girl (Jacobs), 65
indirection, 62, 72, 111, 121–123, 140, 153
individualism, 49, 60, 62, 146
in medias res beginnings, 45, 53, 58–59, 74, 90–91, 114–115, 121
intergenerational dialogue, 12–13, 69–70, 112
interiority, 4–5, 17, 62, 67–68, 84, 110, 164; at intersection of the already and the not yet, 68; third spaces of interior life, 38, 49, 53–54, 144
interstitial spaces, 26, 57, 61, 64, 70, 113, 139; Black subjectivity created in, 50; and home, 135–136; in *Jazz*, 78, 84–85; reader in, 88–89, 171; reader's navigation of, 97;

of "the quality of being," 104. *See also* both/and spaces; third spaces
"in the break," 26, 59
"in the wake," 75–76, 79
"Invisible Ink: Reading the Writing and Writing the Reading" (Morrison), 20, 172

Jacobs, Harriet, 65
Jameson, Fredric, 24
jazz: both/and nature of aesthetic, 81; "break" in, 84; "discredited" narratives from "discredited people," 78; improvisation as central to, 78; as "race music," 83; as site of contestation, 78; third thing created by, 59
Jazz (Morrison), 14, 19, 74–89, 169; alternation between past and present in, 84, 86; city personified in, 81–83; "future thoughts," 81–82; improvisational narrative play in, 80, 83–84; *in medias res* beginning, 74, 76; interstitial space in, 78, 84–85; italics as device in, 84, 86; jazz style and poetics of, 79–81; memory in, 106; second-guessing in, 19, 88; sites of memory in, 84. *See also Beloved* (Morrison); *Paradise* (Morrison)

Kaplan, Caren, 143
"keeping room," 107–108
Kelley, Robin, 62
King, Martin Luther, Jr., 66
Kirby, Kathleen M., 90, 102, 116, 146, 166
Korean War, 120, 189n38; as "police action," 123; treatment of returning Black veterans, 126–127, 130–131
Ku Klux Klan, 124

lament, 172–173; sorrow songs, 72
Larkin, Lesley, 21, 106–107, 171–172, 188n11
liberation narratives, 173
Lipsitz, George, 41
literacy, 23–24, 119, 165, 171, 181n2
literary archaeology, 9, 62, 113, 155
literary criticism, 2; African American, 5; author's participation in, 18; displacement of traditional, 6–7; in "Unspeakable Things Unspoken," 18
literary encounter, 106–107, 171
The Location of Culture (Bhabha), 25
Locke, Alain, 78

Loffreda, Beth, 95
Lorain, Ohio, 25
Lose Your Mother (Hartman), 149
Louvre, 162–163
love: desire for, 72–73; excesses of, 74, 90, 96; multiple interpretations of, 96–97. *See also* self-love
Love (Morrison), 143
lynching, 107, 108, 122

Martin, Trayvon, 179n30
masculinity, 128–129, 131–132; *the dozens* as safe site for, 132
Massey, Doreen, 15
McDowell, Deborah, 9, 60
McKittrick, Katherine, 14, 34, 58, 65, 95, 117
medicine: medical abuse of Black women, 120, 133, 136–137; "medical apartheid," 134; mistreatment of Black people in mental health system, 120
melancholia, 70–71, 87
The Melancholy of Race: Psychoanalysis, Assimilation, and Hidden Grief (Cheng), 33
memory, 19–20; enigma of presence and absence, 107; and healing, 109–110, 154, 172–173; history connected to identity, 49–50; narrative shaped by, 112–113; paradox of engagement with and avoidance of, 111–113; paradox of remembering and forgetting, 109, 112–113; physical strategies of, 107, 110–111; psychology of, 108–109; as "repository of trauma," 110; shared, 110, 169, 171. *See also* narrative rememory; rememory; sites of memory
mental illness, intersection of with racism, 124–127
A Mercy (Morrison), 19, 113–120; Bacon's Rebellion in, 113–114; critique of European greed in, 116–117; home interrogated in, 113, 116–119, 141–143; *in medias res* beginning, 114; narrative rememory in, 105, 113; "slave codes" in, 124
metacognition, 108, 109
metanarrative, 12, 28, 80, 88–89, 122–123, 135, 174
metanoia, 149
Metzel, Jonathan M., 127
Middle Passage, 19, 70, 112
migration narrative, 79, 91. *See also* Great Migration

Mitchell, Angelyn, 105, 110, 173
Morrison, Toni: ability to speak to reader, 1; bildungsroman in works of, 34, 45, 121, 144; censorship of, 22, 178n8; Chloe as birth name of, 51; on choice and subjectivity, 24, 73, 138–139, 153; "discourses of race," 147; discursive mediation practiced by, 172; engaged in self-spatialization, 89; four narrative strategies of, 17, 166; intentional use of memory, 106–107; italics as device, 84, 86, 122–123, 128, 135–136, 139; lecture on "whiteness and the literary imagination," 146; Lorain, Ohio birthplace, 25; master's thesis on alienation, suicide, and death, 33; metanarrative used by, 12, 28, 80, 88–89, 122–123, 135, 174; narrative strategies of, 1–4; Nobel Prize lecture, 2, 7, 11–12, 111, 114, 161; nonfiction collection, 161; *The Pieces I Am* (film), 173; public participation of, 6–7, 9, 16, 17–18, 20, 172, 175; on reasons for writing *Beloved*, 105; seventieth birthday, 27; on unexplored approaches to her work, 1–2; Works: *The Black Book* (edited collection), 132; "The Foreigner's Home," 3, 20, 141, 161–162; "God's Language," 20; "Goodbye to All That: Race, Surrogacy, and Farewell," 3–4; "Home," 20, 86, 141–142; "Invisible Ink: Reading the Writing and Writing the Reading," 20, 172; lecture on "whiteness and the literary imagination," 146, 165; *Love*, 143; *The Origin of Others*, 20, 153; "Peril," 149; *Playing in the Dark*, 16; "Recitatif," 20, 165–168; "Rootedness: The Ancestor as Foundation," 173; *The Source of Self-Regard*, 3, 20, 59, 161–162; "Wartalk," 123. *See also* authorial intention; *Beloved* (Morrison); *The Bluest Eye* (Morrison); *The Foreigner's Home* (Louvre exhibit); *God Help the Child* (Morrison); *Home* (Morrison); *Jazz* (Morrison); *A Mercy* (Morrison); *Paradise* (Morrison); "The Site of Memory" (Morrison); *Song of Solomon* (Morrison); *Sula* (Morrison); *Tar Baby* (Morrison); "Unspeakable Things Unspoken" (Morrison)
The Morrison Case (play), 129
Moten, Fred, 26, 59, 79

mother-daughter relationship, 68, 147–149, 155; infanticide, act of, 10–11, 19, 68, 70–71, 109, 111–112; as site of memory, 149, 166
Muhammad, Khalil Gibran, 11

names: Black naming traditions, 41, 50; and meaning, 51
narrative: emancipatory, 105; linear sequencing destabilized, 45–46, 76, 79, 111, 121, 173; shaped by memory, 112–113. *See also* storytelling; text
narrative rememory, 9–11, 17, 19–20, 49; of Bacon's Rebellion, 113–114; in *Beloved*, 10, 104–107; "circling the subject," 10, 110, 116–120, 140, 155, 173; in *God Help the Child*, 152–154; home, interrogation of, 105, 121, 128–129, 132, 144, 148; lament, 172–173; in *A Mercy*, 105, 116–122. *See also* geopoetics; imagination
nation's narrative, 8, 113, 119–133; nation as space of home, 143; seventeenth-century origins of, 113–114
nature: disruptions in, 53; as sacred space, 62, 64
Nobel Prize lecture (Morrison), 2, 7, 11–12, 111, 114, 161
"nomadic subjectivity," 61
nommo (power of the word), 13

Obama, Barack, 64
official narratives, 24–25, 46, 61–62, 124
Onadaatje, Michael, 162
"order of things," 53
The Origin of Others (Morrison), 20, 153
"orthography of the wake," 36
othering, 39–40, 153

Paradise (Morrison), 19, 20, 74, 89; biblical parodies in, 99; Convent as emancipatory space in, 97–99; Convent as home, interrogation of, 142–143; excesses of religious love in, 90, 96; *in medias res* beginning, 90–91; intergenerational shift in, 92; "Old Fathers" in, 91–92; "Out There," 92, 100; Oven, shift in meanings of, 91–93; Oven as third space in, 93; patriarchy in, 95, 98, 102, 142; ritual of healing in, 101–102; sacred-secular social continuum in, 93–94; title of *War* rejected by editor, 123. *See also Beloved* (Morrison); *Jazz* (Morrison)
passing, 150–152
"Peril" (Morrison), 149
personification, 53, 81, 144
Philip, M. Nourbese, 66
The Physics of Blackness: Beyond the Middle Passage Epistemology (Wright), 140
The Pieces I Am (film), 173
place, 4; de-spatialization of sense of, 34; excess as affirmation of, 29; "location of culture," 15; meaning of to Black subjects, 45; multiscale meanings of, 28; race linked with, 16, 82; "scenes of subjection," 15, 23, 111, 144–145; shift from exterior places to interior spaces, 58; space as experience of, 15; space distinguished from, 15, 42; and trauma, 108. *See also* geography; house and home; space
Playing in the Dark (Morrison), 16
poetics. *See* aesthetics; geopoetics
primers, 22–26
The Protest Psychosis: How Schizophrenia Became a Black Disease (Metzel), 127

Quashie, Kevin, 14, 58, 71

race, 4; Black female subjectivity shaped by intersection of with gender and class, 30, 34, 37; commonsense connotations of, 16; "discourses of," 147; and geographic space, 35; global scale of, 157–158; intersectional analysis of mental health and, 126–127; intersection of with capitalism, 23–24; spatial realities of, 124–126
Race Matters (West), 11
"Race Matters Conference" (Princeton University, 1994), 141, 161
racial dynamics, 7, 10–11, 34, 55, 82; complicity of white women in, 135
racial imaginary, 16–17, 20, 54; Black, as narrative of healing and belonging, 148; Black female children, effects on, 146–147, 167; destabilizing effects of, 170; hatred for other turned to hatred for self, 33–34; intersectionality of, 170; male, patriarchal perspective, 95; racism on daily basis, 152
racialization: of literacy, 23–24, 171, 181n2; of space, 41, 44, 125–126

racism: as about money, 155; colorism as internalized, 147, 150, 152; internalized, 142, 152; pedagogy of, 22, 25; psychic toll of, 34; in public space, 108; spatial, 106
"radical imagination," 62
The Raft of the Medusa (Gericault), 162
Rankine, Claudia, 16, 95
reader: and belonging, 16–17; and Black aesthetic tradition of the 1960s, 77; both/and framework, orientation toward, 52, 97; as co-conspirator with author, 3; community of readers, 27, 34, 182n21; conflict between seeing and believing, 52; and dialogism, 8; difficulty with *Beloved*, 2, 180n40; discursive mediation of racial markers, 166–172; disorienting experience for, 19–20; disrupted by *in medias res* beginnings, 45–46, 53, 58–59, 74, 76, 90–91; as eavesdropper, 69; effect of *Beloved* on women readers, 179n28; expectations of disrupted, 53, 57, 59–61, 70, 77, 80, 85, 90–91, 123–124; experience of mourning and loss, 71; geographical location, coming to terms with, 51; healing space for, 139; "hostile readership," 188n11; imagination required of, 80; as interloper, 55; interpretive communities, 7; in interstitial space, 88–89, 171; listener-reader, 2; metanarrative as challenge to, 28, 80, 122–123, 135; "modes of interaction" with text, 166; and narrative indirection, 111, 121–123, 140, 153; and narrative rememory, 109; narrative sequencing desired by, 45–46; openness required of, 122; participatory goal for, 1–3, 24–25, 172; reader-response critics, 2; "reading encounters," 21; reimagination of relationships, 11, 74, 103; self-interrogation, 61; in space of exile, 3; in space of recognition, 51, 71; and structure of novel, 77; "tar baby" experience of, 53; as witness to Black subjectivity, 51. *See also* authorial intention; discursive mediation; emancipatory spaces
reading, 186n52; Black ways of, 62; destabilization of, 3, 46, 88, 115, 175; dialogic method of, 9; doubling of complication of, 170–171; making meaning in places where Black subjects find themselves, 17, 30, 90–91, 114, 140, 168; protocols of, 61, 77; public consequences and responsibility of, 90; racialized for African Americans, 144, 180–181n2; "reading encounters," 21, 172
"Recitatif" (Morrison), 20, 165–171
recitative, as term, 171
redlining, 35, 145, 152
Red Scare, 129
reimagination: by artists of color, 163; of belonging, 11, 15, 18, 19, 88, 101–102, 161, 165; of Black female subjectivity, 76, 102; of home, 20, 41, 101–102, 121, 137, 141, 161–162; of relationships, 11, 74, 103; of self, 19, 63, 74, 87, 101–103, 161–162; of space for reader, 18, 89, 103, 121, 138, 144; of unsafe space as safe, 95. *See also* imagination
rememory, 9–10, 49; as dialogic process, 110; introduced as term in *Beloved,* 9–10, 106–107; as mnemonic and spatial phenomenon, 107; spaces of belonging created by, 17. *See also* narrative rememory
resistance: to internalized oppression, 62–64; sacred strategy, 64; sorrow songs as, 72; to white notions of beauty, 31–32
respectability politics, 145
Rich, Adrienne, 113
Ricoeur, Paul, 107
Robinson, Bill "Bojangles," 31
"Rootedness: The Ancestor as Foundation" (Morrison), 173
Rose, Gillian, 76
Rose, Tricia, 67–68
Rowe, Sheila Wise, 106
Rushdie, Salman, 78

scapegoating, 39, 44, 106, 147
scenes of subjection, 15, 23, 111, 144–145
Scholes, Robert, 61
Schreiber, Evelyn Jaffe, 108, 143
Seattle Red Scare, 129–130
self: communal, 62; interior mindscape, 67; interrogation of, 60–61, 67, 85–86; racial and racialized, 59; reimagination of, 19, 63, 74, 87, 101–103, 161–162; spatialization of, 58, 62, 64, 74, 86, 88; spiritual, 149; textual matters within consciousness, 61
self-loathing, racial, 5, 31–32, 37, 66, 126, 153, 174; hatred for other turned to hatred for self, 33–34; internalization of, 34, 63; shift to fraudulent love, 33; and white ideals of beauty, 31–32

self-love, 11, 64–68; communal, 66; in emancipatory spaces, 64–65; as survival strategy, 65–68. *See also* love
self-regard, geopoetics of, 32, 35–37, 49, 174
seventeenth century, 113–114
Shabazz, Rashad, 41, 58, 124, 125
Sharpe, Christine, 4, 36, 75, 76, 86
signifying, 4, 23, 36, 41, 46, 80, 94, 133
Silverblatt, Michael, 77
"The Site of Memory" (Morrison), 4, 9, 61–62
sites of memory, 3, 46, 84, 120, 124; archival, 25, 48, 51, 62, 76, 113, 130, 166; colorism as, 34; Green Book, 130, 190n48; literary archaeology, 9, 62, 113, 155; mother-child relationship as, 149, 166; nonfictional, 75, 129; return to, 48–49
"slave codes," 124
slave narratives, 111, 112
slavery. *See* enslavement/slavery
Smith, Neil, 8
social justice struggles, 179n30
Song of Solomon (Morrison), 18, 38, 154; birth and freedom as sites of identity, 47; folklore and myth in, 44–45; historical memories in, 106; *in medias res* beginning, 45–46; male protagonist in, 123–124; privilege in, 49–50
"Song of Solomon" (Old Testament), 51
sorrow songs, 72
Souls of Black Folk (Du Bois), 66, 72
The Source of Self-Regard (Morrison), 3, 20, 59, 161–162
space: aesthetics of, 24; "between the legs," 66, 150; of body and ideology, as site of violence, 90; communal, 72; of exile, 3, 16, 142, 145, 162; as experience of place, 15; of global audience of readers, 12; intersubjective, 171; intimate, 38; male productions and uses of, 98; marginalized, 12; material and metaphorical, mutuality of, 8; melancholia as, 70–71; multiple meanings of, 97–99; originary, 25; place distinguished from, 15, 42; poetics of, 38; production of, 95, 117; and production of identities, 58; racialization of, 41; for reader to bear witness, 51; "reforming the spaces of the subject," 102; shift from exterior places to interior spaces, 58; "spaces for the reader," 1; spaces of belonging, 13–14, 17, 72, 145, 148, 171.

See also both/and spaces; diaspora, African; emancipatory spaces; interstitial space; place; third spaces
spatialization: de-spatialization of sense of place, 34; narrative, 76; of self, 58, 62, 64, 74, 86, 88; and train trope, 131
Spatializing Blackness (Shabazz), 41, 124
spatial literary studies, 14
spatial racism, 106
spatial realities of race, 124–126
spatial turn, 2–3
spatial turn in humanities, 7, 14, 172
"speakerly text," 80
Spillers, Hortense, 9, 16, 23, 60
spiritual resources, 72
Spivak, Gayatri, 6
structures of feeling, 4, 13, 17, 107
subjectivity: binary oppositional dimensions of, 39–40; and choice, 24, 73, 138–139, 153; hybrid, 70; interspersed with contested sites of being and belonging, 45; liminal spaces between dominant and marginalized, 23; nomadic, 61; received notions of self, 23; "reforming the spaces of the subject," 102; third space of, 112, 116, 166
subjectivity, Black: as beyond white gaze, 2, 5, 13, 92, 95, 141, 172; Black subjects regarded as bodies only, 146, 167; both interior and exterior, 169; at center of own narrative, 24, 47, 73, 138, 153; in conflict with itself, 34; connection between sense of self and sense of place, 35–37; constructed through racial violence and indifference, 47, 145; created in interstices, 50; during enslavement, 108–109; under enslavement, 10; existential dimensions of, 146; explored through imagination of characters, 59; making meaning in places where subjects find themselves, 17, 30, 90–91, 114, 140, 168; multiple sites of, 140–141; plenitude of cultural formations, 17; reader as witness to, 51; and reading of skin color, 34; rereading history through, 19; resistance to internalization racism, 62–64
subjectivity, Black female, 23, 37–38, 50, 113, 166; beyond stereotypical representations, 41–42, 48, 58–60; and colorism, 34, 146–152, 160; conditions of enslavement foreclosed on, 67; discursive

subjectivity (*continued*)
  mediation of, 23–27, 32–33; education and reeducation, 39; and enslavement, 102, 104, 108–109, 111–112, 115, 117–118; friendship, 42–44, 60, 133; and gender divisions, 43; interiority of, 67–69; as on the margin, 59; and marriage, 43; reimagining, 76, 102; shaped by intersection of race, gender, and class, 30, 34, 37. *See also* women, Black, communal network of
subjectivity, Black male: coming into manhood, 48–49; as house assaulted by outside forces, 38–39; in relation to Black female subjectivity, 45
Sula (Morrison), 9, 18, 38, 41–44; binary oppositional forces in, 42, 44; Black female friendship in, 42–44, 60, 106; marriage and gender divisions in, 43–44
Summers, Brandi Thompson, 124–125
surveillance, racialization of, 125–126
survival strategies, 62

Tar Baby (Morrison), 18, 51–57; binary oppositional forces in, 52–53, 56–59; colorism in, 34; critique of race, gender, and class inequities in, 52–53; interrogative voice in, 55–56; *in medias res* beginning, 53; tar baby figure as "sticky mediator," 52, 57; tar baby figure in, 52–53, 55–57
Tate, Claudia, 8, 16, 179n29
Taylor, Charles, 13, 17
Taylor, Quintard, 129–130
Temple, Shirley, 29, 31–32, 38
text: counternarrative produced by, 8–9; destabilization of, 3, 88, 111, 170, 175. *See also* narrative
third spaces, 7–8; of belonging, 13, 72, 145, 171; in *Beloved*, 25; books as, 89–90; church as, 95–96; desire for love as, 72–73; disputes over meaning as, 93; of dissociation, 124; and imagination, 108, 112–113; of innocence and guilt, 169; of interior life, 38, 49, 53–54, 144; of longing, 80–81; mind as "keeping room," 107–108; mutual creation of, 13, 42; between narratives of Jazz Age and Harlem Renaissance, 78; paradisiacal, 100; reading of by Black subjects, 7–8; "space between the legs," 66, 150; within spiritual self, 149; in *Sula*, 42–44. *See also* emancipatory spaces; space
third thing, concept of, 59, 136
Thurman, Howard, 165
Tometi, Opal, 179n30
Toni Morrison Society (TMS), 182n21
train, trope of, 131
trauma: emotional reluctance and fear of victims, 73; home as site of, 144–145; memory as "repository of," 110; and place, 108
trauma victims: operations of memory in, 108
Tuan, Yi-Fu, 15
Tulsa bombing (1921), 91
Turner, Victor W., 104

Underground Railroad, 70, 112
United Negro Improvement Association (UNIA), 82
United States: primers as racialized educational tool in, 22–24; as racialized and race-conscious society, 16; as space, 7
unity, historical claims for, 11
unspeakable things unspoken, 27, 39, 71, 87, 104, 149, 152, 161
"Unspeakable Things Unspoken" (Morrison), 1–2, 18, 24

"vagrancy," 125
Van Der Zee, James, 74–76
vernacular, Black, 41; call-and-response tradition, 7, 95, 150; *dozens (the dozens)*, 132; first-person plural pronoun, 65; signifying, 4, 23, 36, 41, 46, 80, 94, 133

war, 123–124; atrocities of, 128–129; destabilization of meanings of, 123–124, 164
The Warmth of Other Suns: The Epic Story of America's Great Migration (Wilkerson), 79
"Wartalk" (Morrison), 123
Weisenberger, Steven, 112
West, Cornel, 11, 16
what and how, distinction between, 1–2
White, Kenneth, 4, 5
white gaze, 126; Black subjectivity as beyond, 2, 5, 13, 92, 95, 141, 172

white supremacy, Black male memory of, 124
why and how, distinction between, 1, 28, 157
Wilkerson, Isabel, 79, 148–149
Williams, Patricia, 32
Williams, Raymond, 4
Winfrey, Oprah, 2, 180n40
women, Black: healing by communal network of, 71–72, 97–102, 112–113, 121, 137–139, 146; "rooted," 159; spaces mapped by, 19; wisdom of elders, 63–66, 159–160

women, Black, communal network of: healing by, 98, 113, 121, 137–139, 146; "mean" love, 137. *See also* community, Black; subjectivity, Black female
Woolf, Virginia, 121
word-work, 2, 12, 21
World War I, 130
Wright, Michele M., 121, 140

Yancy, George, 126

Zornberg, Avivah Gottlieb, 109

Marilyn Sanders Mobley is Emerita Professor of English and African American Studies at Case Western Reserve University in Cleveland, Ohio. She is the author of *Folk Roots and Mythic Wings in Sarah Orne Jewett and Toni Morrison: The Cultural Function of Narrative* and a spiritual memoir, *The Strawberry Room, and Other Places Where a Woman Finds Herself.*

www.ingramcontent.com/pod-product-compliance
Lightning Source LLC
Chambersburg PA
CBHW021757230426
43669CB00006B/105